Publisher's note

Ancient Chinese classic poems are exquisite works of art. As far as 2,000 years ago, Chinese poets composed the beautiful work *Book of Poetry* and *Elegies of the South*. Later, they created more splendid Tang poetry and Song lyrics. Such classic works as *Thus Spoke the Master* and *Laws Divine and Human* were extremely significant in building and shaping the culture of the Chinese nation. These works are both a cultural bond linking the thoughts and affections of Chinese people and an important bridge for Chinese culture and the world.

Mr. Xu Yuanchong has been engaged in translation for 70 years. He won the Lifetime Achievement Award in Translation conferred by the Translators Association of China (TAC) in 2010, and won the "Aurora Borealis" Prize for Outstanding Translation of Fiction Literature, conferred by the Federation of International Translators (FIT) in 2014. He is honored as the only expert who translates Chinese poems into both English and French. After his excellent interpretation, many Chinese classic poems have been further refined into perfect English and French rhymes. This collection of Classical Chinese Poetry and Prose gathers his most representative English translations. It includes the classic works *Thus Spoke the Master*, *Laws Divine and Human* and dramas such as *Romance of the Western Bower*, *Dream in Peony Pavilion*, *Love in Long-life Hall* and *Peach Blooms Painted with Blood*. The largest part of the collection includes the translation of selected poems from different dynasties. The selection includes various types of poetry. The selected works start from the pre-Qin era to the Qing Dynasty, covering almost the entire history of classic poems in China. Reading these works is like tasting "living water from the source" of Chinese culture.

We hope this collection will help English readers "understand, enjoy and delight in" Chinese classic poems, share the intelligence of Confucius and Lao Tzu (the Older Master), share the gracefulness of Tang poems, Song lyrics and classic operas and songs and promote exchanges between Eastern and Western culture. We also sincerely invite precious suggestions from our readers.

出版前言

中国古代经典诗文是中国传统文化的奇葩。早在两千多年以前,中国诗人就写出了美丽的《诗经》和《楚辞》;以后,他们又创造了更加灿烂的唐诗和宋词。《论语》《老子》这样的经典著作,则在塑造、构成中华民族文化精神方面具有极其重要的意义。这些作品既是联接所有中国人思想、情感的文化纽带,也是中国文化走向世界的重要桥梁。

许渊冲先生从事翻译工作70年,2010年荣获"中国翻译文化终身成就奖",2014年荣获国际译联颁发的"北极光"杰出文学翻译奖。他被称为将中国诗词译成英法韵文的唯一专家,经他的妙手,许多中国经典诗文被译成出色的英文和法文韵语。这套"许译中国经典诗文集"荟萃许先生最具代表性的英文译作,既包括《论语》《老子》这样的经典著作,又包括《西厢记》《牡丹亭》《长生殿》《桃花扇》等戏曲剧本,数量最多的则是历代诗歌选集。这些诗歌选集包括诗、词、散曲等多种体裁,所选作品上起先秦,下至清代,几乎涵盖了中国古典诗歌的整个历史。阅读和了解这些作品,即可尽览中国文化的"源头活水"。

我们希望这套许氏译本能使英语读者对中国经典诗文也"知之,好之,乐之",能够分享孔子、老子的智慧,分享唐诗、宋词、中国古典戏曲的优美,并以此促进东西文化的交流。也敬请读者朋友提出宝贵意见。

PROJECT FOR TRANSLATION AND PUBLICATION
OF CHINESE CULTURAL WORKS

中国文化著作翻译出版工程项目

CLASSICAL CHINESE POETRY AND PROSE

THUS SPOKE THE MASTER

TRANSLATED BY XU YUANCHONG

许译中国经典诗文集

论语 | 许渊冲 译

五洲传播出版社
China Intercontinental Press

中华书局
Zhonghua Book Company

CONTENTS
目 录

Preface 1
Chapter I 8
Chapter II 13
Chapter III 19
Chapter IV 26
Chapter V 31
Chapter VI 38
Chapter VII 45
Chapter VIII 52
Chapter IX 57
Chapter X 64
Chapter XI 70
Chapter XII 78
Chapter XIII 86
Chapter XIV 94

序 145
学而篇第一 150
为政篇第二 163
八佾篇第三 180
里仁篇第四 196
公冶长篇第五 207
雍也篇第六 224
述而篇第七 241
泰伯篇第八 259
子罕篇第九 270
乡党篇第十 285
先进篇第十一 300
颜渊篇第十二 317
子路篇第十三 330
宪问篇第十四 346

Chapter XV 104	卫灵公篇第十五 368
Chapter XVI 112	季氏篇第十六 384
Chapter XVII 119	阳货篇第十七 394
Chapter XVIII 126	微子篇第十八 409
Chapter XIX 131	子张篇第十九 418
Chapter XX 138	尧曰篇第二十 429

CLASSICAL CHINESE POETRY AND PROSE

THUS SPOKE
THE MASTER

TRANSLATED BY XU YUANCHONG

China Intercontinental Press   Zhonghua Book Company

PREFACE

Confucius (551—479 BC) is the most influential sage in China. This book is a record of the dialogues between the sage and his disciples. In answering their questions, he does not tell them what the answer is, but how he would solve the question, so his answer has an everlasting transcendental value. He teaches his disciples how to cultivate the mind and thinks it a delight to acquire knowledge and to behave in accordance with what is right. In this book politics, ethics and religion are combined into one, but he replaces religion by aesthetics or the sense of delight, which becomes the essence of life. His way of thinking might not be logical, deductive or inductive but intuitive, associative and analogical. He has exercised great influence on forming and molding national character and social behavior, and given guidance to public and private life.

Seventy-five Nobel Prize winners who gathered together at Paris in 1988 made a statement to the effect that mankind should seek wisdom from Confucius if they wished to live a peaceful and happy life in the 21st century. What is the wisdom of Confucius? It consists in the maxim saying, "Do not do to others what you would not have others do to you." There is a similar maxim in the *Bible*, saying, "Do to others what you would have others do to you" or "Do as you would be done by." What is the difference between these two maxims? The Biblical maxim is positive, while the Confucian is negative. For instance, in the Middle Ages, religious wars between the Catholics and the Protestants lasted for long, long years, because the Catholics believed in Catholicism and the Protestants in Protestantism, the former called the latter pagans and would put some of them to death. Here we see the influence of this Biblical maxim. As the Catholics believed in Catholicism and would have the Protestants believe in Catholicism too, so war broke out. On the other hand, in ancient China Confucianism co-existed with Buddhism and Taoism peacefully for thousands of years, because Chinese emperors would not convert Buddhists nor Taoists into Confucians, so no religious war ever broke out in China. Here we see the influence of this Confucian maxim and the wisdom of Confucius.

Confucius was a great master in ancient China. He taught his disciples to be good men. What was a good man?

Preface

It is said in this book that a good man should cultivate and develop five qualities, that is, reverence, lenience, confidence, diligence and benevolence. What do they mean? It is meant by reverence that a man should respect others as himself; by lenience one should understand and tolerate others; by confidence one should believe in others and be trustworthy; by diligence one should be devoted to others heart and soul; and by benevolence one should do good to others. In a word, a good man should do to others what he would do to himself and would not force others to do what they will not.

Confucius also taught his disciples ritual and music. Ritual would bring order and music would afford delight; ritual imitated the order of the universe and music the harmony of nature. It would be interesting to compare Confucius with Plato in their teachings. Plato said in his *Republic* that every young man should receive physical and musical education. Here we see both Confucius and Plato thought it necessary to be educated in music, but Confucius lay emphasis on ritual service and Plato on physical education. If music could make man wise, then ritual would make men good and keep society in order, and physical education would make men strong and brave. Here we see the difference between the two sages: one emphasized ritual and order and the other strength and bravery.

Plato's philosophy reflects the views of Homer's epics *Iliad* and *Odyssey*: the one extols the strength and bravery of Achilles and Hector, while the other extols the intellect and wisdom of Ulysses. Hector's heroism is typically illustrated by the following verse:

Where heroes war, the foremost place I claim.

The first in danger as the first in fame.

But Confucius did not approve the bravery of his disciples. For instance, when Zi Lu said, "If I were entrusted with a state of a thousand war chariots, though situated among big powers and invaded by hostile armies, I would teach its people to be courageous by the end of three years." Confucius laughed at him to show his disapproval of his rash courage.

The disciple whom Confucius appreciated most was Yan Hui who was so wise as to be able to infer ten things from one, so eager to learn as not to commit the same mistake again, and so contented as not to complain of the humble life with only a handful of rice to eat and a gourdful of water to drink. How could he be happy in poverty? As said in the beginning of this book, it is a delight to acquire knowledge and put it into practice. Yan Hui is an example to show delight in learning could make a man forget hunger and neglect sorrow and not perceive the coming of old age. Thus we may say the basic feeling in Confucian philosophy is delight. As said in this book, it is good to know truth, better to love it and best to delight in it. Here we can see wisdom in the sense of delight. How can delight yield wisdom? Confucius said, "A man may be inspired by poetry, established by rites and perfected by music." So we may say poetry, rites and music would combine to make a man wise. And Confucius said, "The wise are free from doubt, the good from worry and the brave from fear." He approved the wise and the good, but not the strong and the brave, with the result that wise good men are more highly honored in China than brave strong men.

In the West, it is said in the Bible that God created Adam and Eve, but drove them out of the Garden of Eden because they had eaten of the forbidden fruit of Wisdom, that is to say, God did not approve man and woman to be wise, and man and woman had a sense of sin for they had done what God forbade them to do. Plato also said in his *Republic* that poets should be driven out of the Republic, this shows that the Greek philosopher did not approve wise poets either. When religion and philosophy joined hands to banish the wise, wisdom fell into the hands of the clergymen.

If the clergymen believed in one sect of religion, they would deem it a sin to be a pagan and would burn him alive for he had sinned against God. When wisdom yielded its place to strength and violence, war broke out, followed by the dark ages. What is more, religious wars turned into Crusades against another religion. It was not until the Renaissance that the West, awakened from the sense of sin, began to enjoy the forbidden fruit of wisdom and rebuild Western countries into big powers.

In the East, the Han emperors worshipped Confucius and Confucian philosophy almost became national religion. As Confucius preached against monstrosities, violence, disorder and divinities, there was no religious war in Chinese history, and China became the most civilized country in the world from the first century down to 1820 when China's GDP was the highest (30%) in the world. If the preaching of Confucius could be put into practice in the West as in the East, then the world would become more civilized and peaceful. If all the world preached and practised against violence and disorder, then even the conflicting sides in the world could be reconciled. That is the reason, I think, why the seventy-five Nobel Prize winners would seek wisdom from Confucius to put the world in good order.

PREFACE

On the other hand, Confucius had his weakness. As a result of his disapproval of strong men and brave men, heroes were not so highly honored as sages in China and the country weakened for lack of strong and brave men. That is one of the reasons why the country was often invaded by barbarian tribes from within and without and became a semi-colony during the first half of the 20th century. In order to become strong, China should honor heroism as the West does. Confucianism should be modernized to make the people wise, good and brave, then mankind would live a happy, peaceful life in the 21st century.

Superior and alone, Confucius stood,
Who taught that useful science, to be good. —*A. Pope*

Xu Yuanchong
April 10, 2005

CHAPTER I

Chapter I

1.1. Is it not a delight, said the Master, to acquire knowledge and put it into practice? Is it not a pleasure to meet friends coming from afar? Is he not an intelligentleman, who is careless alike of being known or unknown?

1.2. Few who respect their parents and their elders, said Master You, would do anything against their superiors. None who do nothing against their superiors would rise in revolt. An intelligentleman should be fundamentally good. A fundamentally good man will behave in the right way. Respect for one's parents and elder brothers is the fundamental quality for a good man.

1.3. A good man, said the Master, would rarely say what he does not believe, or pretend to appear better than he is.

1.4. I ask myself, said Master Zeng, three questions everyday. In dealing with others, have I not thought of their interests? In making friends, have my deeds not agreed with my words? In teaching students, have I not put into practice what I teach them?

1. 5. In a country of a thousand war-chariots, said the Master, the ruler should be respectful in deed and faithful in word, thrifty in expenditure and affectionate towards the people and tell them to labor at the proper times of the year.

1. 6. A young man, said the Master, should be filial at home and respectful abroad, cautious and trustworthy, affectionate towards all and intimate with the good. If he has time to spare when his duties are done, he may use it to learn arts.

1. 7. If a man, said Zi Xia, loves virtue above beauty, does his best to serve his parents, devotes his life to the service of the prince and keeps his words in making friends, though he is not learned as people may say, I will say he is cultured.

1. 8. An intelligentleman, said the Master, should not be frivolous, or he would lack solemnity in his behavior and solidity in his learning. He should be truthful and faithful, and befriend his equals. He should not be afraid of admitting and amending his faults.

1. 9. If a ruler regrets the death of his parents, said Master Zeng, and never forgets his ancestors, then people would follow him in doing good.

1.10. Zi You said to Zi Gong, "When our Master comes to a country, he would make inquiry into the way how the state is governed. Is the inquiry made on invitation or on his own initiative?" Zi Gong said, "Our Master makes inquiry in a good way, moderate and temperate, modest and humble. Is it not different from other ways of inquiry? What matters if it is made on invitation or on his own initiative?"

1.11. Judge a man by what he will do to his father who is alive, said the Master, and by what he has done to his father who is dead. A son who does not alter his father's ways three years after the father's death may be called filial.

1.12. In performing the rites, said Master You, propriety is important. That is the fair way how former kings dealt with matters great or small. But it will not do to observe propriety without the regulation of the rites.

1.13. If you make a promise, said Master You, in accordance with what is right, your promise can be carried out. If you respect a man in accordance with the rites, you will be far from dishonor. If you are not discredited by your kin, you will be reliable.

1.14. An intelligentleman, said the Master, eats to live, and not lives to eat. He may dwell in comfort, but not seek comfort in dwelling. He should be prompt in action and cautious in speech. He should seek good company and amend his faults. Such a man may be said to be good at learning.

1.15. Zi Gong said. "What do you think of a poor man who does not flatter and a rich man who does not swagger?" The Master said, "Not bad, but not so good as a poor man who is cheerful and a rich man who is respectful." Zi Gong said, "Are such men *like polished ivory and stone and jade refined*, as said in the *Book of Poetry*?" The Master said, "My dear Zi Gong, now I may begin to talk with you about *Poetry*. For when I told you about the past, you can anticipate the future."

1.16. I care less, said the Master, to be understood and recognized by other people than to understand and recognize others.

CHAPTER II

2.1. A prince, said the Master, should rule his state by virtue as the polar star which keeps its place among the stars turning around it.

2.2. There are three hundred poems in the *Book of Poetry*, said the Master. In a word, there is nothing improper.

2.3. If the people are governed by laws, said the Master, and order is kept by punishment, they would be obedient but not conscientious. If they are led by virtue and order is kept by the rites, they would be conscientious and act in agreement with what is right.

2.4. At fifteen, said the Master, I was fond of learning. At thirty, I was established. At forty, I did not waver. At fifty, I knew my sacred mission. At sixty, I had a discerning ear. At seventy, I could do what I would without going beyond what is right.

2.5. When Meng Yi Zi asked about filial duty, the Master said, "Do nothing in disagreement with the rites." When Fan Chi was driving his carriage for him, the Master told him how he answered the question of Meng Yi Zi. When Fan Chi asked for an explanation, the Master said, "Parents should be served in agreement with the rites while alive; when dead, they should be buried and the sacrifice be offered in agreement with the rites."

2.6. When the son of Meng Yi Zi asked about filial duty, the Master said, "Do not let your parents worry about their health!"

2.7. When Zi You asked about filial duty, the Master said, "Filial sons of today only take care their parents are well fed. But even dogs and horses are well fed now. What is the difference if their parents are fed without reverence?"

2.8. When Zi Xia asked about filial duty, the Master said, "It is difficult to appear happy in trouble. If the young serve the old and feed them with wine and food before themselves, but with troubled looks, could they be called filial sons?"

2.9. When I talked with Yan Hui all day long, said the Master, he never disagreed with me as if he were stupid. When he retired to do his work all by himself, I found nothing in disagreement with my teaching. Hui is not stupid at all.

2.10. See what a man does, said the Master, examine why he has done so, and observe whether he is content. Can his character remain hidden? Can it remain hidden?

2.11. One who can learn something new while reviewing what he has learned, said the Master, is fit to be a teacher.

2.12. An intelligentleman, said the Master, is not a mere implement.

2.13. When Zi Gong asked about the intelligentleman, the Master said, "One whose deeds precede his words."

2.14. An intelligentleman, said the Master, cares for the whole more than for the parts, while an uncultured man cares for the parts rather than for the whole.

2.15. To learn without thinking, said the Master, risks to be blind, while to think without learning risks to be impractical.

2.16. To antagonize a different view, said the Master, would reveal one's own weakness.

2.17. Shall I teach you what knowledge is? said the Master to Zi Lu, to admit what you know and what you do not know, that is knowledge.

2.18. When Zi Zhang asked about official emolument, the Master said, "Hear much and put aside what is doubtful, and be cautious in speaking of the rest, then you would be less to blame. See much and put aside what is risky, and be cautious in doing the rest, then you would regret the less. If your words are seldom blamed and your deeds seldom regretful, then you need not worry about official emolument."

2.19. When Duke Ai asked how to win the support of the people, the Master replied, "If honest men are employed and dishonest ones discarded, then people will support you. If dishonest men replace the honest, you will lose the support of the people."

2.20. When Ji Kang Zi asked how the people could be induced to be respectful and faithful, the Master replied, "If you maintain dignity, people will respect you. If you are dutiful towards your parents and kind towards all, they will have faith in you. If the worthy are employed and the incompetent are trained, they will be induced to be respectful and faithful."

2.21. When asked why he is not occupied with state affairs, Confucius answered, "It is said in the *Book of History* about filial duty that respect for parents and fraternity towards brothers are family affairs. If these are practised in the state towards the old and the young, it is state affair. Thus engaged in family affairs, am I not occupied with state affairs too?"

2.22. How can an untrustworthy man be employed? said the Master. Could a large cart go without a yoke-bar or small cart without a cross-bar?

2.23. When Zi Zhang asked if the ritual systems of ten generations to come could be foreseen, the Master said, "The Yin dynasty followed and modified the ritual system of the Xia, and its modified system was known. The Zhou dynasty followed and altered the ritual system of the Yin, and its altered system is also known. So we may predict the system of the successors of the Zhou can be foreseen even a hundred generations later."

2.24. To worship other ancestors than one's own, said the Master, reveals pretentious. Not to right the wrong shows the lack of courage.

CHAPTER III

3.1. Confucius said of the lord of Ji Family, "The royal dance of eight teams are performed in his courtyard. If this can be tolerated, what cannot?"

3.2. At the end of the Three Families' sacrifice, King Wu's prayer to King Wen was sung: "*The princes at the side Of the king dignified,*" The Master said, "What has the royal prayer to do with the Three Families? How could it be sung in their hall?"

3.3. If a man is not good, said the Master, what is the use for him to perform the rites? If a man is not good, what is the use for him to perform music?

3.4. Lin Fang asked about the fundamental of the rites. "A significant question!" said the Master. "In ritual performance, it would be better to be thrift than lavish; in mourning service, it would be better to be deep in grief than minute in observance."

3.5. The barbarian tribe with a sovereign, said the Master, is not so good as a civilized state without one.

3.6. The lord of Ji Family was going to perform the royal ceremony of sacrifice to Mount Tai. The Master asked Ran You if he could prevent it, and Ran You

CHAPTER III

answered he could not. Then the Master said, "Alas! does Mount Tai not know what Lin Fang does about the rites?" (Could it accept the royal sacrifice offered not by a prince but by a lord?)

3.7. Cultured men do not contest, said the Master. Even in archery, the archers bow and make way for each other before the contest and drink after it. Such is the rivalry between cultured men.

3.8. Zi Xia asked about the meaning of the following verse: "*Ah! Dark on white her speaking eyes, Her cheeks with smiles and dimples glow. Colored designs are made on plain silk.*" The Master said, "Colors should be put on the plain ground." Zi Xia asked if the rites should be performed on some ground. The Master said, "It is Zi Xia who understands me. Now I have someone with whom to talk about poetry."

3.9. The rites of the Xia dynasty, said the Master, can be described, but I do not rely on the evidence supplied by its descendants of Qi. The rites of the Yin dynasty can be described, but I do not rely on the evidence supplied by its descendants of Song. For there are no sufficient documents. Otherwise, the rites of Qi and Song can be described.

3.10. At the ancestral sacrificial service of the Duke of Lu, said the Master, I would not attend after the libation, for the royal ceremony should not be performed by a duke.

3.11. Asked about the imperial sacrifice, the Master said, "I do not know it. Those who know it may see an empire as clearly as his palm."

3.12. Sacrifice to the dead as if they were living, and to the divinities as if they were present. If I do not think they are present, said the Master, I had better not sacrifice at all.

3.13. Wangsun Jia asked if it would be better to pray to home divinities than to those in Heaven. "No," said the Master, " if you sin against Heaven, what is the use of praying?"

3.14. The Zhou dynasty, said the Master, has profited from the two preceding dynasties. What a wealth of culture it has accumulated! I would rather follow the Zhou system.

3.15. When the Master entered the grand temple, he asked about everything there. Someone remarked, "Who would say this son of a villager from Zou knows the rites? When he entered the grand temple, he asked about everything." Hearing of this, the Master said, "This is just a part of the rites."

3.16. In archery, said the Master, the principal thing is to hit, not to pierce through. Such is the way of the ancients. For archers are not equal in strength.

3.17. Zi Gong wanted to do away with the sacrificial sheep on the first day of each moon. The Master said, "Zi Gong, you care for a sheep while I care for the rites."

3.18. One who serves his prince nowadays in strict accordance with the rites, said the Master, would be considered as a sycophant.

3.19. When Duke Ding asked how a prince should employ his ministers and how ministers should serve their prince, Confucius replied, "The prince should employ his ministers in accordance with the rites and the ministers should be devoted to the prince."

3.20. *Cooing and Wooing* (the first song in the *Book of Poetry*), said the Master, tells us pleasure and grief should not go to excess.

3.21. When Duke Ai asked Zai Wo what symbol was used in the altar, Zai Wo replied, "The Xia rulers used the pine, the Yin rulers used the cypress, and the Zhou rulers used the chestnut, which means to chase the people off their nut." Hearing of this, the Master said, "What is done cannot be undone; what is accomplished need not be criticized, what is bygone need not be blamed."

3.22. The Master said, "Guan Zhong was not a great

minister." When asked if Guan Zhong was frugal, the Master said, "Guan Zhong had three granaries while his official duties were not performed, how could he be considered frugal?" When asked if Guan Zhong knew the rites, the Master said, "Only the prince may build a wall to screen the gate of his mansion, but Guan Zhong had one before his. Only the prince may use a stand for cups to entertain his guests, but Guan Zhong used one. If he knew the rites, who does not?"

3.23. Talking about music with the great master of the State of Lu, the Master said, "It is not difficult to perform music. In the beginning all the musical instruments should be played in high spirit. Then the music should be harmonious, distinct and flowing without breaking up to the end."

3.24. The guardian of the border at Yi asked to be presented to the Master, saying, "When a man of renown has come here, I have never been denied an interview." A follower of the Master presented him. After the interview, he said to two or three of the followers, "Why are you distressed at your master's unemployment? The world has gone out of the right way for long. Heaven would employ your master as an alarm bell."

3.25. The Master said of the Inauguration Music as perfectly beautiful and perfectly good, and the Martial Dance as perfectly beautiful but not perfectly good.

3.26. High office filled without generosity, said the Master, ceremony performed without reverence, and mourning observed without grief, how can I bear to see such things!

CHAPTER IV

Chapter IV

4.1. Good neighborhood, said the Master, adds beauty to life. If a man does not choose good neighborhood, how can he be called wise?

4.2. A man without virtue, said the Master, cannot endure adversity nor enjoy prosperity for long. A good man is content to be good; a wise man knows it pays to be good.

4.3. Only a benevolent man, said the Master, can love the good and dislike the wrong.

4.4. If a man, said the Master, has made up his mind to be good, he will do no wrong.

4.5. Wealth and rank, said the Master, are what men desire. If they could be attained only in an improper way, they should be relinquished. Poverty and obscurity are what men dislike, if they could be avoided only in an improper way, they should be endured. If a man had no virtue, how could he be worthy of his fame? A cultured man cannot do anything contrary to virtue even for the shortest time of a meal. He must do nothing contrary to virtue even in haste or in distress.

4.6. I have not seen anyone, said the Master, who really loves virtue and abhors vice. If one really loves virtue, how could anyone else be better than he? If one abhors vice, it is because he is afraid that vice would do harm to him. Is there anyone who has practised virtue with all his might all the day long? I have not seen one. Perhaps there are some, but I have seen none.

4.7. A man's faults, said the Master, may reveal what kind of man he is. A man may be judged by his faults.

4.8. If a man knows in the morning the right way of living, said the Master, he may die in the evening without regret.

4.9. If an intellectual, said the Master, has made up his mind to find out the right way of life but feels ashamed of plain clothes and plain food, I do not think he is worth talking with.

4.10. A cultured man, said the Master, does not set his heart for or against anything in the world. He only does what is right.

4.11. A cultured man cares for virtue, said the Master, and an uncultured man for the land. The former cares for order and the latter for favor.

4.12. Those who do everything only in their own interest, said the Master, would arouse discontent.

Chapter IV

4.13. If a country can be governed, said the Master, in accordance with the ritual system, what more need I to say? If not, what is the use of the ritual system?

4.14. Be more concerned, said the Master, with your mission than your position. Fear not that you are unknown, but that you are unworthy to be known.

4.15. The Master said, "Shen, you know how my principles can be simplified." Master Zeng Shen answered, "Yes." When the Master was out, other disciples asked what the Master meant. Master Zeng said, "Our Master's principles can be simplified into loyalty and leniency."

4.16. A cultured man cares for what is proper and fit while an uncultured man cares for the profit.

4.17. When you see a man better than you, said the Master, you should try to equal him. When you see a man doing wrong, you should ask yourself if you have done the same.

4.18. In serving one's parents, said the Master, one may make remonstrance. If it is rejected, the son should show no discontent, but resume an attitude of deference and reiterate his remonstrance without complaint.

4.19. When father and mother are alive, said the Master, a good son should not go afar. If he does, they should be informed where he is going.

4.20. A son, said the Master, who does not alter his father's ways three years after his death may be called filial.

4.21. The age of one's parents, said the Master, should not be forgotten. Old age may bring comfort on the one hand and worry on the other.

4.22. The ancients, said the Master, would not say what they could do, for they would be ashamed if their deeds disagreed with their words.

4.23. Few would make mistakes, said the Master, who could control themselves in accordance with the rules of propriety.

4.24. A cultured man, said the Master, may be slow in word but prompt in deed.

4.25. A good man never feels lonely, said the Master, good neighbors will come up to him.

4.26. Zi You said, "Repetition of remonstrances would lead to loss of favor in the service of a prince, and to estrangement in friendship."

CHAPTER V

5.1. The Master said, "Gongye Chang might be a good husband, though he was once put in jail, but it was not through his fault." And the Master married his daughter to him.

5.2. The Master said, "Nan Rong would not be unemployed in a well-governed country, nor would he be punished in an ill governed one." And the Master married his niece to him.

5.3. Zi jian, said the Master, is a cultured man. If there were no cultured men in the state of Lu, how could he have learned to be one?

5.4. Zi Gong asked the Master, "What do you think of me, sir?" The Master said, "You are a vessel." Zi Gong said, "What sort of vessel?" The Master said, "The best jade vessel for food, used in ancestral sacrifice."

5.5. Someone said, "Yong is virtuous, but he is not eloquent." The Master said, "What is the use of eloquence? Eloquence to the point of imposition would often cause disgust. I do not know whether Yong is virtuous. But what is use of his being eloquent?"

5.6. The Master asked Qidiao Kai to serve as an officer. Qidiao Kai replied, "I am not sure how I can fulfill an office." The Master was pleased.

5.7. The Master said, "If the truth I preach were not followed, I would float on the sea by a raft, who would then follow me but Zi Lu?" On hearing of this, Zi Lu was glad. Then the Master said, "Zi Lu is more courageous than I, but I am afraid his courage is reckless."

5.8. Meng Wu asked whether Zi Lu was a man of men. The Master said, "I do not know." When asked again, he said, "In a country of a thousand chariots, Zi Lu might serve in the military field, but I do not know how he could be a man of men." When asked about Ran Qiu, the Master said, "In a city of a thousand families or a baronial house of a hundred chariots, Qiu might serve as an administrator, but I do not know how he could be a man of men." When asked about Gongxi Chi, the Master said, "Standing at court with a sash around the waist, Chi might serve in the intercourse with honorable guests, but I do not know how he could be a man of men."

5.9. The Master asked Zi Gong, "Which one do you think is better, you or Yan Hui?" Zi Gong replied, "How can I compare with Hui? He may infer ten from one, while I can only infer two." The Master said, "You cannot match with him. Neither you nor I can match with him."

5.10. Zai Yu often slept by day. The Master said, "Rotten wood cannot be carved; a wall of dried dung cannot be whitewashed. What is the use of my blaming him?" Again the Master said, "At first when I dealt with people, I listened to what they said and believed they would do likewise. Now when I deal with people, I will not only listen to what they say but also see what they do. It is from Zai Yu that I have learned to make this change."

5.11. The Master said, "I have never seen a man steady and strong." When Shen Chang was mentioned, the Master said, "Chang is at the mercy of his desires. How could he be steady and strong?"

5.12. Zi Gong said, "What I would not have others do to me, I would not do to them." The Master said, "Zi Gong, you have not yet attained to that."

5.13. Zi Gong said, "We may have heard our Master's views on culture, but not on human nature and divine law."

5.14. Zi Lu would put into practice what he had learned, otherwise, he would not learn anything more.

5.15. When Zi Gong asked why Kong Wen Zi was called

a civilized man, the Master said, "He was curious and fond of learning and not ashamed to learn from his inferiors, so he was called a civilized man."

5.16. The Master said of Zi Chan, "He is a cultured man in four respects: modest in his conduct, respectful in serving his superiors, beneficial to the people and just in employing his inferiors."

5.17. Yan Pingzhong, said the Master, knows how to make friends. The longer their friendship lasts, the more they respect him.

5.18. Zang Wenzhong, said the Master, kept a divine tortoise in a hall with hill patterns on its pillars and duckweed patterns on its beams. What did he know of the rites?

5.19. Zi Zhang asked what the Master would say of Zi Wen who was not overdelighted when thrice appointed minister, and not disappointed when thrice deposed, and who informed his successors how he had governed the state. The Master said, "He was loyal." When asked whether he was a man of men, the Master said, "I do not know how he could be a man of men." Zi Zhang said, "When Cui Zi murdered the prince of Qi, Chen Wen Zi who had a fief of ten chariots gave it up and left for another state. Arrived there, he said the ruler was as bad as

Cui Zi, and left for a third. Arrived there, he said the same and left it again. What would you say of him?" The Master said, "He is free from blame." When asked whether he was a man of men, the Master said, "I do not know how he could be a man of men."

5.20. Ji Wen Zi would not take action until he thought it over thrice. Hearing of this, the Master said, "Twice is enough."

5.21. Ning Wu Zi, said the Master, showed wisdom when the country was well governed, but pretended to be dull when it was ill governed. His wisdom may be equalled, but not his dullness.

5.22. Why not return? said the Master in the State of Chen, why not return? The youth in my own country are thoughtless and careless, but they write well. How can I leave them uneducated?

5.23. Bo Yi and Shu Qi, said the Master, who would not accede to the trone, bore no old grudge, so few bore a grudge against them.

5.24. Who says Wei Shenggao is honest? said the Master. Someone asked him for vinegar, he begged it from his neighbor and then gave it as his own.

5.25. Flowery words, hypocritical deeds, excessive respect, said the Master, are shameful in the eyes of Zuo

Chapter V

Qiuming, so are they in mine. To befriend those whom one resents is shameful in the eyes of Zuo Qiuming, so is it in mine.

5.26. The Master said to Yan Yuan and Zi Lu in attendance, "Will each of you tell me what you wish?" Zi Lu said, "I would have carriage and horses, clothes and fur dress to share with my friends till these things are outworn, and I would feel no regret." Yan Hui said, "I would not show the good I have done nor the trouble I have taken for others." Zi Lu asked what the Master's wish was. The Master said, "I would comfort the old, be trusted by my friends and be loved by the young."

5.27. In vain, said the Master, have I looked for one who could find out his own faults and blame himself.

5.28. In a hamlet of ten houses, said the Master, there must be someone as faithful and as trustworthy as I am, but he may not be so fond of learning.

CHAPTER VI

Chapter VI

6.1. Ran Yong, said the Master, might be made a leader setting his face to the south.

6.2. When Ran Yong asked about Master Zi Sang Bo, the Master said, "He will do, for he is lenient." Ran Yong said, "Severe with oneself and lenient with others, one may become a good ruler. Lenient with oneself as with others, will one not become negligent?" The Master said, "Yong, you are right."

6.3. Duke Ai of Lu asked Confucius, "Which of your disciples are eager to learn?" Confucius said, "There was Yan Hui who was eager to learn. He did not shift the blame on to others, nor would he make the same mistake again. But it was a pity that he died early. Now there is none like him. I have never again heard of anyone so eager to learn."

6.4. When Gongxi Hua was sent on a mission to the state of Qi, Ran You requested grain for Gongxi's mother. The Master said, "Give her a measure." Ran You asked for more. The Master said, "Give her two measures." But Ran You gave her ten measures. The Master said, "When Gongxi Hua went to Qi, he drove sleek horses and wore light furs. I have heard that a cultured man will help those in need but not those who are rich."

6.5. Yuan Si, when made a governor, was given a salary of nine hundred litres of grain, but he declined. The Master said, "Do not decline it. Why not share it with your neighbors, villagers and townsfolk?"

6.6. Would mountain gods and river gods, said the Master, reject the sacrifice of a calf because it is brindled and horned?

6.7. Yan Hui, said the Master, would not do anything against humanism for three months on end. Others may do so, but only for a day or at most for a month.

6.8. When Ji Kang Zi asked whether Zi Lu was fit to be employed as an officer, the Master said, "Zi Lu is courageous. Why can he not be employed as an officer?" When asked about Zi Gong, the Master gave the same reply because Zi Gong was efficient. When asked about Ran Qiu, the Master said the same again because Ran Qiu was versatile.

6.9. When the usurper sent to ask Min Zi Qian to be governor of Fei, Min said, "Would you please decline that office for me? If anyone should come again, I would go far, far beyond the River Wen."

6.10. When Bo Niu was ill, the Master went to inquire

after him. Grasping his hand through the window, the Master said, "It is all over. Alas! it is fatal for such a good man to have such a fatal illness. Such a good man should have such a fatal illness."

6.11. How good Yan Hui was, said the Master, living in a humble lane with only a handful of rice to eat and a gourdful of water to drink! Others could not bear such a wretched life, but Yan Hui was as happy as ever. How good Yan Hui was!

6.12. Ran Qiu said, "It is not that I am not delighted to follow your way, but that I lack the power." The Master said, "Those who lack power may stop on the midway, but you have not yet started."

6.13. The Master said to Zi Xia, "You should be an intellectual of the higher class, not one of the lower class."

6.14. When Zi You was governor of the town of Wu, the Master asked him whether he had got any helping hand. Zi You answered, "There is Tantai Mieming who never takes a shortcut in walking and never comes to my office unless on business."

6.15. Meng Zi Fan, said the Master, was no boaster. Once defeated, he was the last to retreat. Whipping up his horse near the city gate, he said, "I am the last to retreat, not because I am brave, but because my horse is slow."

6.16. Without the eloquence of the priest Tuo, said the Master, and the beauty of Prince Chao of Song, it would be hard to get through with the world of today.

6.17. Who, said the Master, could go out but by the door? Why not go this way?

6.18. More natural than cultured, said the Master, one would appear rustic. More cultured than natural, one would appear artificial. An intelligentleman should appear both cultured and natural.

6.19. A man should live an honest life, said the Master. It is by luck that a dishonest man can escape punishment.

6.20. To know the truth is good, said the Master, to love it is better, and to delight in it is best. (To understand is good, to enjoy is better and to delight is best.)

6.21. We may talk about what goes beyond the understanding of the average, said the Master, with those who are above mediocrity, not with those who are below.

6.22. When Fan Chi asked about wisdom, the Master said, "A wise man should do what is good for the people, respect spiritual beings and keep away from them." When asked about a good man, the Master said, "A good man will do hard work before he reaps. So may he be called a good man."

6.23. The wise, said the Master, delight in water while the good delight in mountains. The wise love mobility while the good love tranquillity. The wise live happy while the good live long.

6.24. After reformation, said the Master, the strong state of Qi might advance to a moral state, and the moral state of Lu might advance to an ideal state.

6.25. The wine cup, said the Master, looks unlike a cup. Can it be called a cup? Can it be called a cup?

6.26. Zai Wo asked whether a good man, when told another man was fallen into a well, should go down after him. The Master said, "Why should he go down? A good man might be told to go near the well, but not to go into it. He might be deceived, but not befooled."

6.27. A cultured man, said the Master, if wide read in literature and restrained by the rites, would not overstep what is right.

6.28. When Zi Lu was displeased with the Master's visit to the beautiful but ill-famed Princess Nan Zi, the Master swore, "If I had done anything wrong, may Heaven reject me! May Heaven reject me!"

6.29. How useful is the Golden Middle Way! said the Master. It is the highest virtue, but it has not been followed for a long time.

6.30. Zi Gong asked whether it could be called virtue to do good to people and benefit them. The Master said, It is more than virtue; it is the accomplishment of a sage. Even the earliest emperors could not boast of such accomplishment. What is virtue? To establish others as you would establish yourself, and help others to develop as you would help yourself to. To judge of others by what is in yourself, that is the way towards virtue.

CHAPTER VII

7.1. I narrate, said the Master, but not create. I believe and delight in the ancients, and make bold to compare myself to the Old Master.

7.2. If I can learn by heart, said the Master, not tired of learning nor of teaching, what more shall I need?

7.3. Virtue uncultivated, said the Master, knowledge unpropagated, the right undone, and the wrong unrighted, these are my worries.

7.4. Unoccupied, the Master took it easy and looked pleased.

7.5. How decrepit have I grown! said the Master. For long have I not dreamed of the sage.

7.6. Aim at truth, said the Master, depend on virtue, rely on the good and delight in the arts.

7.7. I would teach, said the Master, any student above fifteen who would bring me a bundle of dried flesh.

7.8. I will not instruct. said the Master, those who are not eager to learn, nor enlighten those who are not anxious to discover. If I show a man one corner of the table and he cannot infer the other three, I will not repeat the lesson.

CHAPTER VII

7.9. Taking a meal by the side of a mourner, the Master would never eat to the full.

7.10. The Master would not sing after he had wept at a funeral.

7.11. The Master said to Yan Hui, "Ride when employed and hide when unemployed, that is what you and I would do." Zi Lu asked the Master, "Who would you employ if you were in command of three armies?" The Master said, "I would not employ one who would fight a tiger with bare hands or cross a river with broken legs and die without regret and remorse. I would employ one considerate when confronted with difficulties, and deliberate when accomplishing a task."

7.12. If wealth is attainable, said the Master, I would condescend to be a gate-keeper of the market. With wealth unattainable, I would do what I like.

7.13. The Master was cautious before the sacrifice, in war and in sickness.

7.14. Hearing the music of succession in Qi, the Master did not know the taste of meat for three months, saying, "I did not realize that music could have been so delicious,"

7.15. Ran You said, "Is our Master on the side of the Prince of Wei who contended for the throne with his father?" Zi Gong said, "I do not know. I will ask him." Coming in, he asked the Master, "What do you think of the two Yin brothers who yielded the crown?" The Master said, "They were two worthy ancients." Zi Gong asked, "Did they regret?" The Master said, "They sought to be worthy men. Why should they regret?" Coming out, Zi Gong said, "Our Master is not on the side of the Prince."

7.16. There is delight, said the Master, in plain food and water while pillowing the head on the arm. I would keep ill-gotten wealth and rank as far away as floating cloud.

7.17. Give me a few more years, said the Master, to study the *Book of Change* after fifty, I may be free from error.

7.18. The Master used fine language in reading *Poetry* and *History*, and in performing the rites. All these are written in fine language.

7.19. The Duke of She asked Zi Lu about Confucius. Zi Lu made no reply. Then the Master said, "Why did you not tell him that I am a man who forgets his hunger while thirsty for knowledge, and neglects his sorrow while drowned in delight so as not to perceive the coming of old age?"

7.20. I was not born with innate knowledge, said the

Chapter VII

Master. Fond of history, I am eager in pursuit of the experience accumulated in it.

7.21. The Master never talked of monstrosity, violence, disturbance and divinity.

7.22. When three men walk together, said the Master, there must be one worthy to be my teacher. I will choose what is good in him to follow, and avoid what is not good.

7.23. I have the innate virtue in me, said the Master. What have I to fear for the Minister of War?

7.24. Two or three of you, said the Master, may think I have secret from you. In fact, I have no secret at all. I have done nothing which I should keep secret from you. Otherwise, how could I be myself?

7.25. The Master taught four things: culture, conduct, faithfulness and trustworthiness.

7.26. I cannot hope, said the Master, to see a sage, but only a cultured man, nor can I hope to see a man of men, but only a consistent one. A consistent man will not take nothing for something, nor the empty for the full, nor the poor for the rich. Otherwise, he cannot be called a consistent man.

7.27. The Master fished with a line, but not with a net. He shot at birds, but not at roosting ones.

7.28. There are those, said the Master, who do what they do not understand. but I am not among the number. I would learn again and again and choose and follow what is good and bear it in mind. Knowledge acquired is only next to innate gift.

7.29. The people of Hu Village were difficult to approach. One day when a young man of Hu Village came for an interview with the Master, the disciples doubted whether he should be accepted. The Master said, "When a man comes forward, he is welcome. When he retrogrades, we should not go backwards with him. Be not too particular! A purified man is acceptable. Let bygones be bygones!"

7.30. Are we far from benevolence? said the Master. If we wish to be benevolent, then benevolence is within our reach.

7.31. When the Minister of Crime of the State of Chen asked whether Duke Zhao of Lu knew the ritual system, Confucius answered, "Yes." When Confucius withdrew, the Minister motioned Wuma Qi to come forward and said to him, "I have heard that an intelligentleman should not be partial. How could your Master be partial to Duke Zhao who married a daughter of the same clan but called her a different name? If the Duke knew the ritual system, then who does not?" Wuma Qi told this to the Master, who

CHAPTER VII

said, "How fortunate I am! When I have made a mistake, the people are sure to know it."

7.32. When the Master liked a song, he would make the singer repeat it and then sang it together with him.

7.33. In word, said the Master, perhaps I am no better than others. In deed, I dare not say that I am an accomplished intelligentleman.

7.34. The Master said, "The sage and his benevolence are beyond me. What I claim is only the untiring effort to learn and to teach." Gongxi Hua said, "That is just what we disciples are incapable of."

7.35. When the Master was very ill, Zi Lu asked leave to pray for him. The Master said, "Did the ancients pray?" Zi Lu said, "Yes, it is said in the *Book of Prayer* that we may pray to the divinities above and below." The Master said, "Then I have been praying for a long time."

7.36. Extravagance, said the Master, leads to insubordination, and frugality to obstinacy. But it would be far better to be obstinate than to be insubordinate.

7.37. An intelligentleman, said the Master, is carefree while an uncultured man is careworn.

7.38. The Master was mild but firm, dignified but unaggressive, respectful but equanimous.

CHAPTER VIII

Chapter VIII

8.1. Tai Bo, said the Master, might be said to have the highest virtue, for he had thrice renounced the throne. He was beyond the praise of the people.

8.2. Beyond propriety, said the Master, respect would lead to labor lost, caution to timidity, courage to violence, and even frankness would hurt. If cultured men are affectionate to their kin, then people will be inspired to do good. If old friends are not forgotten, then people will not be negligent.

8.3. When Master Zeng was ill, he summoned his disciples around him and said, "Uncover my feet and uncover my hands! It is said in the *Book of Poetry: 'Be careful as if you did stand On the brink of the gulf of vice Or tread upon the ice!'* From now on, I need not be so careful, my young friends."

8.4. When Master Zeng was ill, Meng Jing Zi came to inquire after him. Master Zeng said, "When a bird is about to die, its song is mournful. When a man is about to die, what he says is good. In performing the rites, a cultured man will pay attention to three things: how to look inoffensive and respectful, appear trustworthy, and be free from vulgarity in speech. As to sacrificial service, he will leave it to officials in charge."

8.5. Master Zeng said, "The capable may consult the incapable, the possessor of much may consult those of little; those who have may appear to have not, those who are full may appear empty; a man may take no care even when he is offended. Such was the way of one of my former friends."

8.6. Master Zeng said, "Is he not an intelligentleman who can be entrusted with a helpless orphan prince and the fate of a state, and who dare to face danger without fear? Yes, he is."

8.7. Master Zeng said, "An intellectual should be strong and steady, for his duty is heavy and his journey will be long. Is it not a heavy duty to be a man of men? Is his journey not long which will not end until his death?"

8.8. A man, said the Master, may be inspired by poetry, established in performing the rites, and perfected by music.

8.9. The common people, said the Master, may be made to follow, but not to understand the reason why.

8.10. If a daring man, said the Master, suffers from poverty, he will disobey the order. If he hates to excess those who are unkind, he will rise in revolt.

CHAPTER VIII

8.11. If a man, said the Master, is arrogant and narrow-minded, what could we learn from him even if he is gifted as the Duke of Zhou?

8.12. It is not easy, said the Master, to find one who has studied for three years without thinking of reward.

8.13. Be firm in belief and fond of learning, said the Master. Do not fear to die for truth. Do not enter a tottering state nor dwell in one in disorder. Appear where truth is followed and disappear where it is not. It is a shame to be poor and dishonored in a well-governed state as to be rich and honored in an ill-governed one.

8.14. Do not interfere, said the Master, into the matter you are not in a position to.

8.15. How pleasant to the ear, said the Master, are the Prelude played by the Music Master of Lu and the Chorus of *Cooing and Wooing*! What a flood of music!

8.16. What can I do, said the Master, with such persons as are proud and not frank, dull and not true, incapable and untrustworthy?

8.17. Be eager to acquire knowledge, said the Master, as if it were beyond reach, as if you were afraid to lose it even when it is acquired.

8.18. How sublime, said the Master, were Emperors Shun

and Yu, who ascended the throne without striving for it!

8.19. How great, said the Master, was Emperor Yao as sovereign of the state! How sublime was he who imitated the boundless Heaven! So majestic was he that people could not find a name for him! How glorious were his achievements! How dazzling was his culture!

8.20. Emperor Shun had five ministers and the empire was well-governed. King Wu said, "I have ten able ministers." Confucius said, "It is difficult to find talents, is it not so? During the Tang and Yu Dynasties, it was particularly true. During the reign of King Wu there was a woman among his ministers, so there were only nine men in his service. King Wen of Zhou had two-thirds of the Realm of Yin, yet he served the Yin Emperor. Zhou may be said to attain the highest point of submission."

8.21. As for Emperor Yu, said the Master, I have nothing to say against him. He took plain food and drink for himself, but offered plentiful sacrifice for the divinities. He wore poor garment but put on magnificent dress in ritual ceremonies. He lived in a humble house but spared no effort to dig ditches and canals for the people. So what can I say against him?

CHAPTER IX

9.1. The Master seldom talked about what was profit or fate or benevolence.

9.2. A villager from Daxiang said, "Great is Confucius! He possesses wide general knowledge but no special knowledge to make a name." Hearing of this, the Master said to his disciples, "What shall I specialize in? In chariot-driving or in archery? I should like to drive a chariot."

9.3. The linen cap, said the Master, is prescribed by the rules of ceremony, but now a silk one is worn. It is economical, and I follow the common practice. Bowing below the hall is prescribed by the rules, but now the common practice is bowing after ascending the hall. It is presumptuous, so I still bow below the hall against the general practice.

9.4. The Master was entirely free from four things, namely, supposition, predetermination, obstination and self-assertion.

9.5. When detained at Kuang, the Master said, "After the death of King Wen. I am entrusted with keeping culture from perishing. If Heaven would destroy culture, how could those who die after King Wen know what culture is. If Heaven would not destroy it, what harm could the people of Kuang do to me?"

9.6. A high officer asked Zi Gong whether his Master was a sage and how he could be so versatile. Zi Gong said that his Master was born a sage, so he was versatile in many arts. Hearing of this, the Master said, "Does the high officer know me? While young, I was poor and humble, so I had to be versatile to earn a living. Does an intelligentleman need to be versatile in arts? No, there is no need."

9.7. It was said by Lao that the Master said, "Not employed as an officer, I had to be versatile in arts."

9.8. Am I endowed with knowledge? said the Master. I am not. When a simpleton came to ask me a question, I was as empty as he was. But when I considered the props and the cons of the question, I got an answer in the end.

9.9. No prodigious phoenix would appear, said the Master, nor would the picturesque portant emerge on the River. What could I do?

9.10. Seeing a man in mourning or in ceremonial dress, or meeting with a blind man, though they were young, the Master would rise. Passing by them, he would quicken his steps.

9.11. Yan Yuan said with a deep sigh, "Looking up, I find our Master high above. Digging into his word, I find it firm down below. His image appears before me, but suddenly it emerges behind. Our Master leads us forward step by step, broadens our mind with culture and regulates our conduct with the rules of propriety. How could I stop learning from him? When I have made the most of my ability, it seems that I could stand, but when I try to follow him, I find myself at a loss far behind."

9.12. When the Master was very ill, Zi Lu asked some disciples to act as official mourners. Convalescent, the Master said, "Zi Lu has deceived me for long. Pretending to have official mourners when I am not qualified to, whom could I deceive? Could I deceive Heaven? Would it be better to die in the hands of official mourners than in those of my disciples? Even if I cannot get an official burial, could I be abandoned by the roadside?"

9.13. Zi Gong said, "If there is a beautiful gem here, should I hide it in a box or sell it to a connoisseur?" The Master said, "Sell it, sell it! I am one waiting for a connoisseur."

9.14. The Master wanted to settle among the nine barbarian tribes. When asked how he could settle among such backward people, the Master said, "How could a place be backward where settled an intelligentleman?"

9.15. Since my return from Wei to Lu, said the Master, I have revised the *Book of Music* and put *Odes* and *Hymns* in their proper place.

9.16. At court, said the Master, I have served the duke and his ministers; at home, my father and elders. I dare not neglect the mourning service, nor am I indulged in wine. What else should I care?

9.17. Standing by a stream, the Master said, "Time passes away night and day like running water."

9.18. I have never seen a man, said the Master, who loves his duty more than beauty.

9.19. If ordered, said the Master, to stop bringing the last basketful of earth to raise a mound, I would stop. If ordered to proceed after bringing the first basketful of earth to level a ground, I would proceed.

9.20. It was only Yan Yuan, said the Master, who would listen to me without getting tired.

9.21. The Master said of the death of Yan Yuan, "Alas! I saw him ever advance, and never stop in his progress."

9.22. There are shoots, said the Master, which spring up but do not flower, and others which flower but do not bear fruit.

9.23. Respect the young, said the Master. How can you foretell they will not do better than you? If they have no achievement at forty or fifty, then you need not be afraid of them.

9.24. Can we not follow, said the Master, the rules of propriety? It is important to change our ways when they are against the rules. Can we not be pleased with good advice? But it is important to analyse it. What can I do with a man pleased without analysis, or following without reform?

9.25. It is essential, said the Master, to be truthful and faithful, to befriend one's equals and be not afraid to admit and amend one's faults. (Cf. 1. 8.)

9.26. The three armies, said the Master, may be deprived of their commander-in-chief, but the common people cannot be deprived of his opinion.

9.27. The Master said, "It is Zi Lu who is not ashamed to stand in rags beside one in furs." Zi Lu recited the following verse all his life long: "*For nothing would he long. Will he do what is wrong?*" The Master said, "The truth contained in this verse is not worth treasuring so much."

9.28. Only in the coldest weather, said the Master, can we realize that the pine and the cypress are the last to lose their leaves.

Chapter IX

9.29. The wise, said the Master, are free from doubt; the good, from worry; and the brave, from fear.

9.30. One who studies together with you, said the Master, may not put what he studies into practice; another who puts it into practice may not get established; and a third who gets established may not share weal and woe with you.

9.31. "*Cherry flowers in view so swift back and forth sway. Do I not think of you? Your house is far away.*" The Master said, "He did not think of his friend, or how can it be so far away?"

CHAPTER X

CHAPTER X

10.1. In his native village Confucius looked simple and unassuming as if he were not fluent. At court or in the ducal ancestral temple he spoke readily and chose his words with care.

10.2. When he talked with his colleagues at court, he spoke freely. With his superiors, he spoke formally with restraint. In the presence of the prince, he spoke respectfully with unease but with self-possession.

10.3. When summoned by the prince in the reception of an honorable guest, he looked solemn, quickened his steps, and saluted his colleagues standing left and right, with his robe evenly adjusted before and behind. He advanced to the guest with his arms like the wings of a bird. When the guest had retired, he would report to the prince, "The guest is gone without looking back."

10.4. Entering the palace gate, he bent his body as if there were no room enough for him to strengthen up. Halting, he never stood in the middle of the gate. Passing by the vacant throne, his face turned solemn, his pace quickened and his words seemed chocked. Ascending the audience hall, he held up the hem of his robe and bent his body as if he dared not breathe. Coming out, he began to relax after descending the first step and appeared relieved. At the bottom of the steps, he quickened his pace with his sleeves like two wings. Regaining his place, he looked respectfully and wary.

10.5. Holding the tablet of jade, he seemed to bend his body under an unbearable weight. Holding it high, he seemed to bow; holding it low, he seemed to offer a gift. His face seemed wary and he went straightforward. Presenting the ritual gift, he looked placid. At the private audience, he looked happy.

10.6. A cultured man does not wear a black-collared dress with grey-hemmed sleeves nor a reddish or purple undress. In hot weather he wears an unlined gown of fine thread loosely woven, but put on an outside garment before going out-of-doors. He wears a black robe over lambskin a white robe of undyed silk over fawn's fur, or a yellow robe over fox's fur. On the fur robe of his undress the right sleeve is shorter than the left. His bedcloth must be half as long again as his body. Thick furs of fox or badger are used as cushions at home. He may wear all his girdle-ornaments after the mourning. His under-garment must be cut short, except his court apron. Black-dyed lambskin and hat must not be worn on a visit of condolence. On the first day of the moon he must go to court in full court dress.

10.7. Before sacrifice, he must wear bathrobe made of lenin cloth. He must change his food and live in another bedroom not together with his wife.

10.8. He did not reject finely cleaned rice or minced meat. He did not eat rice affected by weather or turned sour, nor rotten fish and putrid flesh, nor discolored or bad-smelling meat. He did not eat over-or under-cooked food, nor vegetables out of season or improperly cut, nor meat or food without its proper sauce. He must not eat more meat than rice. There was no limit for wine, but he must not get drunken. He must not buy wine or dried meat in the market. He might eat ginger food, but not much.

10.9. The sacrificial flesh he received from the ducal palace must not be kept overnight. The sacrificial flesh of the family must not be kept over three days, or it is uneatable.

10.10. While eating, he did not talk. In bed, he did not speak.

10.11. Even coarse rice and vegetables may be respectfully offered as sacrificial food.

10.12. He did not sit in improper order.

10.13. He did not leave the villagers' drinking party before the staff-carrying elders left.

10.14. At the villagers' evil-driving ceremony, he put on his court robe and stood on the eastern steps.

10.15. When sending inquiry after a friend in another state, he bowed twice and saw the messenger off.

10.16. When Ji Kang Zi sent him some medicine, he bowed and accepted it, saying, "As I am not acquainted with its properties, I dare not taste it."

10.17. His stable was burned down when he was at court. On his return he asked if anybody was hurt without asking about his horses.

10.18. When the prince sent him food, he would sit in his place and taste it. When undressed meat was sent, he would cook it and offer it to his ancestors. When a live animal was sent, he would rear it. When he attended the prince at a meal while the prince was making a sacrificial offering, he would taste the dishes.

10.19. If he received the prince's visit while ill, he would lie with his head towards the east, his court robe spread over his body and his girdle across his robe.

10.20. When summoned by the prince, he would go at once without waiting for the carriage to be yoked.

10.21. When he entered the Grand Temple, he asked about everything there. (Cf. 3. 15.)

10.22. If a friend died without any relative, he would say, "I will take care of his funeral."

10.23. He would not bow on receiving a gift from a friend, be it a carriage with horses. He would only bow on receiving a sacrificial flesh.

10.24. He would not lie in bed like a corpse nor sit at home like a guest.

10.25. He would change his attitude on seeing a mourner, or a man in sacrificial dress, or a blind man, though they were his friends or in undress. He would bow even in his carriage when he met with a man in mourning dress or on official duty. He would rise with altered facial expression at a sumptuous feast or on hearing sudden thunder or a violent gale.

10.26. He would stand straight in his carriage, holding the cord. He would not turn round, nor speak hastily, nor point with his fingers.

10.27. His face changed color on seeing birds hover and settle. He read the verse: *Hen-pheasants at their prime Know how to bide their time.* Zi Lu made an offering to them, but they sniffed thrice and flew away.

CHAPTER XI

Chapter XI

11.1. The villagers, said the Master, performed ritual and music before townsfolk. So I would employ the villagers in practising ritual and music.

11.2. Those who followed me in the states of Chen and Cai when I was in difficulty, said the Master, are not with me now.

11.3. Among them Yan Yuan, Min Zi Qian, Ran Bo Niu and Zhong Yong were distinguished in virtue; Zai Wo and Zi Gong in eloquence; Ran You and Zi Lu in talent; Zi You and. Zi Xia in letters.

11.4. Yan Yuan, said the Master, was of little help to me. He was delighted in whatever I said.

11.5. Min Zi Qian was a good son, said the Master. None could disagree with his parents and brothers about their praise of him.

11.6. Nan Rong recited the following verse again and again: *A flaw in white jade found, Away it may be ground, A flaw in what you say, Its influence will stay.* Confucius married his niece to Nan Rong. (Cf. 5. 2.)

11.7. Ji Kang Zi asked, "Which of your disciples are eager to acquire knowledge?" Confucius answered, "There was Yan Yuan who was eager to learn, but it was a pity that he died early. Now there is none like him." (Cf. 6. 3.)

11.8. When Yan Yuan died, his father begged Confucius to sell his carriage in order to buy an outer coffin for Yan Yuan. The Master said, "Our sons may be gifted or ungifted. When my son died, he had a coffin without the outer one. I could not sell my carriage to buy an outer coffin for your son, because I could not go on foot to follow other officials who ride in their carriages."

11.9. At Yan Yuan's death, the Master said, "Alas! Heaven has bereaved me, Heaven has bereaved me."

11.10. Deeply grieved at Yan Yuan's death, the Master wept bitterly. His follower said, "Master, you are too deeply grieved." The Master said, "Am I so deeply grieved? For whom should I be grieved if not for him?"

11.11. After Yan Yuan's death his fellow disciples would bury him reverently. The Master said that would not do. But the disciples still buried him reverently. The Master said, "O Yan Yuan who looked on me as his father! But I could not look on him as my son. It is not my fault. It is yours, my disciples."

11.12. When Zi Lu asked how to serve the spirits and the divinities, the Master said, "If you do not know how to serve the living, could you know how to serve the dead?" Then Zi Lu asked about death, the Master said, "How can you know about death if you do not know about life?"

11.13. Standing by the side of the Master, Min Zi Qian looked respectful, Zi Lu seemed energetic, Ran You and Zi Gong were mild and cheerful. The Master was pleased, but he said, "A man like Zi Lu could never die in his bed."

11.14. The minister of Lu was to rebuild the Long Treasury. Min Zi Qian said, "Why not repair it? I see no need to replace the old by the new." The Master said, "Min Zi Qian seldom speaks, but when he does, he hits the point."

11.15. The Master did not like Zi Lu playing on lute at his door, so the disciples did not respect Zi Lu. The Master said, "Zi Lu has entered my hall but not my inner room."

11.16. Zi Gong asked about Zi Zhang and Zi Xia, "Which of them is better?" The Master said, "Zi Zhang has overdone and Zi Xia underdone." Zi Gong asked, "Is Zi Zhang better?" The Master said, "To overdo is no better than to underdo."

11.17. The lord of the Ji Family was richer than the Duke of Zhou, yet Ran You collected revenues for him and increased his wealth. The Master said, "Ran You is no follower of mine. Dear disciples, you may beat your drum and assail him."

11.18. "Gao Cai is simple; Zen Shen is dull; Zi Zhang is queer; Zi Lu is bold."

11.19. Yan Yuan, said the Master, is nearest to an ideal man, but he is often in want. Zi Gong does not obey the order, but he has enriched himself and often hit the mark in his calculation.

11.20. Zi Zhang asked how to learn from a good man. The Master said, "If you do not follow his trace, you cannot enter his room."

11.21. One's solemnity, said the Master, may be taken for granted. But is he a cultured man or does he simply appear to be solemn as a cultured one?

11.22. When Zi Lu asked whether he should put into practice the principle he had heard, the Master said, "You should first consult your father and your elder brother." When Ran You asked the same question, the Master said, "You may put it into practice." When Gongxi Hua heard this, he said, "I do not understand why you gave different answers to the same question." The Master said, "Ran You is timid, so I encourage him; Zi Lu is rash, so I discourage him."

11.23. The Master was detained at Kuang and Yan Yuan did not come till the Master was released. The Master said, "I thought you were dead." Yan Yuan said, "How dare I die when you are alive?"

11.24. Ji Zi Ran asked whether Zi Lu and Ran Qiu could be called ministers. The Master said, "I thought you were talking about other officials than Zi Lu and Ran Qiu. What is a minister but one who serves his prince according to the principle and will resign if it is not followed? If so, they may be called qualified ministers." Ji Zi Ran said, "Will they always follow orders?" The Master said, "Not when they are told to murder their prince or father."

11.25. Zi Lu got Zi Gao appointed governor of Fei. The Master said, "That would do wrong to the people." Zi Lu said, "He might learn from the peasants and the altar. Why should he acquire knowledge only from books?" The Master said, "It is on this account that I do not like glib talkers."

11.26. Zi Lu, Zeng Xi, Ran You and Gongxi Hua sitting in attendance, the Master said, "Never mind I am older than you. Do not say your abilities are not recognized. What if they were?" Zi Lu replied straightforwardly, "If I were entrusted with a state of a thousand chariots, though situated among bigger powers and invaded by hostile armies, and suffering from famine and draught, I would teach its people to be courageous and know what is right by the end of three years." The Master smiled at him and said to Ran You, "What about you?" Ran You said, "If I were entrusted with a state of sixty or seventy square leagues, I could give its people plenty to live on by the end of three years. As for ritual and music, I would leave them to cultured men." "What about you, Gongxi Hua?" Gongxi Hua said, "I do not think I am capable, but I would like to learn. In ceremonies at the ancestral temple and at the conference of princes, I would like to act as an assistant in black gown and hat," "What about you, Zeng Xi?" Zeng Xi, pausing as he was playing on his twanging lute, put it aside and said, "My answer is quite different from theirs." The Master said, "What matters? Just say what you would like to do." Then Zeng Xi said, "In late spring I would put on my newly made spring dress and go with five or six grown-ups and six or seven young men to purify ourselves in River Yi, enjoy the breeze at the Rain Altar and come back singing." The Master said with a sigh, "I would like to go with you." When the three disciples were out, Zeng Xi remained behind and asked, "What do you, dear Master, think of

Chapter XI

what my fellow disciples have just said?" The Master said, "They have said what they would like to do." Zeng Xi asked, "Why did you smile at what Zi Lu said?" The Master said, "A state should be governed in accordance with what is right. Zi Lu was not modest, so I smiled at him." "Did not Ran You talk about the governance of a country?" "Is a state of sixty or seventy square leagues not a country to be governed?" "Did not Gongxi Hua talk about the governance of a country?" "What are services at the ancestral temple and conferences of the princes if not performance of a country? If Gongxi Hua could only act as an assistant, then who could be the master in ceremony?"

CHAPTER XII

Chapter XII

12.1. Yan Yuan asked about benevolence. The Master said, "A benevolent man will control himself in conformity with the rules of propriety. Once every man can control himself in conformity with the rules of propriety, the world will be in good order. Benevolence depends on oneself, not on others." Yan Yuan asked about the details. The Master said, "Do not look at anything nor listen to anything nor speak of anything nor do anything against the rules of propriety." Then Yan Yuan said, "Dull as I am, I would put your instruction into practice."

12.2. Zhong Gong asked about benevolence. The Master said, "Behave out-of doors as if you were before a very important person. Serve the people as if you were attending a very important sacrificial service. Do not do to others what you would not have others do to you. Do nothing to bring a complaint against you at home or abroad." Zhong Gong said, "Dull as I am, I would put your instruction into practice."

12.3. Sima Niu asked about benevolence. The Master said, "A benevolent man is cautious in speaking."

Sima Niu said, "Is it benevolence to be cautious only in speaking?" The Master said, "Could a benevolent man not be cautious in speaking when he finds it difficult to put what he says into practice?"

12.4. Sima Niu asked about an intelligentleman. The Master said, "An intelligentleman has no worry and no fear." Sima Niu said, "Can he be an intelligentleman, who simply has no worry and no fear?" The Master said, "If a man finds nothing wrong on looking within himself, what is there to worry about and to fear?"

12.5. Sima Niu said worriedly, "Other men have brothers, but I have none." Zi Xia said, "I have heard that life and death are decided by fate, and wealth and honor depend on Heaven. A cultured man will respect others and will not go beyond what is right. If he is respectful and observes the rules of propriety, then all men within the four seas will be fraternal to him. Why need he worry about having no brothers?".

12.6. Zi Zhang asked about clear sight. The Master said, "Invulnerable to soaking slander and burning pain, one may be said to be clear-sighted. Proof against soaking slander and burning pain, one may be said to be long-sighted."

12.7. Zi Gong asked about the art of ruling. The Master said, "A country must have enough food, enough forces, and faith of the people." Zi Gong said, "Which of the three may be dispensed with if obliged to?" The Master said, "Military forces." Zi Gong asked, "Which of the two remaining may be dispensed with if obliged to?" The Master said, "Food. Though people will die without food, yet it is so since the olden days. But without the faith of the people, a country cannot stand."

12.8. Ji Zi Cheng said, "What a cultured man needs is only the inner matter. What is the use of the outer manner?" Zi Gong said, "It is a pity that you should have said that! Four steeds cannot overtake your words. The manner is as important as the matter and the matter is as important as the manner. If a tiger had not its yellow skin and black stripes or a leopard had not its yellowish coat and dark spots, what is the difference between their hide and the sheepskin?"

12.9. Duke Ai inquired of Master You, saying, "In the year of famine, the state has not enough for its needs. What can I do?" Master You said, "Why not tithe the people?" The duke said, "With two-tenths I have not enough, What could I do with one-tenth?" Master You said, "If the people have enough, the prince will not be in want. If the people are in want, how can the prince have enough?"

12.10. Zi Zhang asked how to promote virtue and solve a dilemma. The Master said, "Be sincere and faithful and follow what is right, that is the way to promote virtue. If you love a man and wish him to live, and then hate him and wish him to die, you are in a dilemma." It is said in the Book of Odes: "*I can't bear your disdain, So I go back with pain,*" (Disdain shows your hate and pain reveals your love.)

12.11. Duke Jing of the State of Qi asked about the art of ruling. The Master said, "In a country the prince should be a prince, the minister a minister, the father a father, the son a son." The duke said, "How true it is! If prince, minister, father, son do not do their duty, how can I enjoy my revenue though I have plenty?"

12.12. The Master said, "It is Zi Lu who could settle a lawsuit with half a word." Zi Lu did not put off what he had promised till the next day.

12.13. As a judge in the court, said the Master, I am no better than other judges. But I would like nobody to go to law.

12.14. Zi Zhang asked about the art of ruling. The Master said, "Be indefatigable in office and sincere in practice."

12.15. A cultured man, said the Master, if wide read in

literature and restrained by the rites, would not overstep what is right. (Cf. 6, 27.)

12.16. A cultured man, said the Master, will help others in doing good, not in doing wrong. An uncultured man will do the contrary.

12.17. Ji Kang Zi asked Confucius about the art of ruling. Confucius said, "To rule is to do what is right. If the ruler only does what is right, how dare the ruled do wrong?"

12.18. Troubled by the thieves, Ji Kang Zi asked Confucius how to do away with them. Confucius replied, "If you were not covetous, none would steal even if paid to."

12.19. Asking about the art of ruling, Ji Kang Zi said to Confucius, "What do you think of killing the evil-doer to protect the good people?" Confucius replied, "Why should you kill to rule? If you rule in the right way, people will be good. The relation between the ruler and the ruled is like that between the wind and the grass. When the wind blows, the grass will bend down."

12.20. Zi Zhang asked, "How can an intellectual be influential?" The Master said, "What do you mean by 'influential'?" Zi Zhang replied, "To be wellknown in the state and in the house of his lord." The Master said, "Then what you mean is renown, not influence. An influential man should do and love what is right.

He should examine the people's countenance and observe their expressions, and think of others before himself. Then he will be influential in the state and in the house of his lord. A man of renown may appear good but do the contrary. He may think of himself before others without doubting about himself. So he becomes only wellknown in the state and in the house of his lord."

12.21. Fan Chi asked the Master while taking a walk with him at Rain Altar, "May I venture to ask how to promote virtue, amend faults and distinguish right from wrong?" The Master said, "Good questions! If you do your work before you get your reward, is it not to promote virtue? If you criticize your own shortcomings instead of those of others, is it not to amend your faults? If you are outrageous beyond yourself in a fit of anger, to the detriment of your parents, can you distinguish right from wrong?"

12.22. Fan Chi asked about a good ruler. The Master said, "A good ruler loves the ruled." Fan Chi asked about a wise ruler. The Master said, "A wise ruler knows the ruled." Fan Chi did not quite understand. The Master said, "Put the straight above the crooked, the crooked will be straightened." Fan Chi withdrew and said to Zi Xia, "I have just asked our Master about the wise ruler, our Master said, 'Put the straight above the crooked, the crooked will be straightened.' What does he mean?" Zi Xia said, "How rich in meaning his words are! When Shun ruled over the country, he selected Gao Tao as his minister and those who were not good were kept away. When Tang ruled over the country, he selected Yi Yin as his minister, and those who were not good were kept away."

12.23. Zi Gong asked how to make friends. The Master said, "Give earnest advice in good terms. Stop if it is rejected, lest you be insulted."

12.24. Master Zeng said, "A cultured man will make friends with men of letters, and his friends will help him to promote virtue."

CHAPTER XIII

Chapter XIII

13.1. Zi Lu asked about the art of ruling. The Master said, "Lead the people and labor together with them." Zi Lu asked for more. The Master said, "Labor indefatigably."

13.2. Zhong Gong who became minister of the Ji Family asked about the art of ruling. The Master said, "Lead your subordinate officials, pardon their minor faults and promote those who have talent." Zhong Gong asked how to discover talents. The Master said, "Select those whom you know. As for those whom you know not, do you think others will neglect them?"

13.3. Zi Lu said, "The Prince of Wei is waiting for you to rule over his country. What will you do first?" The Master said, "First of all, things must be properly named." Zi Lu said, "How can you be so far from reality? Why should things be properly named first of all?" The Master said, "How rude you are, Zi Lu! A cultured man will keep silent on what he does not know. If things are not properly named, then what you say about them cannot be right. If what you

87

say is not right, how can you accomplish a task? If you cannot accomplish a task, how can ritual and music be properly performed? If ritual and music cannot be properly performed, how can punishment be adequately carried out? If punishment cannot be adequate, how can people know right from wrong? Therefore, a cultured man will first of all name the things properly so that what he says may be right. If what he says is right, then it can be properly carried out. Whatever a cultured man says must not be improper and incorrect, that is all I mean."

13.4. When Fan Chi asked about farming. The Master said, "I am no better than an old farmer." When asked about gardening, the Master said "I am no better than an old gardener." When Fan Chi had gone out, the Master said, "Fan Chi is indeed an uncultured man. If the ruler loves the rites, no people would be disrespectful. If the ruler loves what is right, no people would be disobedient. If the ruler loves the truth, no people would disregard reality. If such is the case, then people from all the corners of the earth would come to him with their babies strapped on their back. Why need he learn farming?"

13.5. If a man versed in three hundred poems, said the

Chapter XIII

Master, cannot discharge the office entrusted to him, nor can he fulfill the mission when sent abroad, what then is the use of being wide read?

13.6. An upright ruler, said the Master, will be obeyed though he gives no order. If he is not upright, he will not be obeyed though he gives orders.

13.7. Lu and Wei, said the Master, are brother states. Neither is better nor worse than the other in politics.

13.8. The Master said of Jing, a scion of the ducal family of Wei, "He knew well how to lead an economic life. When he began to have means, he said that he had almost enough. When he had a little more, he said that he was almost full. When he was rich, he said that it could not be better."

13.9. The Master went his way to Wei and Ran You drove the carriage for him. The Master said, "What a large population!" Ran You said, "What should be done to such a large population?" The Master said, "Enrich them!" Ran You said, "What should be done when they are enriched?" The Master said, "Educate them!"

13.10. If any prince should employ me, said the Master, one year would be enough to show what I can do, and three years would show what I can accomplish.

13.11. If good men, said the Master, were to rule the state for a hundred years, violence and slaughter would be done away with. But how could it come true?

13.12. Even a truly royal ruler, said the Master, would need a generation to make virtue prevail among the people.

12.13. If the ruler is right, said the Master, he need not worry about how to rule the state. If he is not right, how can he put other people right?

13.14. Once when Ran You came back from court, the Master said, "Why are you so late?" Ran You said, "There were political affairs." The Master said, "It must have been only administrative business. If there had been political affairs, I should have been consulted though I am not in office now."

13.15. Duke Ding asked whether there was a word which could make a country prosperous. Confucius said, "A word could hardly do that. But I have heard that it is difficult to be a prince and not easy to be a minister. If a ruler really understands that, can we not say that a word may nearly prosper a country?" Duke Ding asked then whether there was a word which could ruin a country. Confucius said, "A word could hardly do that. But I have heard that a prince finds no pleasure but in that none oppose to what he says. If what he says is right and opposed by none, it is very good. But if what he says is wrong and opposed by none, then is it not a word which may nearly ruin a country?"

13.16. The Duke of She asked about the art of ruling. The Master said, "Make the near happy to stay and the far-off happy to come."

13.17. Zi Xia who became governor of Jufu asked about the art of ruling. The Master said, "Be neither hasty nor partial! For haste makes waste, and partiality loses entirety."

13.18. The Duke of She said to Confucius, "A straightforward man in my country accused his father when he had stolen a sheep." Confucius said, "A straightforward man in mine is different. The father would conceal his son's misconduct and the son would conceal his father's. In this we see the relation of a family."

13.19. Fan Chi asked about the good man. The Master said, "A good man respects himself in private life, and respects others in public life. Trustworthy in business, he remains the same though among uncivilized tribes."

13.20. Zi Gong asked what kind of man may be called an official. The Master said, "A man ashamed of his misbehavior and loyal to the prince's commission when sent abroad may be called an official." Zi Gong said, "May I venture to ask what kind of man may rank next?" The Master said, "A man commended by his relatives for filial piety and by his fellow villagers for deference to the elders." When asked what ranks still next, the Master said, "A man faithful in word and in deed, busy all day long like common. people of lower class may perhaps rank next." When asked how about the officials in the government, the Master said, "Pooh! They are mere thimblefuls, not worth taking into account."

13.21. If I cannot find men, said the Master, who follow the middle way, I would rather have the radical and the moderate. The radical would advance and the moderate would not do anything wrong.

13.22. The Master said, "It is said in the south that a man without constancy cannot make a good witch-doctor. Well said!" It is said in the *Book of Change* "Inconstancy will lead to disgrace." The Master said, "This simply discourages the inconstant from initiating into witchcraft."

13.23. A cultured man, said the Master, may disagree to reach an agreement, while an uncultured man dare not disagree but agrees without understanding.

13.24. Zi Gong asked, "What do you think of a man loved by all his countrymen?" The Master said, "I do not think he is good enough." When asked about a man disliked by all his countrymen, the Master said, "I am not sure he is bad. I would prefer a man loved by the good countrymen and disliked by the bad ones."

13.25. It is easy to serve, said the Master, but difficult to please a cultured man, for he will not be pleased but in the right way, and he employs men according to their abilities. It is difficult to serve, but easy to please un uncultured man, for he may be pleased though not in the right way, but he expects the employed equal to everything.

13.26. A cultured man, said the Master, is dignified and not proud, while an uncultured man is proud and not dignified.

13.27. Strong and steady, said the Master, wooden and wordless, such a man is nearly a good man.

13.28. Zi Lu asked what kind of man might be called a cultured man. The Master said, "He should be helpful and peaceful: helpful to friends and peaceful among brothers."

13.29. The people, said the Master, trained by good teachers for seven years, may be employed in war.

13.30. It would be a useless sacrifice, said the Master, to employ untrained people in war.

CHAPTER XIV

CHAPTER XIV

14.1. Yuan Xian asked about shame. The Master said, "It would be a shame to get the same pay when the state goes on the wrong way as when it goes on the right way." When asked whether it is benevolent to control oneself and not to boast of oneself, and to be free from resentment and greediness, the Master said, "It would be difficult to do so, but I do not know whether it could be called benevolence."

14.2. An intellectual, said the Master, indulged in a comfortable life could not be called an intellectual.

14.3. When the state goes on the right way, said the Master, one should be honest in word and in deed. When it goes on the wrong way, one should be honest in deed but cautious in word.

14.4. A virtuous man, said the Master, will say what is right, but one who says what is right may not be a virtuous man. A benevolent man will be brave, but a brave man may not be benevolent.

14.5. Nangong Kuo asked Confucius why the best archer and the hero who overturned a boat both died a tragical death, while the two cultivators of the land became the rulers of the state. The Master made no reply. When Nangong Kuo was out, the Master said, "This is indeed a cultured man. He loves virtue above strength."

14.6. A cultured man, said the Master, may fall short of virtue, but none of the uncultured men will love virtue.

14.7. Could there be love, said the Master, which demands no work? Could there be loyalty which demands no instruction?

14.8. Before an order is issued, said the Master, Bi Chen made the draft, Shi Shu checked it, Zi Yu the diplomat amended it, and Zi Chan of the East Village elaborated it.

14.9. When asked about Zi Chan, the Master said, "He is a kind man." When asked about Zi Xi, he merely said, "That man, that man!" When asked about Guan Zhong, he said, "He is a personage. For he has deprived the Bo family of three hundred villages and the head of the Bo family lived on coarse food without a word of complaint till he grew old and toothless."

14.10. Poverty without complaint, said the Master, is more difficult than wealth without pride.

14.11. Meng Gong Chuo would be a better official in such big families as Zhao and Wei than a minister in such small states as Teng or Xue.

Chapter XIV

14.12. When Zi Lu asked what an accomplished man should be like, the Master said, "A man wise as Zang Wu Zhong, desire-free as Meng Gong Chuo, brave as Bian Zhuang Zi, and artful as Ran Qiu may be considered as an accomplished man if he is cultivated in ritual and music." He then added, "What is the need for an accomplished man of today to have all these things? If he should prefer the proper to the profit, risk his life in face of danger, and never forget a promise made long ago, I think he is good enough to be called an accomplished man."

14.13. The Master asked Gongming Jia about his master Gong Shu Wen Zi, "Is it true that your master neither spoke nor laughed nor took?" Gong-ming Jia said, "The man who told you that was exaggerating. My master spoke when people were not tired of what he said; he laughed when he was happy and people were not tired of his laughter; he took what was right to take when people were not displeased with what he took." The Master said. "Was it so? Can it have been so?"

14.14. Zang Wu Zhong, said the Master, occupied the fief of Fang and demanded the Duke of Lu to allow his brother Wei to take over the fief. Though he said no pressure was used, yet I do not believe it.

14.15. Duke Wen of Jin, said the Master, was tactful and not upright, while Duke Huan of Qi was upright and tactless.

14.16. Zi Lu said, "Duke Huan of Qi asked the State of Lu to put to death his elder brother Jiu, Jiu's master Zhao Hu followed Jiu in death, but Guan Zhong did not. Was Guan Zhong not short of virtue?" The Master said, "Duke Huan assembled nine times the rulers of all the states without resorting to his war chariots, and it was on the strength of Guan Zhong. What is virtue if this is not?"

14.17. Zi Gong said, "Was Guan Zhong not short of virtue? When Duke Huan put Prince Jiu to death, he did not die with him, but became prime minister to Duke Huan?" The Master said, "When Guan Zhong was prime minister, he helped Duke Huan to rule over all the princes of the state, unify the kingdom and benefit the people up to the present day. Without Guan Zhong, we might have been conquered by uncivilized tribes with disheveled hair and in barbarian dress. Would you expect from him as ordinary people to die in a ditch without leaving a name behind?"

14.18. Gong Shu Wen Zi had an officer called Xun promoted to the rank of minister as high as himself

CHAPTER XIV

and through his own recommendation. Hearing of this, the Master said, "Gong Shu Wen Zi is worthy of his name of a cultured man ('wen')."

14.19. The Master was speaking about the corruption of Duke Ling of Wei, when Ji Kang asked how the duke did not lose his state since he was so corrupt. The Master said, "He had three good ministers: Zhong Shu Yu in charge of foreign affairs, Shi Tuo in charge of civil service and Gong Sun Jia in command of his armies. How could he lose his state?"

14.20. One who exaggerates, said the Master, will find it difficult for his deeds to agree with his words.

14.21. When Chen Heng Zi murdered Duke Jian of Qi, Confucius took a bath and went to court to inform Duke Ai of Lu that Chen Heng Zi had slain his prince and begged that forces be sent to punish him. The duke said, "Inform the chiefs of the three families." Confucius said, "As I am in the retinue of His Highness, I consider it my duty to inform him of the murder. But I was told to inform the chiefs of the three families." Then he went to the three chiefs and informed them of the matter, but they refused the petition. Confucius said, "As I am in the retinue of the duke, I consider it my duty to inform them."

14.22. Zi Lu asked how to serve the prince. The Master

said, "Do not say what is contrary to your thoughts, but you may openly express your disagreement."

14.23. A cultured man, said the Master, goes up while an uncultured man goes down.

13.24. In old days, said the Master, men learned to improve themselves; nowadays, they learn to impress others.

14.25. Qu Bo Yu sent a messenger to inquire after Confucius. Confucius bade him to be seated and asked what his master was doing. The messenger said, "My master is trying to lessen his failings and not yet quite successful." When the messenger was out, Confucius said, "What a messenger! What a messenger!"

14.26. The Master said, "Do not interfere into the matter you are not in a position to!" Master Zeng said, "Even in his thoughts, an intelligentleman should not interfere into the matter he is not in a position to."

14.27. An intelligentleman, said the Master, is ashamed that his words outrun his deeds.

14.28. The Master said, "An intelligentleman is three in one, but I am none. A good man should be carefree, a wise man should be doubt-free and a brave man should be fearless." Master Zeng said, "Our Master has told us what he is."

14.29. Zi Gong was always criticizing others. The Master

Chapter XIV

said, "Zi Gong, are you good enough? As for me, I have no leisure to criticize others."

14.30. Be not afraid, said the Master, that you are unknown, but that you are unable.

14.31. Do not think in advance, said the Master, that people are deceiving you nor that they do not believe you. Undeceived and believed at once, you would be sagacious.

14.32. Weisheng Mu said to Confucius, "What are you busy about here and there? Are you a glib talker?" Confucius said, "Not that I am glib, but that I do not like to be stiff."

14.33. A steed is good, said the Master, not for its strength, but for its quality.

14.34. When asked whether good should be returned for evil, the Master said, "What then should be returned for good? Justice should be returned for evil and good for good."

14.35. The Master said, "It is a pity that none understands me." Master Zeng asked "Why?" The Master said, "I do not complain against Heaven and lay no blame on man. I only learn laws human and divine. But only Heaven understands me."

14.36. Gong Bo Liao spoke against Zi Lu to the chief of the Ji family. Zi Fu Ying Bo told the Master that the chief was deluded by Gong Bo Liao, and that he still had power to put Gong Bo Liao to death. The Master said, "It is Heaven's will whether my way will be followed or not. What could Gong Bo Liao do against Heaven's will?"

14.37. The Master said, "A good man would retire first from a bad society, next from a bad place, next from bad looks, next from bad words." Then he added, "There are seven good men who have already done so."

14.38. Zi Lu passed one night at the Stone Gate. Next morning the gate keeper asked him where he came from. He said, "From Confucius." The gatekeeper said, "Is it the man who would try the impossible?"

14.39. The Master was playing on a musical stone in the State of Wei when a man bearing a basket passed by his door. The man said, "His heart must be full to beat the musical stone in such a way." Then he said. "Is it worthwhile to show oneself off? What matters if one is unknown or unrecognized? *'If water's shallow, leap; And strip if it is deep!'*" The Master said, "If so, it would not be difficult to find a way out,"

14.40. Zi Zhang said, "It is said in the *Book of History* that the High Emperor of Yin did not talk in the shed of mourning for three years. What does this mean?" The Master said, "Why should the High Emperor be mentioned in particular when all the ancients did in the same way? After the sovereign's death, all the officials continued to hold their office and took orders from the the prime minister for three years."

14.41. So long as the ruler observes the ritual said the Master, the people will be obedient.

14.42. When Zi Lu asked about an intelligentleman, the Master said, "He should cultivate himself and do his duty with respect." When asked whether it was all, the Master said, "He should cultivate himself so as to make others live in comfort." When asked again whether it was all, the Master said, "He should cultivate himself so as to make people live in comfort. Such is the end the sagacious emperors would have attained."

14.43. Yuan Rong waited for Confucius, squatting on the heels. The Master said, "Immodest in youth, unaccomplished in manhood and useless in old age, such a man would be a pest." He struck him on the slank with his staff.

14.44. A young man carried a message for Confucius from his native village. When asked whether the messenger was good at learning, the Master said, "I have seen him occupy the place of an adult and walk side by side with his elders. He is not good at learning but would become a grown-up before his time."

CHAPTER XV

Chapter XV

15.1. Duke Ling of Wei asked Confucius about battle array, Confucius replied, "I know only something about ritual, but nothing about military affairs." He left Wei the next day.

15.2. Confucius was not supplied with food in the state of Chen, his followers became too weak to rise to their feet. Dissatisfied, Zi Lu came and said, "How can an intelligentleman fall in want?" The Master said, "An intelligentleman will do nothing wrong even if he is in want, while an uncultured man in want will break loose from all restraints."

15.3. The Master said to Zi Gong, "Do you think I am a man who knows many things and keeps them in memory?" Zi Gong said, "Yes, is it not so?" The Master said, "No, I know only one in many and many in one."

15.4. The Master said to Zi Lu, "Few know what virtue is."

15.5. Emperor Shun ruled by non-interference, said the Master. Was it not so? What did he do but occupy the imperial throne reverently?

15.6. When Zi Zhang asked about good behavior, the Master said, "Sincere in what you say and trustworthy in what you do, you would behave well even among uncivilized tribes. Insincere in word and untrustworthy in deed, could you behave well in your native village? Standing, you should see these words before your eyes. Sitting in the carriage, you should see them inscribed on the yoke. Then you can behave well." Zi Zhang wrote these words on his sash.

15.7. How straightforward was the historian Yu, said the Master, who served as a straight arrow the state in good order or in disorder! What an intelligentleman was Qu Bo Yu who served as an official when the state was in good order, and who concealed himself and hid away when the state was in disorder!

15.8. Not to talk to a worthy man, said the Master, is to lose the man, and to talk to an unworthy man is to waste words. The wise will neither lose a man nor waste words.

15.9. A wise good man, said the Master, will do no wrong to preserve his own life but sacrifice his life to do what is right.

15.10. Zi Gong asked how to render good service. The Master said, "A craftsman who wishes to do his work well must first sharpen his tools. You who serve in a state must act in agreement with its good officers and befriend its good intellectuals."

15.11. Yan Yuan asked how to serve in a state. The Master said, "Use the calendar of Xia, ride the carriage of Yin, wear the ceremonial dress of Zhou, play the music of Emperor Shun and dance to the tune of the Martial King. Reject the songs of Zheng which are licentious and keep away from flatterers who are dangerous."

15.12. If you have no long sight, said the Master, trouble will be near at hand.

15.13. In vain, said the Master, have I looked for one who loves his duty more than beauty.

15.14. Was not Zang Wen Zhong, said the Master, a stealer of ranks? He knew Liu Xia Hui gifted but did not give the rank due to him.

15.15. Severe with oneself and lenient with others, said the Master, one will be far from their complaint.

15.16. I do not know what to do, said the Master, with a man who never says, "What to do? What to do?"

15.17. It is difficult, said the Master, to deal with those who gather together all day long without saying what is right but try to show their tact in trifling matters.

15.18. An intelligentleman, said the Master, thinks it his duty to do what is right, carries it out according to the rules of propriety, speaks with modesty and accomplishes it faithfully. Such is an intelligentleman.

15.19. An intelligentleman, said the Master, regrets that he is incapable, and not that he is unknown.

15.20. An intelligentleman, said the Master, dislikes the age of decadence when names belie facts.

15.21. An intelligentleman, said the Master, relies on himself while an uncultured man relies on others.

15.22. An intelligentleman, said the Master, is dignified, but not quarrelsome he is sociable, but not partisan.

15.23. An intelligentleman, said the Master, will not recommend anyone simply because of his good words, nor reject the good words of anyone.

15.24. Zi Gong asked whether there was a word practicable all the life long. The Master said, "Perhaps 'forbearance' is the word. Do not do to others what you would not have others do to you."

15.25. Of those people I have dealt with, said the Master, whom have I praised or blamed? If I have praised someone, I must have tested him. Such is the straightforward way how people were dealt with during the three ancient dynasties.

15.26. In my early days, said the Master, I had seen historian leave a blank in his text, and a horseman leave his horse for another to ride. But now there is none like them.

15.27. Sweet words, said the Master, may sour the deeds. Impatience in minor matter may cause failure in main matter.

15.28. If a man is disliked by all, said the Master, inquiry must be made. If a man is liked by all, inquiry must also be made.

15.29. It is man, said the Master, that can amplify laws, but laws cannot amplify man.

15.30. Not to mend a fault, said the Master, is to make a fault.

15.31. Once, said the Master, I spent a whole day and a whole night in thinking, without eating and sleeping. I got no result and found it better to learn.

15.32. An intelligentleman, said the Master, seeks after truth instead of food. Ploughing, he will not worry about hunger; learning, he may win rank. An intelligentleman is more eager for truth than worried about poverty.

15.33. Wise enough to attain, said the Master, but not good enough to maintain, he will lose what is gained. Wise enough to attain and good enough to maintain, he will not be respected by people if he rules without dignity. Wise enough to attain and good enough to maintain, and ruling with dignity, he is still not a perfect ruler if he does not act in accordance with the ritual system.

15.34. An intelligentleman, said the Master, may not know minor matters, but he can be entrusted with major duties. An uncultured man cannot be entrusted with major duties, but he may know minor matters.

15.35. The people need virtue, said the Master, more than water and fire. I have seen people drowned in water or burned to death in fire, but none die in virtue.

15.36. A good man, said the Master, should not withdraw from being a better man than his teacher.

15.37. An intelligentleman, said the Master, is consistent, but not obstinate.

15.38. In serving the prince, said the Master, a man should do his duty before he gets his reward.

15.39. In education, said the Master, there should be no distinction of classes.

15.40. You cannot take counsel, said the Master, with those who follow a different way.

15.41. Words are good, said the Master, if only they can express the idea.

15.42. The blind music master Mian called on Confucius. When he came to the steps, the Master said, "Here are the steps." When he came to the mat for the

Chapter XV

guests to sit on, the Master said, "Here is the mat." When all the guests were seated, the Master told him, "So and so is here, so and so is there." When the music master was out, Zi Zhang asked whether it was the way to deal with a music master. The Master said, "Yes, this is the way to lead a blind man."

CHAPTER XVI

CHAPTER XVI

16.1. The head of the Ji family was going to attack Zhuanyu. Ran You and Zi Lu came to see Confucius and said, "Our chief is going to attack Zhuanyu." Confucius said, "Ran You, is it not your fault? Long ago Zhuanyu was appointed by former kings to preside over the sacrifice to the Eastern Meng. Moreover, it lies within the boundaries of our state, and it is a vassal state to safeguard our land. How can such an attack be justified?" Ran Yu said, "It is our chief who wishes the attack. Neither of us wishes it, but we are only his officials." Confucius said to Ran You, "The historian Zhou Ren said, 'Take the office if you can display your ability, or decline it if you cannot!' What is the use of a minister if he cannot support a state in stake or prop up a tottering state? Moreover, what you say is wrong. If a tiger or wild bull should escape from its cag, or a tortoise shell or gem be broken in its box, whose fault is it if not the keeper's?" Ran You said, "At present Zhuanyu is a vassal state strongly fortified near the chief fief of Fei. If our chief does not take it now, it would become a pest to his posterity." Confucius said, "Ran You, a cultured man dislikes those who try to find a pretext for taking what they want. I have heard that the chief of a state or of a family need not care for scarcity but for inequality, nor for poverty but for security. There would be no poverty if wealth is equally shared, no scarcity if people live in harmony, no danger if people live in security. If people do not pay homage from afar, then culture must be enhanced to attract them. When won over, they must be comfortably installed. Now, Ran You and Zi Lu, advisors as you are to your chief, you cannot help him to subdue nor attract people from afar, nor restore the state to order out of chaos, but plan hostile activities within the state. I am afraid the trouble with the Ji family may not arise from Zhuanyu but from the sovereign behind the scene."

16.2. Confucius said, "When the world goes the right way, the orders on ritual and music and military expeditions are issued by the sovereign of the state. When it goes the wrong way, they are issued by feudal princes, but few princes could maintain their rule for ten generations. If such orders are issued by ministers, few ministers could maintain their rule for five generations. If they are issued by officials, few officials could maintain theirs for three generations. When the world goes the right way, the state will not be governed by officials, When the world goes the right way, the people will not dispute with the government."

16.3. Confucius said, "The ducal house of Lu has lost power for five generations, and government has been in the hands of the ministers for four generations. No wonder the descendants of the three Lu families are fast losing their power."

16.4. Three kinds of friend will do you good, said Confucius, and other three will do you harm. To make friends with the upright, the faithful and the well-informed will do you good; to make friends with the prejudicial, the insidious and the hypocritical will do you harm.

16.5. Three delightful things, said Confucius, will do you good: delight in ritual and music, in speaking well of others and in making good friends. Three pleasures will do you harm: extravagant pleasure, lascivious pleasure and sumptuous pleasure.

16.6. In the presence of a cultured man, said Confucius, three mistakes should be avoided: to speak before called on to speak is rash; not to speak when called on to is unfrank; to speak without observing the expression of his face is blind.

16.7. A cultured man, said Confucius, should beware of three things. He should beware of lust in youth when his vigor is uncouth, of strife in his prime when he is full of vigor, and of greed in old age when his vigor is on the decline.

16.8. Three things, said Confucius, inspire a cultured man with awe: Heaven's will, great men and words of the sage. An uncultured man does not know Heaven's will, so he does not stand in awe. He respects no great men, and makes light of the sage's words.

16.9. Highest are those born wise, said Confucius, next come those who become wise by learning, still next those who strive to learn, and last come those people who will not strive at all.

16.10. An intelligentleman, said Confucius, should be considerate in nine respects: he should see clearly, hear distinctly, look mild, appear respectful, speak sincerely, act carefully, ask questions when in doubt, think of the consequences when in anger, and bear in mind what is right in sight of gain.

16.11. I have heard, said Confucius, of those who would lose no time to do what is good when they see it, and to shrink from what is harmful as from boiling water, and I have seen such men. I have heard of those who would retire so as not to go on the wrong way and then come out so as to go on the right way, but I have not seen such men.

16.12. Duke Jing of the state of Qi had a thousand chariots with four steeds, but nobody praised him on the day of his death for he had done no good for the people. Bo Yi and Shu Qi, two loyal brothers, starved at the foot of the Sunny Mountain, but people praise them down to the present day. Is this not an illustration of what is said above?

16.13. Chen Kang asked Bo Yu, son of Confucius, whether he had heard from his father anything different from what the others had. Bo Yu said, "No. One day my father was standing alone in the hall when I passed by respectfully. He asked me whether I had studied Poetry. When I replied, 'Not yet,' he said, 'You cannot speak well if you have not.' Then I retired and studied Poetry. Another day he was again standing in the hall when I passed by respectfully. He asked me whether I had studied the rituals. When I replied, 'Not yet,' he said, 'You cannot be established in society if you have not.' Then I retired and studied rituals. These two things are what I have heard from him." Delighted, Chen Kang came away and said, "Asking one thing, I have learned three. I have heard about poetry, rituals and impartiality of an intelligentleman towards his son."

16.14. The prince of a state calls his wife "Madame." She calls herself "Your humble servant." The people of the state call her "Madame Princess." When speaking of her to guests of another state, the prince calls her "My humble princess." The guests also call her "Madame Princess."

CHAPTER XVII

17.1. Yang Huo in power wished Confucius to call on him, but Confucius would not, so he sent a sucking pig to Confucius, and Confucius paid him a visit when he was not at home. But unexpectedly they met on the way. Yang Huo said to Confucius, "Come, I have something to tell you. Is it good for a talent to leave his state in chaos? No. Is it wise for a candidate to lose an opportunity? No, The days and months pass by. The years will wait for no man." Confucius said ironically, "Yes, how could I not serve!"

17.2. Men are born, said the Master, nearly alike by nature, but become different by practice.

17.3. Only the wisest man and the most foolish, said the Master, cannot be changed.

17.4. The Master came to the small town of Wu where Zi You was the ruler. When he heard sacred songs and stringed music, he said with a smile, "Is it necessary to kill a chicken with an ox-knife?" Zi You said, "Formerly, I heard you say that a cultured man well-bred in music would do good to the people, and an uncultured man well-bred in music would be easy to employ." The Master said to two or three disciples, "Zi You is right. I have just said that for fun."

17.5. Gongshan Furao, holding the fief of Fei in revolt, sent for the Master who was inclined to go. Displeased, Zi Lu said, "Why would you like to go to him of all people?" The Master said, "Could he send for me without reason? If anyone were to employ me, I would make ritual and music prosper in his state as in the Eastern Zhou."

17.6. Zi Zhang asked Confucius, "What is a good ruler?" Confucius said, "One who can develop the five qualities in the world could be a good ruler." When Zi Lu begged to know which five, the Master said, "Reverence, lenience, confidence, diligence and benevolence. Reverent, he would not hurt; lenient, he would win support; confident, he would be trusted; diligent, he would succeed; and benevolent, he could employ people."

17.7. When the Master was inclined to visit Bi Xi who sent for him, Zi Lu said, "I have heard you say that a cultured man would not enter the house of an evil-doer. Now Bi Xi holds the fief of Zhongmu in rebellion. How could you think of visiting him?" The Master said, "Yes, I have told you that. But, do you not know that a really hard thing cannot be thinned by grinding? A really white thing cannot be blackened even in black dye? Am I a bitter gourd only fit to be hung up and not fit to eat?"

17.8. The Master said to Zi Lu, "Have you heard of six virtues may lead to six defects?" Zi Lu replied, "No." The Master said, "Come, I will tell you. Without the love of knowledge, a lover of virtue may become a fool, a lover of wisdom may become wanton, a faithful man may be cheated, a frank man may become rash, a brave man may make a riot, and a strong man may become arrogant."

17.9. My dear disciples, said the Master, why do you not like to study poetry? Poetry may serve to inspire, to reflect, to communicate and to complain. It may help you to serve your father at home and your prince at court. Moreover, it may tell you names of birds, beasts, plants and trees.

17.10. Have you studied, said the Master to his son Bo Yu, the *Songs on Man and Wife*? If not, you would be like a man standing in face of a wall without seeing anything beyond it.

17.11. Ritual, ritual! said the Master, does it only mean the gifts of jade and silk? Music, music! Does it only mean bells and drums?

17.12. If an inwardly weak man, said the Master, pretends to look strong outwardly, is he not like a thief who bores a hole or climbs over a wall?

Chapter XVII

17.13. A yesman, said the Master, is a thief of virtue.

17.14. To spread the rumor you have heard on the way, said the Master, is to neglect your duty.

17.15. Could we serve the prince, said the Master, together with such pitiable people as are anxious to get what they have not and afraid to lose what they have? What would not they do if they are afraid to lose what they have got?

17.16. In old days, said the Master, people had three faults which are perhaps not to be found now. Then arrogance showed little consideration for others; now it goes beyond bounds. Then pride was formal; now it is quarrelsome. Then stupidity was straightforward; now it is deceitful.

17.17. A good man, said the Master, would rarely say what he does not believe, or pretend to appear better than he is. (Cf. 1. 3.)

17.18. I hate, said the Master, to see the royal red usurped by the ducal purple, to hear the imperial music corrupted by licentious local songs, and to know a state or a kingdom overturned by sharp tongues.

17.19. The Master said, "I would prefer to say nothing." Zi Gong said, "If you, dear Master, say nothing, what could we disciples record?" The Master said, "What has Heaven said? Yet the four seasons follow their courses and all things come into being. What has

Heaven said?"

17.20. Ru Bei sent a messenger to see Confucius, who declined to see him under the pretext of ill health. When the messenger was out, Confucius took his lute and sang so that the messenger might hear him.

17.21. Asking about the three years' mourning for parents, Zai Wo said, "One year would be long enough, for ritual and music would be lost if a cultured man did not put them into practice for three years. In one year the old grain would be exhausted and the new would spring up. So would fire be made from spring to winter. Therefore, I think the mourning may stop at the end of one year." The Master said, "Would you feel at ease to eat good rice and wear silk dress after one year of mourning?" Zai Wo said "Yes." "If you feel at ease, you may stop mourning at the end of one year. A cultured man in mourning would not enjoy nice food, sweet music and comfortable bed. If you could feel at ease, you might enjoy them." When Zai Wo was out, the Master said, "Zai Wo is not a good son. A child would not leave its parents' arms until three years old. So three years' mourning is a universal practice. How could Zai Wo belie the three years' affection of his parents?"

17.22. Difficult are those, said the Master, who cram

themselves with food all the day long without applying their mind to anything good. Are there not gamesters and chess- players? It would be better to play chess or games than to do nothing at all.

17.23. Zi Lu asked whether a cultured man valued valour. The Master said, "A cultured man values virtue above valour. Valiant without virtue, a cultured man would rise in revolt and an uncultured man would commit robbery."

17.24. Zi Gong asked whether a cultured man had dislikes. The Master said, "Yes, a cultured man dislikes those who speak ill of others, those inferior men who slander their superiors, those who are bold beyond what is right, those who take obstination for resolution." Then the Master asked Zi Gong whether he also had his dislikes. Zi Gong replied, "I dislike those who take cunning for wisdom, immodesty for bravery, and indiscretion for honesty."

17.25. It is difficult, said the Master, to deal with women and servants. If you are familiar with them, they will be immodest; if you keep your distance, they will complain.

17.26. If a man is disliked at the age of forty, said the Master, he would not change for the better till the end of his life.

CHAPTER XVIII

Chapter XVIII

18.1. The lord of Wei fled from the tyrant of Yin, the lord of Ji became the tyrant's slave, and Bi Gan was slain for his remonstrances. Confucius said, "The Yin dynasty had three men of virtue."

18.2. Liuxia Hui was thrice dismissed from his post of chief judge. Someone said, "Is it not better to leave the state of Lu?" Hui said, "If I continue to serve men in an honest way, how could I not be dismissed thrice more? If I choose to serve in a crooked way, why should I leave the state of my parents?"

18.3. Duke Jing of the state of Qi said of the treatment of Confucius, "I cannot treat him as the chief of the Ji family, but between the chiefs of Ji and Meng." Seeing Confucius, he said, "I am old and have no use for you." Confucius left the state of Qi.

18.4. The state of Qi sent to Lu a band of musicians and songstresses. Ji Huan Zi accepted them, and no court was held for three days. Confucius left the state of Lu.

18.5. A hermit of Chu passed by the carriage of Confucius and sang, "Oh, phoenix, oh phoenix, How unfortunate you are! The past cannot be repaired, But the future can be remedied. Done with it! Done with it! What can be done with the government?" Confucius descended from his carriage in order to speak with the hermit, who hastened away so as to avoid talking with him.

18.6. Two riverside men were ploughing the field when Confucius passed by and sent Zi Lu to ask where the river could be forded. The first riverside man said, "Who is the man holding the reins in the carriage?" Zi Lu said, "It is Confucius." "Is it Confucius of the state of Lu?" "Yes, it is he." "Then he should have known where the ford is." Zi Lu asked the second riverside man, who said, "Who are you?" "I am Zi Lu." "Are you not the follower of Confucius of Lu?" "Yes." "The world is overwhelmed with a flood of bad men. Who could stem it? Would it not be better to withdraw from the world than from the flood?" He went on covering the seed. On hearing the report of Zi Lu, the Master said with a sigh, "Unable to get along with birds and beasts, with whom could I get along if not with men? If nothing is wrong with the world, what should I be busy about?"

18.7. Zi Lu lagged behind the Master on the way when he met with an old man shouldering a staff and a weeder. Zi Lu asked, "Have you seen my master?" The old man said, "Unable to toil with four limbs and to choose from among five grains for seeding, how can you ask me to tell who your master is?" Then he planted his staff on the ground and began to weed. Zi Lu stood respectfully by the roadside. The old man kept him for the night, killed a fowl and prepared millet for the supper, and introduced him to to his two sons. Next day, Zi Lu pursued his way, overtook his master and told him all. The Master said, "He is a recluse." He told Zi Lu to call on the old man again. But when Zi Lu got there, the old man was already gone. Zi Lu said, "It is not right to refuse to serve one's country. If the relation between old and young cannot be neglected, how could that between sovereign and subjects? How could personal purity be maintained if social relationship should be subverted? If a cultured man serves his state, he is only doing his duty, though he knows he cannot put his principles into practice."

18.8. The following good men who would not serve the state: Bo Yi, Shu Qi, Yu Zhong, Yi Yi, Zhu Zhang, Liuxia Hui, Shao Lian. The Master said, "Bo Yi and Shu Qi would not surrender mentally and physically. Liuxia Hui and Shao Lian would, but they were reasonable and prudent in words and in deeds, but that is all. Yu Zhong and Yi Yi were free of speech in seclusion, pure in action and tactful in retirement. As for me, I am different from them. There is nothing I must do, nor anything I must not."

18.9. Zhi, chief musician, went to Qi; Gan, musician of the second meal, went to Chu; Liao, musician of the third meal, went to Cai; Que, musician of the fourth meal, went to Qin; Fang Shu, drummer, went to the riverside; Wu, hand-drummer, went to River Huai; Yang, assistant master, and Xiang, chime-player, went to the seaside. (None of them would stay in the state of Lu.)

18.10. The Duke of Zhou told his son, "A good ruler should not neglect his kinsmen, nor let his ministers complain of distrust. He should not dismiss his old relations from their offices without grave cause. He should not expect one man to be capable of everything."

18.11. The Zhou dynasty had eight men of virtue: eldest brothers Da and Kuo, elder brothers Tu and Hu, younger brothers Ye and Xia, youngest brothers Sui and Gua.

CHAPTER XIX

19.1. Zi Zhang said, "An intellectual is not afraid of giving up his life in face of danger. He thinks of what is right in face of a gain, of reverence in sacrifice and of grief in mourning. Such may be said to be an intellectual."

19.2. Zi Zhang said, "If a man holds what is right only in a narrow sense and believes in right principles but not firmly, could he be said to hold and believe in what is right? Or could he not?"

19.3. A disciple of Zi Xia asked Zi Zhang how to make friends. Zi Zhang said, "What did Zi Xia tell you?" The disciple said, "Zi Xia told us to make friends with those who are worthy and refuse those who are unworthy." Zi Zhang said, "This is different from what I have learned. A cultured man should respect the good man and bear with others, praise the capable and help the incapable. Am I so good as not to bear with others? If I am not good enough, others will refuse to make friends with me. How could I refuse them?"

19.4. Zi Xia said, "Even a minor art has an importance of its own. But it may hinder one's major occupation, so a cultured man would not practise a minor art."

19.5. Zi Xia said, "If a man knows what he has not yet learned everyday and does not forget what he has learned every month, he may be said to be a lover of knowledge."

19.6. Zi Xia said, "If a man studies in a wide range and with an unswerving aim, if he asks questions earnestly and reflects on closely related problems, he may be said to have good qualities in him."

19.7. Zi Xia said, "Hundreds of artisans complete their work in the workshop; an intelligentleman should learn to attain his ideal."

19.8. Zi Xia said, "An uncultured man would certainly gloss his faults."

19.9. Zi Xia said, "An intelligentleman has three different aspects: when seen from afar, he looks grave; when approached, he looks affable; when listened to, he looks dignified."

19.10. Zi Xia said, "An intelligentleman will not order the people to toil until he is trusted, or they will think they are exploited. He will not criticize the sovereign till he wins his confidence, or the sovereign will think himself vilified."

19.11. Zi Xia said, "In regard to a serious matter of virtue, a man should not go beyond the limit; but in regard to a trifling matter, he may not keep within limit."

19.12. Zi You said, "The disciples and followers of Zi Xia are good at sprinkling water and sweeping floors, answering questions, coming forward and withdrawing, but all these are minor matters. I am afraid they are not so good in dealing with important things, Am I not right?" Hearing of this remark, Zi Xia said, "Alas! Zi You is mistaken. In regard to an intelligentleman's ways, which should be learned first? and which may be learned later? Disciples may be compared to plants and trees; they may be classified. How can an intelligentleman's ways not be learned in order? Who could be one from the beginning to the end? Is it not the sage alone?"

19.13. Zi Xia said, "An official versed in state affairs should amplify his knowledge; an intellectual well equipped with knowledge should serve the state."

19.14. Zi You said, "Mourning should not exceed grief."

19.15. Zi You said, "It is difficult to get a friend as good as Zi Zhang, still he cannot be said to be a benevolent man."

19.16. Master Zeng said, "Zi Zhang is ostentatious. It would be difficult to work together with him."

19.17. Master Zeng said, "I have heard from our Master

that no man should show his feeling to the full unless he is mourning the death of his parents."

19.18. Master Zeng said, "I have heard from our Master that it is possible to be as good a son as Meng Zhuang Zi, but it is difficult to be as good an official as he in employing his father's subordinates and following his father's policy."

19.19. The chief of the Meng family appointed Yang Fu as criminal judge, and Yang Fu consulted Master Zeng. Master Zeng said, "Those above have not followed the right way for a long time, and the people do not support them. If you can find out the reason why the criminals are accused, you should feel sympathy for them instead of joy for yourself."

19.20. Master Zeng said, "King Zhou of Yin might not be so tyrannical as it was reported. That is the reason why an intelligentleman would not stay in a low place, where one would be accused of all the evils of the world."

19.21. Master Zeng said, "The faults of an intelligentleman are like eclipses of the sun or the moon. When he does something wrong, all men can see it. When he has amended his fault, all men look up to him."

19.22. Gongsun Chao of the State of Wei asked Zi Gong, "From whom has Confucius acquired his knowledge?" Zi Gong said, "What the Literary and Martial Kings had taught the people has not been lost on earth. Cultured men have learned to settle main matters and uncultured men to settle minor matters. There is none but has learned something from the Literary and Martial Kings. How could my Master have learned nothing? Why should he have learned from one particular master?"

19.23. Shu Sun Wu Shu said to an official at court, "Zi Gong is more capable than his master Confucius." Zi Fu Jing Bo told Zi Gong what he had heard. Zi Gong said, "Let us use the wall as a comparison. My wall is only as high as my shoulder, so the beauty of my house could be easily perceived from over the wall. But my Master's wall rises many times a man's height. If a man cannot find the door to enter the house, the beauty and magnificence of the temple and halls could not be perceived. But few could enter his house by the door. No wonder the official should have said that about my Master."

19.24. Shu Sun Wu Shu spoke ill of Confucius. Zi Gong said, "It is no use doing wrong to Confucius. Other good men may be vilified, for their height like hillocks or mounds may be surpassed. But Confucius is as high as the sun and the moon. How could he be surpassed? If a man should try to harm him, it would turn to harm himself. What harm could be done to the sun and the moon? It is beyond a man's reach."

19.25. Chen Zi Qin said to Zi Gong, "You are too modest. How could Confucius be superior to you?" Zi Gong said, "By one word an intelligentleman may reveal his wisdom or ignorance. So we should be careful about what we say. It is as hard to catch up with my Master as to ascend the sky by a ladder. If he were in control of a state or a great family, the people would stand when he raised them, they would follow him when he led them, they would come from afar when called on to, and they would work in harmony when taught to. Living, he was glorious; dead, he would be bewailed. How could he be equalled?"

CHAPTER XX

Chapter XX

20.1. Yao said to Shun who succeeded him as emperor, "Oh, Shun! Heaven lays the divine duty on you. You should follow the right way without deviation. If the people in the world suffer poverty and misery, Heaven would no longer bestow favor on you." Shun said the same thing to Yu who succeeded him as emperor. Tang who founded the Yin dynasty said, "I, your humble servant, venture to sacrifice a black ox and declare to my Supreme Sovereign in Heaven that I dare not pardon any sinner nor conceal any guilt of my ministers which is of course clear in your mind. If I myself am guilty, do not lay blame on my people. If my people have done wrong, you may lay blame on me." Zhou had ennobled its lords and enriched its good men. King Wu of Zhou said, "I have bestowed favor on my kinsmen, but less than on good men. If my people are guilty, lay blame on me alone!" When attention was paid to weights and measures, statute and laws were reviewed and disused offices were restored, the government would go on the right way. When fallen states were re-established, descendants of extinguished families were found out, and unemployed good people were employed, the heart of the people would turn to the government. Emphasis should be laid on people, food, mourning and sacrifice. Lenience will win the people, faithfulness will win trust, diligence will win success, and justice will win happiness for the people.

20.2. Zi Zhang asked Confucius, "How could a man become a good ruler?" The Master said, "A man good in five aspects and free from four evils may become a good ruler." Zi Zhang asked, "May I know in which five aspects?" The Master said, "An intelligentleman should do good without waste, make people work without complaint, have desire without greed, uphold justice without pride and inspire respect without awe." Zi Zhang asked, "How could a man do good without waste?" The Master said, "If a ruler only does what will profit the people, is it not doing good without waste? If he orders people to do what they can, how could they complain? If he desires only to do good, how could he become greedy? If he treats all equally, whether there are many people or few, in great matter or small, is it not justice without pride? If he adjusts his clothes and hat and looks dignified, would he not

CHAPTER XX

inspire respect without awe?" Zi Zhang asked, "May I ask about the four evils?" The Master said, "To put people to death without reason is called tyranny. To expect success without due warning is called exaction. To demand timely completion without giving timely orders is called irresponsibility. To reward people in a stingy way is called miserliness."

20.3. Confucius said, "One who does not understand the divine law cannot be called an intelligentleman. One who does not understand the social order cannot stand in society. One who does not understand what wards imply cannot understand men."

许译中国经典诗文集

论语

许渊冲　英译
杨伯峻　中文译注

五洲传播出版社　中华书局

序

孔子（公元前551—前479年）是中国影响最大的、平凡中见伟大的人物。《论语》是孔子言行的真实记录。孔子在言谈中很少说"什么是"的问题，总是回答"如何做"的方法，但却具有超越时空的长久价值。《论语》重视情感教育，以学习本身为乐，从赏心娱目到怡性悦情，从社交行为到礼制道德，都可看出"克己复礼"的乐感。《论语》重视道德，把政治、伦理、宗教三者结合为一，认为政治是公德，伦理是私德，并以乐感或美感代替宗教，可以在日常生活中体验到超道德的宗教境界，领会到人生的本体是如何生活，为什么活，活得怎样。孔子思想的特点是不重逻辑思维，不重归纳演绎，而重直观联想，重类比关系。结果，《论语》在塑造、构成中华民族文化心理结构方面，成了整个社会言行、公私生活、思想意识的指引规范，渗透在政教体制、社会习俗、心理习惯、人的思想行为、言语活动之中。

七十五位荣获诺贝尔奖的科学家1988年在巴黎聚会，发表了一个声明，大意是说：人类如果要过和平幸福的生活，应该回到二千五百年前的孔子那里去寻找智慧。孔子的智慧是什么？如果要用一句话来概括，可以说是："己所不欲，勿施于人。"在《圣经》中，也有一句差不多的话，那就是："己之所欲，亦施于人。"这两句话有什么不同？《圣经》中的名言是积极的，而孔子的话是消极的。《圣经》说自己相信什么，就要别人也信什么；孔子却说自己不愿意做什么，就不要求别人做什么。如果自己相信自由民主，并且要求别人也相信自由民主，这是符合《圣经》的积极思想；如果自己不相信什么宗教，也不强求别人相信什么宗教，这就符合孔子的消极思想。在中世纪，发生了旧教和新教的长年战争，因为旧教徒信仰旧教，并且把不信旧教的新教徒叫作异教徒，甚至要把他们处死，所以发生了宗教战争。而在中国，两千年来，孔子的思想和佛教道教和平共处，统治者既不要求人信佛教或道教，也不勉强佛教徒或道教徒信仰孔子，所以从来没有发生过宗教战争。由此可以看出孔子思想的影响，也可以看出孔子的智慧。

孔子的思想言行，如果要用一个字来概括，那大约是一个"仁"字。什么是"仁"？《论语》第十七章中说："子张问仁于孔子，孔子曰：'能行五者于天下，为仁矣。'请问之。曰：'恭、宽、信、敏、惠。恭则不侮，宽则得众，信则人任焉，敏则有功，惠则足以使人。'"这就是说，"仁"是尊敬，尊重别人像尊重自己一样；仁是宽厚，要严于责己，宽以待人，容忍不同的意见；仁是诚信，言而有信，才能得到别人信任；仁是敏捷，只有行事迅速灵敏，才能得到成功；仁是恩惠，要为人做好事，决不损人利己。总之，就是"仁者爱人"，对待别人像对自己一样，将心比心，己所不欲，勿施于人。

孔子要行仁政，就是礼乐之治。礼乐是"仁"的外化。据冯友兰说，礼模仿自然界外在的秩序，乐模仿自然界内在的和谐。礼可以养性，乐可以怡情。做人要重仁义，治国要重礼乐。这是中国传统文化的精神。如果比较一下古代中国和古代希腊的文化教育，就可以发现，在孔子重视礼乐的时候，西方的柏拉图却在《理想国》中强调体育和音乐。由此可见，无论东方还是西方，都很重视音乐教育，也就是乐育。所不同的，中国更重礼教，就是维持社会秩序，处理人与人的关系；西方更重体育，要使人人体力更强，跑得更快，跳得更高更远。如果说乐育使人耳聪目明，成为智者；礼教却使人循规蹈矩，成为好人；体育则使人身强力壮，成为强人。这就是孔子和柏拉图的异同，他们使东西方的教育走上了不同的发展道路：东方要培养智者仁者，西方要培养智者勇者。

智仁勇三者的关系，不但表明了中西教育哲学的异同，也表现在中西方的文学作品之中。如西方的荷马史诗，《伊利亚特》歌颂了阿喀琉斯和赫克托耳等的英雄主义。《奥德赛》则赞美了奥德修斯的智慧和勇敢。而赫克托耳离开妻子上战场时的临别赠言是个典型的例子：

　　冲锋陷阵我带头，论功行赏不落后。

在中国的《诗经》中，歌颂的是圣君贤臣，对武王伐纣时的军师姜尚，只说了一句：

　　维师尚父，时维鹰扬。

把姜尚比作飞扬的雄鹰，和荷马史诗的描写相比，简直不可同日而语。而在《论语》第十一章中子路说："千乘之国，摄乎大国之间，加之以师旅，因之以饥馑，由也为之，比及三年，可使有勇，且知方也。"对这样的勇士，孔子只是置之一笑。

孔子不赞赏子路的勇敢，而赞美颜回的智慧，因为"回也闻一以知十"，又说："有颜回者好学，不迁怒，不贰过。"这就是赞美他的德行了。还说："贤哉回也！一箪食，一瓢饮，在陋巷，人不堪其忧，回也不改其乐。"这说明了孔子的乐育思想。颜回如何能在贫困中"不改其乐呢"？《论语》开宗明义第一章就说："学而时习之，不亦说乎？有朋自远方来，不亦乐乎？"这说明了好学和乐育的关系，颜回就是一个典型的例子，他"发愤忘食，乐以忘忧，不知老之将至"。由此可以看出孔子哲学思想的基础是乐感。

乐感不但是孔子思想的基础，也是最高的境界，所以他说："知之者不如好之者，好之者不如乐之者。"乐感就是孔子的智慧。乐感如何能产生智慧呢？孔子又说："兴于诗，立于礼，成于乐。"由此可见，诗和礼乐结合起来，就可以培育智者。孔子还说："知者不惑，仁者不忧，勇者不惧。"孔子赞赏知者仁者，却不赞赏勇者强者。这种修文偃武、重德轻才、顺应自然而不是征服自然、天人合一而不是人定胜天的思想，结果造成了中国两千多年以来重柔轻刚的风气，积弱成习的后患。

而在西方，《圣经》上说，上帝创造了男人和女人，却把他们赶出了天堂乐园，因为他们偷吃了智慧的禁果。这就是说，上帝禁止人有智慧，而人违反了上帝的禁令，不是顺应自然，而是征服自然，违抗了上帝的意志，所以人有负罪之感，就是罪感，而不是乐感。这是中西文化不同的一点。柏拉图在他的《理想国》中也说，要把诗人赶出国土，可见希腊哲学也排斥诗人的智慧。当宗教和哲学都不重视智者的时候，智慧的解释权就落到教会神职人员手中。因此，一派神职人员只相信自己的宗派，而把不同的宗派叫作异教，并且要把异教徒活活烧死，因为他们反对上帝，所以有罪。这样用暴力取代了智慧，宗教战争就爆发了，中世纪变成了黑暗时代。更甚的是，宗教战争发展成为对另一种宗教的十字军东征，于是天下大乱。直到文艺复兴时期，盗火者从天上盗来了文明的火种，西方的智者才觉醒了，他们摆脱了偷吃智慧禁果的罪感，重新把西方建设成为繁荣富强的文明国家。

而在东方，汉武帝罢黜百家，独尊孔子，使儒家思想几乎成了国教。由于"子不语：怪，力，乱，神"，所以两千年来，中国没有发生过宗教战争。从公元前一世纪到西方文艺复兴时期，中国一直是世界上最繁荣富强的文明国家。据法国《回声报》的统计，1820年中国国民生产总值为世界第一，占全球总产值百分之三十。假如西方各国能像中国一样宣扬孔子"己所不欲，勿施于人"的思想，并且付之实行，那么，世界可能会变得更加和平，更加文明。假如全世界都能宣扬并且实行孔子反对暴力、反对暴乱的思想，那么，世界上的武装冲突也并不是不能和平解决的。因此，我想，七十五位荣获诺贝尔奖的科学家提出要向孔子吸取智慧，就是为了这个缘故，就是因为孔子的智慧有利于建立世界和平的新秩序。

序

　　但从另一方面看来,孔子的思想也有其局限性,需要与时俱进。由于孔子不赞赏勇士和强者,因此中国历史上只崇尚圣贤,而不太歌颂英雄;重视脑力劳动,而轻视体力劳动。结果"江山代有才人出,各领风骚数百年",却缺少敢于与天斗争、与地斗争、与人斗争而感到其乐无穷的英雄。于是内忧外患,频频发生。到了20世纪上半叶,中国甚至沦落成了半殖民地。直至1970年,中国的国民生产总值还只占全球的百分之一。为了恢复繁荣强盛,中国需要学习西方英雄主义的精神,科学求实的作风。从前有句名言:"半部《论语》治天下",说的是只需要半部《论语》就足够治理国家。到了今天,应该理解为只有半部《论语》可以治国,其他半部已经过时,应向西方取长补短,使《论语》现代化。东西结合,才可以使"知者不惑,仁者不忧,勇者不惧"。如果每个国家都能"己所不欲,勿施于人",和平共处,共同发展,那么,21世纪的人类就可以过上幸福的和平生活。让我们记住英国18世纪诗人蒲伯的诗句作为结束:孔夫子超凡入圣,教我们如何做人。

许渊冲
2005年4月18日

学而篇第一

共十六章

学而篇第一

1.1 子⑴曰:"学而时⑵习⑶之,不亦说⑷乎?有朋⑸自远方来,不亦乐乎?人不知⑹,而不愠⑺,不亦君子⑻乎?"

【译文】孔子说:"学了,然后按一定的时间去实习它,不也高兴吗?有志同道合的人从远处来,不也快乐吗?人家不了解我,我却不怨恨,不也是君子吗?"

【注释】

⑴子——《论语》"子曰"的"子"都是指孔子而言。

⑵时——"时"字在周秦时候若作副词用,等于《孟子·梁惠王上》"斧斤以时入山林"的"以时","在一定的时候"或者"在适当的时候"的意思。王肃的《论语注》正是这样解释的。朱熹的《论语集注》把它解为"时常",是用后代的词义解释古书。

⑶习——一般人把习解为"温习",但在古书中,它还有"实习""演习"的意义,如《礼记·射义》的"习礼乐""习射"。《史记·孔子世家》:"孔子去曹适宋,与弟子习礼大树下。"这一"习"字,更是演习的意思。孔子所讲的功课,一般都和当时的社会生活和政治生活密切结合。像礼(包括各种仪节)、乐(音乐)、射(射箭)、御(驾车)这些,尤其非演习、实习不可。所以这"习"字以讲为实习为好。

⑷说——音读和意义跟"悦"字相同,高兴、愉快的意思。

⑸有朋——古本有作"友朋"的。旧注说:"同门曰朋。"宋翔凤《朴学斋札记》说,这里的"朋"字即指"弟子",就是《史记·孔子世

家》的"故孔子不仕,退而修《诗》、《书》、礼乐,弟子弥众,至自远方"。译文用"志同道合之人"即本此义。

(6) 人不知——这一句,"知"下没有宾语,人家不知道什么呢?当时因为有说话的实际环境,不需要说出便可以了解,所以未给说出。这却给后人留下一个谜。有人说,这一句是接上一句说的,从远方来的朋友向我求教,我告诉他,他还不懂,我却不怨恨。这样,"人不知"是"人家不知道我所讲述的"了。这种说法我嫌牵强,所以仍照一般的解释。这一句和《宪问篇》的"君子病无能焉,不病人之不己知也"的精神相同。

(7) 愠——音运,yùn,怨恨。

(8) 君子——《论语》的"君子",有时指"有德者",有时指"有位者",这里是指"有德者"。

1.2 有子[1]曰:"其为人也孝弟[2],而好犯[3]上者,鲜[4]矣;不好犯上,而好作乱者,未之有也[5]。君子务本,本立而道生。孝弟也者,其为仁之本[6]与[7]!"

【译文】有子说:"他的为人,孝顺爹娘,敬爱兄长,却喜欢触犯上级,这种人是很少的;不喜欢触犯上级,却喜欢造反,这种人从来没有过。君子专心致力于基础工作,基础树立了,'道'就会产生。孝顺爹娘,敬爱兄长,这就是'仁'的基础吧!"

【注释】

(1) 有子——孔子学生,姓有,名若,比孔子小十三岁,一说小三十三岁,以小三十三岁之说较可信。《论语》记载孔子的学生一般称字,独曾参和有若称"子"(另外,冉有和闵子骞偶一称子,又当别论),因此很多人疑心《论语》就是由他们两人的学生所纂述的。但是有若称子，可能是由于他在孔子死后曾一度为孔门弟子所尊重的缘故（这一史实可参阅《礼记•檀弓上》《孟子•滕文公上》和《史记•仲尼弟子列传》）。至于《左传》哀公八年说有若是一个"国士"，还未必是足以使他被尊称为"子"的原因。

(2)孝弟——孝，奴隶社会时期所认为的子女对待父母的正确态度；弟，音读和意义跟"悌"相同，音替，tì，弟弟对待兄长的正确态度。封建时代也把"孝弟"作为维持它那时候的社会制度、社会秩序的一种基本道德力量。

(3)犯——抵触，违反，冒犯。

(4)鲜——音显，xiǎn，少。《论语》的"鲜"都是如此用法。

(5)未之有也——"未有之也"的倒装形式。古代句法有一条这样的规律：否定句，宾语若是指代词，这指代词的宾语一般放在动词前。

(6)孝弟也者，其为仁之本——"仁"是孔子的一种最高道德的名称。也有人说（宋人陈善的《扪虱新语》开始如此说，后人赞同者很多），这"仁"字就是"人"字，古书"仁""人"两字本有很多写混了的。这里是说"孝悌是做人的根本"。这一说虽然也讲得通，但不能和"本立而道生"一句相呼应，未必符合有子的原意。《管子•戒篇》说，"孝弟者，仁之祖也"，也是这意。

(7)与——音读和意义跟"欤"字一样，《论语》的"欤"字都写作"与"。

1.3 子曰："巧言令色[1]，鲜矣仁！"

【译文】孔子说："花言巧语，伪善的面貌，这种人，'仁德'是不会多的。"

【注释】

(1)巧言令色——朱《注》云："好其言，善其色，致饰于外，务以说人。"所以译文以"花言巧语"译巧言，"伪善的面貌"译令色。

1.4 曾子⁽¹⁾曰:"吾日三省⁽²⁾吾身——为人谋而不忠乎?与朋友交而不信⁽³⁾乎?传⁽⁴⁾不习⁽⁵⁾乎?"

【译文】曾子说:"我每天多次自己反省:替别人办事是否尽心竭力了呢?同朋友往来是否诚实呢?老师传授我的学业是否复习了呢?"

【注释】

(1)曾子——孔子学生,名参(音身,shēn),字子舆,南武城(故城在今天的山东平邑县附近)人,比孔子小四十六岁(公元前505—前435)。

(2)三省——"三"字有读去声的,其实不破读也可以。"省"音醒,xǐng,自我检查,反省,内省。"三省"的"三"表示多次的意思。古代在有动作性的动词上加数字,这数字一般表示动作频率。而"三""九"等字,又一般表示次数的多,不要着实地去看待。说详汪中《述学•释三九》。这里所反省的是三件事,和"三省"的"三"只是巧合。如果这"三"字是指以下三件事而言,依《论语》的句法便应该这样说:"吾日省者三。"和《宪问篇》的"君子道者三"一样。

(3)信——诚也。

(4)传——平声,chuán,动词作名词用,老师的传授。

(5)习——这"习"字和"学而时习之"的"习"一样,包括温习、实习、演习而言,这里概括地译为"复习"。

1.5 子曰:"道⁽¹⁾千乘之国⁽²⁾,敬事⁽³⁾而信,节用而爱人⁽⁴⁾,使民以时⁽⁵⁾。"

【译文】孔子说:"治理具有一千辆兵车的国家,就要严肃认真地对待工作，信实无欺，节约费用，爱护官吏，役使老百姓要在农闲时间。"

【注释】

(1)道——动词，治理的意思。

(2)千乘之国——乘音剩，shèng，古代用四匹马拉着的兵车。春秋时代，打仗用车子，所以国家的强弱都用车辆的数目来计算。春秋初期，大国都没有千辆兵车。像《左传》僖公二十八年所记载的城濮之战，晋文公还只七百乘。但是在那时代，战争频繁，无论侵略者和被侵略者都必须扩充军备。侵略者更因为兼并的结果，兵车的发展速度更快；譬如晋国到平丘之会，据叔向的话，已有四千乘了（见《左传》昭公十三年）。千乘之国，在孔子之时已经不是大国，因此子路也说"千乘之国摄乎大国之间"（11.26）的话了。

(3)敬事——"敬"字一般用于表示工作态度，因之常和"事"字连用，如《卫灵公篇》的"事君敬其事而后其食"。

(4)爱人——古代"人"字有广狭两义。广义的"人"指一切人群，狭义的人只指士大夫以上各阶层的人。这里和"民"（使"民"以时）对言，用的是狭义。

(5)使民以时——古代以农业为主，"使民以时"即是《孟子·梁惠王上》的"不违农时"，因此用意译。

1.6 子曰："弟子[1]，入[2]则孝，出[2]则悌，谨[3]而信，泛爱众，而亲仁[4]。行有余力，则以学文。"

【译文】孔子说："后生小子，在父母跟前，就孝顺父母；离开自己房子，便敬爱兄长；寡言少语，说则诚实可信，博爱大众，亲近有仁德的人。这样躬行实践之后，有剩余力量，就再去学习文献。"

【注释】

(1)弟子——一般有两种意义:(甲)年纪幼小的人,(乙)学生。这里用的是第一种意义。

(2)入、出——《礼记·内则》:"由命士以上,父子皆异宫",则知这里的"弟子"是指"命士"以上的人物而言。"入"是"入父宫","出"是"出己宫"。

(3)谨——寡言叫做谨。详见杨遇夫先生的《积微居小学金石论丛》卷一。

(4)仁——"仁"即"仁人",和《雍也篇第六》的"井有仁焉"的"仁"一样。古代的词汇经常运用这样一种规律:用某一具体人和事物的性质、特征甚至原料来代表那一具体的人和事物。

1.7 子夏(1)曰:"贤贤易色(2);事父母,能竭其力;事君,能致(3)其身;与朋友交,言而有信。虽曰未学,吾必谓之学矣。"

【译文】子夏说:"对妻子,重品德,不重容貌;侍奉爹娘,能尽心竭力;服事君上,能豁出生命;同朋友交往,说话诚实守信。这种人,虽说没学习过,我一定说他已经学习过了。"

【注释】

(1)子夏——孔子学生,姓卜,名商,字子夏,比孔子小四十四岁。(公元前507—?)

(2)贤贤易色——这句话,一般的解释是:"用尊贵优秀品德的心来交换(或者改变)爱好美色的心。"照这种解释,这句话的意义就比较空泛。陈祖范的《经咫》、宋翔凤的《朴学斋札记》等书却说,以下三句,事父母、事君、交朋友,各指一定的人事关系;那么,"贤贤易色"也应该是指某一种人事关系而言,不能是一般的泛指。奴隶社会和封建社会把夫妻间关系看得极重,认为是"人伦之始"和"王化之基",这里开始便谈到它,是不足为奇的。我认为这话很有道理。"易"有交换、改变的意义,也有轻视(如言"轻易")、简慢的意义。因之我便用《汉书》卷七十五《李寻传》颜师古《注》的说法,把"易色"解为"不重容貌"。

(3)致——有"委弃"、"献纳"等意义,所以用"豁出生命"来译它。

1.8 子曰:"君子[1]不重,则不威;学则不固。主忠信[2]。无友不如己者[3]。过,则勿惮改。"

【译文】孔子说:"君子,如果不庄重,就没有威严;即使读书,所学的也不会巩固。要以忠和信两种道德为主。不要跟不如自己的人交朋友。有了过错,就不要怕改正。"

【注释】
(1)君子——这一词一直贯串到末尾,因此译文将这两字作一停顿。
(2)主忠信——《颜渊篇》(1,10)也说,"主忠信,徙义,崇德也",可见"忠信"是道德。
(3)无友不如己者——古今人对这一句发生不少怀疑,因而有一些不同的解释。译义只就字面译出。

1.9 曾子曰:"慎终[1],追远[2],民德归厚矣。"

【译文】曾子说:"谨慎地对待父母的死亡,追念远代祖先,自然会导致老百姓归于忠厚老实了。"
【注释】
(1)慎终——郑玄的《注》:"老死曰终。"可见这"终"字是指父母的死亡。慎终的内容,刘宝楠《论语正义》引《檀弓》曾子的话是指附身(装殓)、附棺(埋葬)的事必诚必信,不要有后悔。

(2)追远——具体地说是指"祭祀尽其敬"。两者译文都只就字面译出。

1.10 子禽[1]问于子贡[2]曰:"夫子[3]至于是邦也,必闻其政,求之与?抑与之与?"子贡曰:"夫子温、良、恭、俭、让以得之。夫子之求之也,其诸[4]异乎人之求之与?"

【译文】子禽向子贡问道:"他老人家一到哪个国家,必然听得到那个国家的政事,求来的呢?还是别人自动告诉他的呢?"子贡道:"他老人家是靠温和、善良、严肃、节俭、谦逊来取得的。他老人家获得的方法,和别人获得的方法,不相同吧?"

【注释】

(1)子禽——陈亢(kàng)字子禽。从《子张篇》所载的事看来,恐怕不是孔子的学生。《史记•仲尼弟子列传》也不载此人。但郑玄注《论语》和《檀弓》都说他是孔子学生,不晓得有什么根据。(臧庸的《拜经日记》说子禽就是《仲尼弟子列传》的原亢禽,简朝亮的《论语集注补疏》曾加以辩驳。)

(2)子贡——孔子学生,姓端木,名赐,字子贡,卫人,比孔子小三十一岁。(公元前520—?)

(3)夫子——这是古代的一种敬称,凡是做过大夫的人,都可以取得这一敬称。孔子曾为鲁国的司寇,所以他的学生称他为夫子,后来因此沿袭以称呼老师。在一定的场合下,也用以特指孔子。

(4)其诸——洪颐煊《读书丛录》云:"《公羊》桓六年《传》,'其诸以病桓与?'闵元年《传》,'其诸吾仲孙与?'僖二十四年《传》,'其诸此之谓与?'宣五年《传》,'其诸为其双双而俱至者与?'十五年《传》,'其诸则宜于此焉变矣'。'其诸'是齐鲁间语。"案,总上诸例,皆用来表示不肯定的语气。黄家岱《𡠾艺轩杂著》说"其诸"意为"或者",大致得之。

1.11 子曰:"父在,观其⑴志;父没,观其⑴行⑵;三年⑶无改于父之道⑷,可谓孝矣。"

【译文】孔子说:"当他父亲活着,[因为他无权独立行动,]要观察他的志向;他父亲死了,要考察他的行为;若是他对他父亲的合理部分,长期地不加改变,可以说做到孝了。"

【注释】

⑴其——指儿子,不是指父亲。

⑵行——去声,xìng。

⑶三年——古人这种数字,有时不要看得太机械。它经常只表示一种很长的期间。

⑷道——有时候是一般意义的名词,无论好坏、善恶都可以叫做道。但更多时候是积极意义的名词,表示善的好的东西。这里应该这样看,所以译为"合理部分"。

1.12 有子曰:"礼之用,和⑴为贵。先王之道,斯为美;小大由之。有所不行⑵,知和而和,不以礼节之,亦不可行也。"

【译文】有子说:"礼的作用,以遇事都做得恰当为可贵。过去圣明君王的治理国家,可宝贵的地方就在这里;他们小事大事都做得恰当。但是，如有行不通的地方，便为恰当而求恰当，不用一定的规矩制度来加以节制，也是不可行的。"

【注释】

(1)和——《礼记·中庸》："喜怒哀乐之未发谓之中，发而皆中节谓之和。"杨遇夫先生《论语疏证》说："事之中节者皆谓之和，不独喜怒哀乐之发一事也。《说文》云：'龢，调也。''盉，调味也。'乐调谓之龢，味调谓之盉，事之调适者谓之和，其义一也。和今言适合，言恰当，言恰到好处。"

(2)有所不行——皇侃《义疏》把这句属上，全文便如此读："礼之用，和为贵。先王之道，斯为美。小大由之，有所不行。……"他把"和"解为音乐，说："此以下明人君行化必乐相须。……变乐言和，见乐功也。……小大由之有所不行者，言每事小大皆用礼，而不以乐和之，则其政有所不行也。"这种句读法值得考虑，但把"和"解释为音乐，而且认为"小大由之"的"之"是指"礼"而言，都觉牵强。特为注出，以供大家考虑。

1.13 有子曰："信近于义，言可复⁽¹⁾也。恭近于礼，远⁽²⁾耻辱也。因⁽³⁾不失其亲，亦可宗⁽⁴⁾也。"

【译文】有子说："所守的约言符合义，说的话就能兑现。态度容貌的庄矜合于礼，就不致遭受侮辱。依靠关系深的人，也就可靠了。"

【注释】

(1)复——《左传》僖公九年荀息说："吾与先君言矣，不可以贰，能欲复言而爱身乎？"又哀公十六年叶公说："吾闻胜也好复言……复言非信也。"这"复言"都是实践诺言之义。《论语》此义当同于此。朱熹《集注》云："复，践言也。"但未举论证，因之后代训诂家多有疑之者。童第德先生为我举出《左传》为证，足补古今字书之所未及。
(2)远——去声，音院，yuàn，动词，使动用法，使之远离的意思。此处亦可以译为避免。
(3)因——依靠，凭借。有人读为"姻"字，那"因不失其亲"便当译为"所与婚姻的人都是可亲的"，恐未必如此。
(4)宗——主，可靠。一般解释为"尊敬"，不妥。

1.14 子曰："君子⁽¹⁾食无求饱，居无求安，敏于事而慎于言，就有道而正⁽²⁾焉，可谓好学也已。"

【译文】孔子说："君子，吃食不要求饱足，居住不要求舒适，对工作勤劳敏捷，说话却谨慎，到有道的人那里去匡正自己，这样，可以说是好学了。"

【注释】
(1)君子——《论语》的"君子"有时指"有位之人"，有时指"有德之人"。但有的地方究竟是指有位者，还是指有德者，很难分别。此处大概是指有德者。
(2)正——《论语》"正"字用了很多次。当动词的，都作"匡正"或"端正"讲，这里不必例外。一般把"正"字解为"正其是非""判其得失"，我所不取。

1.15 子贡曰："贫而无谄，富而无骄，何如⁽¹⁾？"子曰："可也；未若贫而乐⁽²⁾，富而好礼者也。"子贡曰："《诗》云：'如切如磋，如琢如磨⁽³⁾，'其斯之谓与？"子曰："赐⁽⁴⁾也，始可与言《诗》已矣，告诸往而知来者⁽⁵⁾。"

【译文】子贡说:"贫穷却不巴结奉承,有钱却不骄傲自大,怎么样?"孔子说:"可以了;但是还不如虽贫穷却乐于道,纵有钱却谦虚好礼哩。"子贡说:"《诗经》上说:'要像对待骨、角、象牙、玉石一样,先开料,再糙锉,细刻,然后磨光。'那就是这样的意思吧?"孔子道:"赐呀,现在可以同你讨论《诗经》了,告诉你一件,你能有所发挥,举一反三了。"

【注释】
(1)何如——《论语》中的"何如",都可以译为"怎么样"。
(2)贫而乐——皇侃本"乐"下有"道"字。郑玄《注》云:"乐谓志于道,不以贫为忧苦。"所以译文增"于道"两字。
(3)如切如磋,如琢如磨——两语见于《诗经·卫风·淇奥篇》。
(4)赐——子贡名。孔子对学生都称名。
(5)告诸往而知来者——"诸",在这里用法同"之"一样。"往",过去的事,这里譬为已知的事;"来者",未来的事,这里譬为未知的事。译文用意译法。孔子赞美子贡能运用《诗经》作譬,表示学问道德都要提高一步看。

1.16 子曰:"不患人之不己知,患不知人也。"

【译文】孔子说:"别人不了解我,我不急;我急的是自己不了解别人。"

为政篇第二

共二十四章

2.1 子曰:"为政以德,譬如北辰⁽¹⁾居其所而众星共⁽²⁾之。"

【译文】孔子说:"用道德来治理国政,自己便会像北极星一般,在一定的位置上,别的星辰都环绕着它。"

【注释】

(1)北辰——由于地球自转轴正对天球北极,在地球自转和公转所反映出来的恒星周日和周年视运动中,天球北极是不动的,其他恒星则绕之旋转。我国黄河中、下游流域,约为北纬36度,因之天球北极也高出北方地平线上36度。孔子所说的北辰,不是指天球北极,而是指北极星。天球北极虽然不动,其他星辰都环绕着它动,但北极星也是动的,而且转动非常快。只是因为它距离地球太远,约782光年,人们不觉得它移动罢了。距今四千年前北极在右枢(天龙座α)附近,今年则在勾陈一(小熊座α)。

(2)共——同拱,与《左传》僖公三十二年"尔墓之木拱矣"的"拱"意义相近,环抱、环绕之意。

2.2 子曰:"《诗》三百⁽¹⁾,一言以蔽之,曰:'思无邪⁽²⁾'。"

【译文】孔子说:"《诗经》三百篇,用一句话来概括它,就是'思想纯正'。"

【注释】

(1)《诗》三百——《诗经》实有三百五篇，"三百"只是举其整数。

(2)思无邪——"思无邪"一语本是《诗经•鲁颂•駉篇》之文，孔子借它来评论所有诗篇。思字在《駉篇》本是无义的语首词，孔子引用它却当思想解，自是断章取义。俞樾《曲园杂纂•说项》说这也是语辞，恐不合孔子原意。

2.3 子曰："道⁽¹⁾之以政，齐之以刑，民免⁽²⁾而无耻；道之以德，齐之以礼，有耻且格⁽³⁾。"

【译文】孔子说："用政法来诱导他们，使用刑罚来整顿他们，人民只是暂时地免于罪过，却没有廉耻之心。如果用道德来诱导他们，使用礼教来整顿他们，人民不但有廉耻之心，而且人心归服。"

【注释】

(1)道——有人把它看成"道千乘之国"的"道"一样，治理的意思。也有人把它看成"导"字，引导的意思，我取后一说。

(2)免——先秦古书若单用一个"免"字，一般都是"免罪""免刑""免祸"的意思。

(3)格——这个字的意义本来很多，在这里有把它解为"来"的，也有解为"至"的，还有解为"正"的，更有写作"恪"，解为"敬"的。这些不同的讲解都未必符合孔子原意。《礼记•缁衣篇》："夫民，教之以德，齐之以礼，则民有格心；教之以政，齐之以刑，则民有遯心。"这话可以看作孔子此言的最早注释，较为可信。此处"格心"和"遯心"相对成文，"遯"即"遁"字，逃避的意思。逃避的反面应该是亲近、归服、向往，所以用"人心归服"来译它。

2.4 子曰:"吾十有⑴五而志于学,三十而立⑵,四十而不惑⑶,五十而知天命⑷,六十而耳顺⑸,七十而从心所欲,不逾矩⑹。"

【译文】孔子说:"我十五岁,有志于学问;三十岁,〔懂礼仪,〕说话做事都有把握;四十岁,〔掌握了各种知识,〕不致迷惑;五十岁,得知天命;六十岁,一听别人言语,便可以分别真假,判明是非;到了七十岁,便随心所欲,任何念头不越出规矩。"

【注释】

⑴有——同又。古人在整数和小一位的数字之间多用"有"字,不用"又"字

⑵立——《泰伯篇》说:"立于礼。"《季氏篇》又说:"不学礼,无以立。"因之译文添了"懂得礼仪"几个字。"立"是站立的意思,这里是"站得住"的意思,为求上下文的流畅,意译为遇事"都有把握"。

⑶不惑——《子罕篇》和《宪问篇》都有"知者不惑"的话,所以译文用"掌握了知识"来说明"不惑"。

⑷天命——孔子不是宿命论者,但也讲天命。孔子的天命,我已有文探讨。后来的人虽然谈得很多,未必符合孔子本意。因此,这两个字暂不译出。

⑸耳顺——这两个字很难讲,企图把它讲通的也有很多人,但都觉牵强。译者姑且作如此讲解。

⑹从心所欲不逾矩——"从"字有作"纵"字的,皇侃《义疏》也读为"纵",解为放纵。柳宗元《与杨晦之书》说"孔子七十而纵心",不但"从"字写作"纵",而且以"心"字绝句,"所欲"属下读。"七十而纵心,所欲不逾矩"。但"纵"字古人多用于贬义,如《左传》昭公十年"我实纵欲",柳读难从。

2.5 孟懿子⁽¹⁾问孝。子曰:"无违⁽²⁾。"樊迟⁽³⁾御,子告之曰:"孟孙问孝于我,我对曰,无违。"樊迟曰:"何谓也?"子曰:"生,事之以礼⁽⁴⁾;死,葬之以礼,祭之以礼。"

【译文】孟懿子向孔子问孝道。孔子说:"不要违背礼节。"不久,樊迟替孔子赶车子,孔子便告诉他说:"孟孙向我问孝道,我答复说,不要违背礼节。"樊迟道:"这是什么意思?"孔子道:"父母活着,依规定的礼节侍奉他们;死了,依规定的礼节埋葬他们,祭祀他们。"

【注释】

(1)孟懿子——鲁国的大夫,三家之一,姓仲孙,名何忌,"懿"是谥号。他父亲是孟僖子仲孙貜。《左传》昭公七年说,孟僖子将死,遗嘱要他向孔子学礼。

(2)无违——黄式三《论语后案》说:"《左传》桓公二年云,'昭德塞违','灭德立违','君违,不忘谏之以德';六年《传》云:'有嘉德而无违心',襄公二十六年《传》云,'正其违而治其烦'……古人凡背礼者谓之违。"因此,我把"违"译为"违礼"。王充《论衡·问孔篇》曾经质问孔子,为什么不讲"无违礼",而故意省略讲为"无违",难道不怕人误会为"毋违志"吗?由此可见"违"字的这一含义在后汉时已经不被人所了解了。

(3)樊迟——孔子学生,名须,字子迟,比孔子小四十六岁。〔《史记·仲尼弟子列传》作小三十六岁,《孔子家语》作小四十六岁。若从《左传》哀公十一年所记载的樊迟的事考之,可能《史记》的"三"系"亖"(古四字)之误。〕

(4)生,事之以礼——"生"和下句"死"都是表示时间的节缩语,所以自成一逗。古代的礼仪有一定的差等,天子、诸侯、大夫、士、庶人各不相同。鲁国的三家是大夫,不但有时用鲁公(诸侯)之礼,甚至有时用天子之礼。这种行为当时叫做"僭",是孔子所最痛心的。孔子这几句答语,或者是针对这一现象发出的。

2.6 孟武伯[1]问孝。子曰:"父母唯其[2]疾之忧。"

【译文】孟武伯向孔子请教孝道。孔子道:"做爹娘的只是为孝子的疾病发愁。"

【注释】
[1]孟武伯——仲孙彘,孟懿子的儿子,"武"是谥号。
[2]其——第三人称表示领位的代名词,相当于"他的"、"他们的"。但这里所指代的是父母呢,还是儿女呢?便有两说。王充《论衡·问孔篇》说:"武伯善忧父母,故曰,唯其疾之忧。"《淮南子·说林训》说:"忧父之疾者子,治之者医。"高诱《注》云:"父母唯其疾之忧,故曰忧之者子。"可见王充、高诱都以为"其"字是指代父母而言。马融却说:"言孝子不妄为非,唯疾病然后使父母忧。"把"其"字代孝子。两说都可通,而译文采取马融之说。

2.7 子游[1]问孝。子曰:"今之孝者,是谓能养[2]。至于[3]犬马,皆能有养[4];不敬,何以别乎?"

【译文】子游问孝道。孔子说:"现在的所谓孝,就是说能够养活爹娘便行了。对于狗马都能够得到饲养;若不存心严肃地孝顺父母,那养活爹娘和饲养狗马怎样去分别呢?"

【注释】
[1]子游——孔子学生,姓言,名偃,字子游,吴人,小于孔子四十五岁。

(2)养——"养父母"的"养"从前人都读去声，音漾，yàng。

(3)至于——张相的《诗词曲语词汇释》把"至于"解作"即使""就是"。在这一段中固然能够讲得文从字顺，可是"至于"的这一种用法，在先秦古书中仅此一见，还难于据以肯定。我认为这一"至于"和《孟子·告子上》的"惟耳亦然。至于声，天下期于师旷，是天下之耳相似也。惟目亦然。至于子都，天下莫不知其姣也"的"至于"用法相似。都可用"谈到""讲到"来译它。不译也可。

(4)至于犬马，皆能有养——这一句很有些不同的讲法。一说是犬马也能养活人，人养活人，若不加以敬，便和犬马的养活人无所分别。这一说也通。还有一说是犬马也能养活它自己的爹娘（李光地《论语札记》、翟灏《四书考异》），可是犬马在事实上是不能够养活自己爹娘的，所以这说不可信。还有人说，犬马是比喻小人之词（刘宝楠《论语正义》引刘宝树说），可是用这种比喻的修辞法，在《论语》中找不出第二个相似的例子，和《论语》的文章风格不相侔，更不足信。

2.8 子夏问孝。子曰："色难⁽¹⁾。有事，弟子⁽²⁾服其劳；有酒食⁽³⁾，先生馔⁽⁴⁾，曾⁽⁵⁾是以为孝乎？"

【译文】子夏问孝道。孔子道："儿子在父母前经常有愉悦的容色，是件难事。有事情，年轻人效劳；有酒有肴，年长的人吃喝，难道这竟可认为是孝么？"

【注释】

(1)色难——这句话有两说，一说是儿子侍奉父母时的容色。《礼记·祭义篇》说："孝子之有深爱者必有和气，有和气者必有愉色，有愉色者必有婉容。"可以做这两个字的注脚。另一说是侍奉父母的容色，后汉的经学家包咸、马融都如此说。但是，若原意果如此话，应该说为"侍色为难",不该简单地说为"色难",因之我不采取。
(2)弟子、先生——刘台拱《论语骈枝》云:"《论语》言'弟子'者七,其二皆年幼者,其五谓门人。言'先生'者二,皆谓年长者。"马融说:"先生谓父兄也。"亦通。
(3)食——旧读去声,音嗣,sì,食物。不过现在仍如字读shí,如"主食""副食""面食"。
(4)馔——音撰,zhuàn,吃喝。《鲁论》作"馂"。馂,食余也。那么这句便当如此读:"有酒,食先生馂",而如此翻译:"有酒,幼辈吃其剩余。"
(5)曾——音层,céng,副词,竟也。

2.9 子曰:"吾与回[1]言终日,不违,如愚。退而省其私[2],亦足以发,回也不愚。"

【译文】孔子说:"我整天和颜回讲学,他从不提反对意见和疑问,像个蠢人。等他退回去自己研究,却也能发挥,可见颜回并不愚蠢。"

【注释】

(1)回——颜回,孔子最得意的学生,鲁国人,字子渊,小孔子三十岁(《史记·仲尼弟子列传》如此。但根据毛奇龄《论语稽求篇》和崔适《论语足征记》的考证,《史记》的"三十"应为"四十"之误,颜渊实比孔子小四十岁,公元前511—前480)。
(2)退而省其私——朱熹的《集注》以为孔子退而省颜回的私,"则见其日用动静语默之间皆足以发明夫子之道",用颜回的实践来证明他能发挥孔子之道,说也可通。

2.10 子曰:"视其所以⁽¹⁾,观其所由⁽²⁾,察其所安⁽³⁾。人焉廋哉⁽⁴⁾?人焉廋哉?"

【译文】孔子说:"考查一个人所结交的朋友;观察他为达到一定目的所采用的方式方法;了解他的心情,安于什么,不安于什么。那么,这个人怎样隐藏得住呢?这个人怎样隐藏得住呢?"

【注释】

(1)所以——"以"字可以当"用"讲,也可以当"与"讲。如果解释为"用",便和下句"所由"的意思重复,因此我把它解释为"与",和《微子篇第十八》"而谁以易之"的"以"同义。有人说"以犹为也"。"视其所以"即《大戴礼·文王官人篇》的"考其所为",也通。

(2)所由——"由","由此行"的意思。《学而篇第一》的"小大由之",《雍也篇第六》的"行不由径",《泰伯篇第八》的"民可使由之"的"由"都如此解。"所由"是指所从由的道路,因此我用方式方法来译述。

(3)所安——"安"就是《阳货篇第十七》孔子对宰予说的"女安,则为之"的"安"。一个人未尝不错做一两件坏事,如果因此而心不安,仍不失为好人。因之译文多说了几句。

(4)人焉廋哉——焉,何处;廋,音搜,sōu,隐藏,藏匿。这句话机械地翻译,便是:"这个人到哪里去隐藏呢。"《史记·魏世家》述说李克的观人方法是"居视其所亲,富视其所与,达视其所举,穷视其所不为,贫视其所不取"。虽较具体,却无此深刻。

2.11 子曰:"温故而知新⁽¹⁾,可以为师矣。"

【译文】孔子说:"在温习旧知识时,能有新体会、新发现,就可以做老师了。"

【注释】

⑴温故而知新——皇侃《义疏》说,"温故"就是"月无忘其所能","知新"就是"日知其所亡"(19.5),也通。

2.12 子曰:"君子不器⑴。"

【译文】孔子说:"君子不像器皿一般,〔只有一定的用途。〕"

【注释】

⑴古代知识范围狭窄,孔子认为应该无所不通。后人还曾说,一事之不知,儒者之耻。虽然有人批评孔子"博学而无所成名"(9.2),但孔子仍说"君子不器"。

2.13 子贡问君子。子曰:"先行其言而后从之。"

【译文】子贡问怎样才能做一个君子。孔子道:"对于你要说的话,先实行了,再说出来〔这就够说是一个君子了〕。"

2.14 子曰:"君子周而不比⑴,小人比而不周。"

【译文】孔子说:"君子是团结,而不是勾结;小人是勾结,而不是团结。"

【注释】

(1)周、比——"周"是以当时所谓道义来团结人,"比"则是以暂时共同利害互相勾结。"比"旧读去声bì。

2.15 子曰:"学而不思则罔⑴,思而不学则殆⑵。"

【译文】孔子说:"只是读书,却不思考,就会受骗;只是空想,却不读书,就会缺乏信心。"

【注释】

(1)罔——诬罔的意思。"学而不思"则受欺,似乎是《孟子•尽心下》"尽信书,不如无书"的意思。
(2)殆——《论语》的"殆"(dǎi)有两个意义,下文第十八章"多见阙殆"的"殆"当"疑惑"解(说本王引之《经义述闻》),《微子篇》"今之从政者殆而"的"殆"当危险解。这里两个意义都讲得过去,译文取前一义。古人常以"罔""殆"对文,如《诗经•小雅•节南山》云:"弗问弗仕,勿罔君子;式夷式已,无小人殆。"("无小人殆"即"无殆小人",因韵脚而倒装。)旧注有以"罔然无所得"释"罔",以"精神疲殆"释"殆"的,似乎难以圆通。

2.16 子曰:"攻⑴乎异端⑵,斯⑶害也已⑷。"

【译文】孔子说:"批判那些不正确的议论,祸害就可以消灭了。"

【注释】

(1)攻——《论语》共用四次"攻"字,像《先进篇》的"小子鸣鼓而攻之",《颜渊篇》的"攻其恶,无攻人之恶"的三个"攻"字都当"攻击"解,这里也不应例外。很多人却把它解为"治学"的"治"。

(2)异端——孔子之时,自然还没有诸子百家,因之很难译为"不同的学说",但和孔子相异的主张、言论未必没有,所以译为"不正确的议论"。

(3)斯——连词,"这就"的意思。

(4)已——应该看为动词,止也。因之我译为"消灭"。如果把"攻"字解为"治",那么"斯"字得看作指代词,"这"的意思;"也已"得看作语气词。全文便如此译:"从事于不正确的学术研究,这是祸害哩。"一般的讲法是如此的,虽能文从字顺,但和《论语》词法和句法都不合。

2.17 子曰:"由[1]!诲女知之乎!知之为知之,不知为不知,是知也[2]。"

【译文】孔子说:"由!教给你对待知或不知的正确态度吧!知道就是知道,不知道就是不知道,这就是聪明智慧。"

【注释】

(1)由——孔子学生,仲由,字子路,卞(故城在今山东平邑县东北仲村)人,小于孔子九岁。(公元前542—前480)

(2)是知也——《荀子·子道篇》也载了这一段话,但比这详细。其中有两句道:"言要则知,行至则仁。"因之读"知"为"智"。如果"知"如字读,便该这样翻译:这就是对待知或不知的正确态度。

2.18 子张[1]学干禄[2]。子曰:"多闻阙疑,慎言其余,则寡尤;多见阙殆⁽³⁾,慎行其余,则寡悔。言寡尤,行⁽⁴⁾寡悔,禄在其中矣。"

【译文】子张向孔子学求官职得俸禄的方法。孔子说:"多听,有怀疑的地方,加以保留;其余足以自信的部分,谨慎地说出,就能减少错误。多看,有怀疑的地方,加以保留;其余足以自信的部分,谨慎地实行,就能减少懊悔。言语的错误少,行动的懊悔少,官职俸禄就在这里面了。"

【注释】

(1)子张——孔子学生颛孙师,字子张,陈人,小于孔子四十八岁。(公元前503—?)

(2)干禄——干,求也;禄,旧时官吏的俸给。

(3)阙殆——和"阙疑"同意。上文作"阙疑",这里作"阙殆","疑"和"殆"是同义词,所谓"互文"见义。

(4)行——名词,去声,xìng。

2.19 哀公⁽¹⁾问曰:"何为则民服?"孔子对曰⁽²⁾:"举直错诸枉⁽³⁾,则民服;举枉错诸直,则民不服。"

【译文】鲁哀公问道:"要做些甚么事才能使百姓服从呢?"孔子答道:"把正直的人提拔出来,放在邪曲的人之上,百姓就服从了;若是把邪曲的人提拔出来,放在正直的人之上,百姓就会不服从。"

【注释】

(1)哀公——鲁君,姓姬,名蒋,定公之子,继定公而即位,在位二十七年。(公元前494—前466)"哀"是谥号。

(2) 孔子对曰——《论语》的行文体例是，臣下对答君上的询问一定用"对曰"，这里孔子答复鲁君之问，所以用"孔子对曰"。
(3) 错诸枉——"错"有放置的意思，也有废置的意思。一般人把它解为废置，说是"废置那些邪恶的人"（把"诸"字解为"众"）。这种解法和古汉语语法规律不相合。因为"枉""直"是以虚代实的名词，古文中的"众""诸"这类数量形容词，一般只放在真正的实体词之上，不放在这种以虚代实的词之上。这一规律，南宋人孙季和（名应时）便已明白。王应麟《困学纪闻》曾引他的话说："若诸家解，何用二'诸'字？"这二"诸"字只能看做"之于"的合音，"错"当"放置"解。"置之于枉"等于说"置之于枉人之上"，古代汉语"于"字之后的方位词有时可以省略。朱亦栋《论语札记》解此句不误。

2.20 季康子⁽¹⁾问："使民敬、忠以⁽²⁾劝，如之何？"子曰："临之以庄，则敬；孝慈，则忠；举善而教不能，则劝。"

【译文】季康子问道："要使人民严肃认真，尽心竭力和互相勉励，应该怎么办呢？"孔子说："你对待人民的事情严肃认真，他们对待你的政令也会严肃认真了；你孝顺父母，慈爱幼小，他们也就会对你尽心竭力了；你提拔好人，教育能力弱的人，他们也就会劝勉了。"

【注释】
(1) 季康子——季孙肥，鲁哀公时正卿，当时政治上最有权力的人。"康"是谥号。
(2) 以——连词，与"和"同。

2.21 或谓孔子曰:"子奚不为政?"子曰:"《书》⑴云:
'孝乎惟孝,友于兄弟,施⑵于有政⑶。'是亦为政,奚其为
为政?"

【译文】有人对孔子道:"你为什么不参与政治?"孔子
道:"《尚书》上说,'孝呀,只有孝顺父母,友爱兄弟,把
这种风气影响到政治上去。'这也就是参与政治了呀,为什么
定要做官才算参与政治呢?"

【注释】

⑴《书》云——以下三句是《尚书》的逸文,作《伪古文尚书》的便从
这里采入《君陈篇》。

⑵施——这里应该当"延及"讲,从前人解为"施行",不妥。

⑶施于有政——"有"字无义,加于名词之前,这是古代构词法的一种
形态,详拙著《文言语法》。杨遇夫先生说:"政谓卿相大臣,以职
言,不以事言。"(说详《增订积微居小学金石论丛•论语子奚不为政
解》)那么,这句话便当译为"把这种风气影响到卿相大臣上去"。

2.22 子曰:"人而无信⑴,不知其可也。大车无輗,小车无
軏⑵,其何以行之哉?"

【译文】孔子说:"作为一个人,却不讲信誉,不知那怎么可
以。譬如大车子没有安横木的輗,小车子没有安横木的軏,如
何能走呢?"

【注释】

⑴人而无信——这"而"字不能当"如果"讲。不说"人无信",而说
"人而无信"者,表示"人"字要作一读。古书多有这种句法,译文

似能表达其意。

(2)輗、軏——輗音倪，ní；軏音月，yuè。古代用牛力的车叫大车，用马力的车叫小车。两者都要把牲口套在车辕上。车辕前面有一道横木，就是驾牲口的地方。那横木，大车上的叫做鬲，小车上的叫做衡。鬲、衡两头都有关键（活销），輗就是鬲的关键，軏就是衡的关键。车子没有它，自然无法套住牲口，那怎么能走呢？

2.23 子张问："十世可知也⁽¹⁾？"子曰："殷因于夏礼，所损益，可知也；周因于殷礼，所损益，可知也。其或继周者，虽百世，可知也。"

【译文】子张问："今后十代〔的礼仪制度〕可以预先知道吗？"孔子说："殷朝沿袭夏朝的礼仪制度，所废除的，所增加的，是可以知道的；周朝沿袭殷朝的礼仪制度，所废除的，所增加的，也是可以知道的。那么，假定有继承周朝而当政的人，就是以后一百代，也是可以预先知道的。"

【注释】

(1)十世可知也——从下文孔子的答语看来，便足以断定子张是问今后十代的礼仪制度，而不是泛问，所以译文加了几个字。这"也"字同"耶"，表疑问。

2.24 子曰："非其鬼⁽¹⁾而祭⁽²⁾之，谄⁽³⁾也。见义不为，无勇也。"

【译文】孔子说:"不是自己应该祭祀的鬼神,却去祭祀他,这是献媚。眼见应该挺身而出的事情,却袖手旁观,这是怯懦。"

【注释】

(1)鬼——古代人死都叫"鬼",一般指已死的祖先而言,但也偶有泛指的。

(2)祭——祭是吉祭,和凶祭的奠不同(人初死,陈设饮食以安其灵魂,叫做奠)。祭鬼的目的一般是祈福。

(3)谄——音产,chǎn,谄媚,阿谀。

八佾篇第三

共二十六章

八佾篇第三

3.1 孔子谓季氏⑴,"八佾⑵舞于庭,是可忍⑶也,孰不可忍也?"

【译文】孔子谈到季氏,说:"他用六十四人在庭院中奏乐舞蹈,这都可以狠心做出来,什么事不可以狠心做出来呢?"

【注释】

⑴季氏——根据《左传》昭公二十五年的记载和《汉书·刘向传》,这季氏可能是指季平子,即季孙意如。据《韩诗外传》,似以为季康子,马融《注》则以为季桓子,恐皆不足信。

⑵八佾——佾音逸,yì。古代舞蹈奏乐,八个人为一行,这一行叫一佾。八佾是八行,八八六十四人,只有天子才能用。诸侯用六佾,即六行,四十八人。大夫用四佾,三十二人。四佾才是季氏所应该用的。

⑶忍——一般人把它解为"容忍""忍耐",不好;因为孔子当时并没有讨伐季氏的条件和意志,而且季平子削弱鲁公室,鲁昭公不能忍,出走到齐,又到晋,终于死在晋国之乾侯。这可能就是孔子所"孰不可忍"的事。《贾子·道术篇》:"恻隐怜人谓之慈,反慈为忍。"这"忍"字正是此意。

3.2 三家⑴者以《雍》⑵彻。子曰:"'相⑶维辟公,天子穆穆',奚取于三家之堂?"

【译文】仲孙、叔孙、季孙三家,当他们祭祀祖先时候,[也用天子的礼,]唱着《雍》这篇诗来撤除祭品。孔子说:"[《雍》诗上有这样的话:]'助祭的是诸侯,天子严肃静穆地在那儿主祭。'这两句话,用在三家祭祖的大厅上在意义上取它哪一点呢?"

【注释】

(1)三家——鲁国当政的三卿。

(2)《雍》——也写作"雝",《诗经·周颂》的一篇。

(3)相——去声,音向,xiàng,助祭者。

3.3 子曰:"人而不仁,如礼何?人而不仁,如乐何?"

【译文】孔子说:"做了人,却不仁,怎样来对待礼仪制度呢?做了人,却不仁,怎样来对待音乐呢?"

3.4 林放⑴问礼之本。子曰:"大哉问!礼,与其奢也,宁俭;丧,与其易⑵也,宁戚。"

【译文】林放问礼的本质。孔子说:"你的问题意义重大呀!就一般礼仪说,与其铺张浪费,宁可朴素俭约;就丧礼说,与其仪文周到,宁可过度悲哀。"

【注释】

(1)林放——鲁人。

(2)易——《礼记·檀弓上》云:"子路曰:'吾闻诸夫子:丧礼,与其哀不足而礼有余也,不若礼不足而哀有余也。'"可以看做"与其易也,宁戚"的最早的解释。"易"有把事情办妥的意思,如《孟子·尽心上》"易其田畴",因此这里译为"仪文周到"。

3.5 子曰:"夷狄之有君,不如⁽¹⁾诸夏之亡⁽²⁾也。"

【译文】孔子说:"文化落后国家虽然有个君主,还不如中国没有君主哩。"

【注释】
(1)夷狄有君……亡也——杨遇夫先生《论语疏证》说,夷狄有君指楚庄王、吴王阖庐等。君是贤明之君。句意是夷狄还有贤明之君,不像中原诸国却没有。说亦可通。
(2)亡——同"无"。在《论语》中,"亡"下不用宾语,"无"下必有宾语。

3.6 季氏旅⁽¹⁾于泰山。子谓冉有⁽²⁾曰:"女弗能救与?"对曰:"不能。"子曰:"呜呼!曾谓泰山不如林放乎?"

【译文】季氏要去祭祀泰山。孔子对冉有说道:"你不能阻止吗?"冉有答道:"不能。"孔子道:"哎呀!竟可以说泰山之神还不及林放[懂礼,居然接受这不合规矩的祭祀]吗?"

【注释】
(1)旅——动词,祭山。在当时,只有天子和诸侯才有祭祀"名山大川"的资格。季氏只是鲁国的大夫,竟去祭祀泰山,因之孔子认为是"僭礼"。
(2)冉有——孔子学生冉求,字子有,小于孔子二十九岁。(公元前522—?)当时在季氏之下做事,所以孔子责备他。

3.7 子曰:"君子无所争。必也射乎!揖让而升,下而饮。其争也君子⑴。"

【译文】孔子说:"君子没有什么可争的事情。如果有所争,一定是比箭吧,[但是当射箭的时候,]相互作揖然后登堂;[射箭完毕,]走下堂来,然后[作揖]喝酒。那一种竞赛是很有礼貌的。"

【注释】

⑴其争也君子——这是讲古代射礼,详见《仪礼•乡射礼》和《大射仪》。登堂而射,射后计算谁中靶多,中靶少的被罚饮酒。

3.8 子夏问曰:"'巧笑倩⑴兮,美目盼⑵兮,素以为绚⑶兮。'何谓也?"子曰:"绘事后素。"曰:"礼后⑷乎?"子曰:"起⑸予者商也!始可与言《诗》已矣。"

【译文】子夏问道:"'有酒窝的脸笑得美呀,黑白分明的眼流转得媚呀,洁白的底子上画着花卉呀。'这几句诗是什么意思?"孔子道:"先有白色底子,然后画花。"子夏道:"那么,是不是礼乐的产生在[仁义]以后呢?"孔子道:"卜商呀,你真是能启发我的人。现在可以同你讨论《诗经》了。"

【注释】

⑴倩——音欠,qiàn,面颊长得好。

⑵盼——黑白分明。

⑶绚——音炫,xuàn,有文采,译文为着协韵,故用"画着花卉"以代之。这三句诗,第一句第二句见于《诗经•卫风•硕人》。第三句可能是逸句,王先谦《三家诗义集疏》以为《鲁诗》有此一句。

(4)礼后——"礼"在什么之后呢,原文没说出。根据儒家的若干文献,译文加了"仁义"两字。

(5)起——友人孙子书(楷第)先生云:"凡人病困而愈谓之起,义有滞碍隐蔽,通达之,亦谓之起。"说见杨遇夫先生《汉书窥管》卷九引文。

3.9 子曰:"夏礼,吾能言之,杞⁽¹⁾不足征也;殷礼,吾能言之,宋⁽²⁾不足征也。文献⁽³⁾不足故也。足,则吾能征之矣。"

【译文】孔子说:"夏代的礼,我能说出来,它的后代杞国不足以作证;殷代的礼,我能说出来,它的后代宋国不足以作证。这是他们的历史文件和贤者不够的缘故。若有足够的文件和贤者,我就可以引来作证了。"

【注释】
(1)杞——国名,夏禹的后代。周武王时候的故城即今日河南的杞县。其后因为国家弱小,依赖别国的力量来延长国命,屡经迁移。
(2)宋——国名,商汤的后代,故城在今日河南商丘县南。国土最大的时候,有现在河南商丘以东,江苏徐州以西之地。战国时为齐、魏、楚三国所共灭。
(3)文献——《论语》的"文献"和今天所用的"文献"一词的概念有不同之处。《论语》的"文献"包括历代的历史文件和当时的贤者两项(朱《注》云:"文,典籍也;献,贤也。")。今日"文献"一词只指历史文件而言。

3.10 子曰:"禘⁽¹⁾自既灌⁽²⁾而往者,吾不欲观之矣。"

【译文】孔子说:"禘祭的礼,从第一次献酒以后,我就不想看了。"

【注释】

(1)禘——这一禘礼是指古代一种极为隆重的大祭之礼,只有天子才能举行。不过周成王曾因为周公旦对周朝有过莫大的功勋,特许他举行禘祭。以后鲁国之君都沿此惯例,"僭"用这一禘礼,因此孔子不想看。

(2)灌——本作"祼",祭祀中的一个节目。古代祭祀,用活人以代受祭者,这活人便叫"尸"。尸一般用幼小的男女。第一次献酒给尸,使他(她)闻到"郁鬯"(一种配合香料煮成的酒)的香气,叫做祼。

3.11 或问禘之说。子曰:"不知也[1];知其说者之于天下也,其如示[2]诸斯乎!"指其掌。

【译文】有人向孔子请教关于禘祭的理论。孔子说:"我不知道;知道的人对于治理天下,会好像把东西摆在这里一样容易罢!"一面说,一面指着手掌。

【注释】

(1)不知也——禘是天子之礼,鲁国举行,在孔子看来,是完全不应该的。但孔子又不想明白指出,只得说"不欲观","不知也",甚至说"如果有懂得的人,他对于治理天下是好像把东西放在手掌上一样的容易"。

(2)示——假借字,同"置",摆、放的意义。或曰同"视",犹言"了如指掌"。

3.12 祭如在,祭神如神在。子曰:"吾不与祭,如不祭[1]。"

【译文】孔子祭祀祖先的时候,便好像祖先真在那里;祭神的时候，便好像神真在那里。孔子又说："我若是不能亲自参加祭祀，是不请别人代理的。"

【注释】

(1) 吾不与祭，如不祭——这是一般的句读法。"与"读去声，音预，yù，参预的意思。"如不祭"译文是意译。另外有人主张"与"字仍读上声，赞同的意思，而且在这里一读，便是"吾不与，祭如不祭"。译文便应改为："若是我所不同意的祭礼，祭了同没祭一般。"我不同意此义，因为孔丘素来不赞成不合所谓礼的祭祀，如"非其鬼而祭之，谄也"，（2.24）孔丘自不会参加他所不赞同的祭祀。

3.13 王孙贾[1]问曰："与其媚于奥，宁媚于灶[2]，何谓也？"子曰："不然；获罪于天，无所祷也[3]。"

【译文】王孙贾问道："'与其巴结房屋里西南角的神，宁可巴结灶君司命，'这两句话是什么意思？"孔子道："不对；若是得罪了上天，祈祷也没用。"

【注释】

(1) 王孙贾——卫灵公的大臣。
(2) 与其媚于奥，宁媚于灶——这两句疑是当时俗语。屋内西南角叫奥，弄饭的设备叫灶，古代都以为那里有神，因而祭它。
(3) 王孙贾和孔子的问答都用的比喻，他们的正意何在，我们只能揣想。有人说，奥是一室之主，比喻卫君；又在室内，也可以比喻卫灵公的宠姬南子；灶则是王孙贾自比。这是王孙贾暗示孔子，"你与其巴结卫公或者南子，不如巴结我"。因此孔子答复他："我若做了坏事，巴结也没有用处；我若不做坏事，谁都不巴结。"又有人说，这不是王孙贾暗示孔子的话，而是请教孔子的话。奥指卫君，灶指南子、弥子瑕，位职虽低，却有权有势。意思是说，"有人告诉我，与其巴结国君，不如巴结有势力的左右像南子、弥子瑕。你以为怎样？"孔子却告诉他："这话不对；得罪了上天，那无所用其祈祷，巴结谁都不行。"我以为后一说比较近情理。

3.14 子曰："周监于二代(1)，郁郁乎文哉！吾从周。"

【译文】孔子说："周朝的礼仪制度是以夏商两代为根据，然后制定的，多么丰富多彩呀！我主张周朝的。"

【注释】

(1)二代——夏、商两朝。

3.15 子入太庙(1)，每事问。或曰："孰谓鄹人之子(2)知礼乎？入太庙，每事问。"子闻之，曰："是礼也。"

【译文】孔子到了周公庙，每件事情都发问。有人便说："谁说叔梁纥的这个儿子懂得礼呢？他到了太庙，每件事都要向别人请教。"孔子听到了这话，便道："这正是礼呀。"

【注释】

(1)太庙——古代开国之君叫太祖，太祖之庙便叫做太庙，周公旦是鲁国最初受封之君，因之这太庙就是周公的庙。

(2)鄹人之子——鄹音邹，zōu，又作郰，地名。《史记·孔子世家》："孔子生鲁昌平乡郰邑。"有人说，这地就是今天的山东省曲阜县东南十里的西邹集。"鄹人"指孔子父亲叔梁纥。叔梁纥曾经作过鄹大夫，古代经常把某地的大夫称为某人，因之这里也把鄹大夫叔梁纥称为"鄹人"。

3.16 子曰:"射不主皮⑴,为⑵力不同科⑶,古之道也。"

【译文】孔子说:"比箭,不一定要穿破箭靶子,因为各人的气力大小不一样,这是古时的规矩。"

【注释】

⑴射不主皮——"皮"代表箭靶子。古代箭靶子叫"侯",有用布做的,也有用皮做的。当中画着各种猛兽或者别的东西,最中心的又叫做"正"或者"鹄"。孔子在这里所讲的射应该是演习礼乐的射,而不是军中的武射,因此以中不中为主,不以穿破皮侯与否为主。《仪礼•乡射礼》云,"礼射不主皮",盖本此。

⑵为——去声,wèi,因为。

⑶同科——同等。

3.17 子贡欲去⑴告朔之饩羊⑵。子曰:"赐也!尔爱⑶其羊,我爱其礼。"

【译文】子贡要把鲁国每月初一告祭祖庙的那只活羊去而不用。孔子道:"赐呀!你可惜那只羊,我可惜那种礼。"

【注释】

⑴去——从前读为上声,因为它在这里作为及物动词,而且和"来去"的"去"意义不同。

⑵告朔饩羊——"告",从前人读梏,gù,入声。"朔",每月的第一天,初一。"饩",音戏,xì。"告朔饩羊",古代的一种制度。每年秋冬之交,周天子把第二年的历书颁给诸侯。这历书包括那年有无闰月,每月初一是哪一天,因之叫"颁告朔"。诸侯接受了这一历书,藏于祖庙。每逢初一,便杀一只活羊祭于庙,然后回到朝

廷听政。这祭庙叫做"告朔",听政叫做"视朔",或者"听朔"。到子贡的时候,每月初一,鲁君不但不亲临祖庙,而且也不听政,只是杀一只活羊"虚应故事"罢了。所以子贡认为不必留此形式,不如干脆连羊也不杀。孔子却认为尽管这是残存的形式,也比什么也不留好。

(3)爱——可惜的意思。

3.18 子曰:"事君尽礼,人以为谄也。"

【译文】孔子说:"服事君主,一切依照做臣子的礼节做去,别人却以为他在谄媚哩。"

3.19 定公⁽¹⁾问:"君使臣,臣事君,如之何?"孔子对曰:"君使臣以礼,臣事君以忠。"

【译文】鲁定公问:"君主使用臣子,臣子服事君主,各应该怎么样?"孔子答道:"君主应该依礼来使用臣子,臣子应该忠心地服事君主。"

【注释】

(1)定公——鲁君,名宋,昭公之弟,继昭公而立,在位十五年。(公元前509—前495)"定"是谥号。

3.20 子曰:"《关雎》⁽¹⁾,乐而不淫⁽²⁾,哀而不伤。"

【译文】孔子说:"《关雎》这诗,快乐而不放荡,悲哀而不痛苦。"

【注释】

(1)《关雎》——《诗经》的第一篇。但这篇诗并没有悲哀的情调,因此刘台拱的《论语骈枝》说:"《诗》有《关雎》,《乐》亦有《关雎》,此章据《乐》言之。古之乐章皆三篇为一。……乐而不淫者,《关雎》《葛覃》也;哀而不伤者,《卷耳》也。"

(2)淫——古人凡过分以至于到失当的地步叫淫,如言"淫祀"(不应该祭祀而去祭祀的祭礼)、"淫雨"(过久的雨水)。

3.21 哀公问社⁽¹⁾于宰我⁽²⁾。宰我对曰:"夏后氏以松,殷人以柏,周人以栗,曰,使民战栗。"子闻之,曰:"成事不说,遂事不谏,既往不咎。"

【译文】鲁哀公向宰我问,作社主用什么木。宰我答道:"夏代用松木,殷代用柏木,周代用栗木,意思是使人民战战栗栗。"孔子听到了这话,[责备宰我]说:"已经做了的事不便再解释了,已经完成的事不便再挽救了,已经过去的事不便再追究了。"

【注释】

(1)社——土神叫社,不过哀公所问的社,从宰我的答话中可以推知是指社主而言。古代祭祀土神,要替他立一个木制的牌位,这牌位叫主,而认为这一木主,便是神灵之所凭依。如果国家有对外战争,还必须载这一木主而行。详见俞正燮《癸巳类稿》。有人说"社"是指立社所栽的树,未必可信。

(2)宰我——孔子学生,名予,字子我。

3.22 子曰:"管仲⑴之器小哉!"或曰:"管仲俭乎?"曰:"管氏有三归⑵,官事不摄⑶,焉得俭?""然则管仲知礼乎?"曰:"邦君树塞门⑷,管氏亦树塞门。邦君为两君之好⑸,有反坫⑹,管氏亦有反坫。管氏而⑺知礼,孰不知礼?"

【译文】孔子说:"管仲的器量狭小得很呀!"有人便问:"他是不是很节俭呢?"孔子道:"他收取了人民的大量的市租,他手下的人员,[一人一职,]从不兼差,如何能说是节俭呢?"那人又问:"那么,他懂得礼节么?"孔子又道:"国君宫殿门前,立了一个塞门;管氏也立了个塞门;国君设宴招待外国的君主,在堂上有放置酒杯的设备,管氏也有这样的设备。假若说他懂得礼节,那谁不懂得礼节呢?"

【注释】
⑴管仲——春秋时齐国人,名夷吾,做了齐桓公的宰相,使他称霸诸侯。
⑵三归——"三归"的解释还有:(甲)国君一娶三女,管仲也娶了三国之女(《集解》引包咸说,皇侃《义疏》等);(乙)三处家庭(俞樾《群经平议》);(丙)地名,管仲的采邑(梁玉绳《瞥记》);(丁)藏泉币的府库(武亿《群经义证》)。我认为这些解释都不正确。郭嵩焘《养知书屋文集》卷一《释三归》云:"此盖《管子》九府轻重之法,当就《管子》书求之。《山至数篇》曰,'则民之三有归于上矣。'三归之名,实本于此。是所谓三归者,市租之常例之归之公者也。桓公既霸,遂以赏管仲。《汉书·地理志》、《食货志》并云,桓公用管仲设轻重以富民,身在陪臣,而取三归。其言较然明显。《韩非子》云,'使子有三归之家',《说苑》作'赏之市租'。三归之为市租,汉世儒者犹能明之,此一证也。《晏子春秋》辞三归之赏,而云厚受赏以伤国民之义,其取之民

无疑也，此又一证也。"这一说法很有道理。我还再举两个间接证据。（甲）《战国策》一说："齐桓公宫中七市，女闾七百，国人非之。管仲故为三归之家以掩桓公，非自伤于民也。"似亦以三归为市租。（乙）《三国志•魏志•武帝纪》建安十五年令曰："若必廉士而后可用，则齐桓其何以霸？"亦以管仲不是清廉之士，当指三归。

(3)摄——兼职。

(4)树塞门——树，动词，立也。塞门，用以间隔内外视线的一种东西，形式和作用可同今天的照壁相比。

(5)好——古读去声，友好。

(6)反坫——坫音店，diàn，用以放置器物的设备，用土筑成的，形似土堆，筑于两楹（厅堂前部东西各有一柱）之间。详全祖望《经史问答》。

(7)而——假设连词，假如，假若。

3.23 子语⁽¹⁾鲁大师⁽²⁾乐，曰："乐其可知也：始作，翕⁽³⁾如也；从⁽⁴⁾之，纯如也，皦⁽⁵⁾如也，绎如也，以成。"

【译文】孔子把演奏音乐的道理告给鲁国的太师，说道："音乐，那是可以晓得的：开始演奏，翕翕地热烈；继续下去，纯纯地和谐，皦皦地清晰，绎绎地不绝，这样，然后完成。"

【注释】

(1)语——去声，yù，告诉。

(2)大师——大音泰，tài，乐官之长。

(3)翕——音西，xī。

(4)从——去声，zòng。

(5)皦——音皎，jiǎo。

3.24 仪封人⁽¹⁾请见⁽²⁾,曰:"君子之至于斯也,吾未尝不得见也。"从者⁽³⁾见之⁽²⁾。出曰:"二三子何患于丧⁽⁴⁾乎?天下之无道也久矣,天将以夫子为木铎⁽⁵⁾。"

【译文】仪这个地方的边防官请求孔子接见他,说道:"所有到了这个地方的有道德学问的人,我从没有不和他见面的。"孔子的随行学生请求孔子接见了他。他辞出以后,对孔子的学生们说:"你们这些人为什么着急没有官位呢?天下黑暗日子也长久了,〔圣人也该有得意的时候了,〕上天会要把他老人家做人民的导师哩。"

【注释】
⑴仪封人——仪,地名。有人说当在今日的开封市内,未必可靠。封人,官名。《左传》有颍谷封人、祭封人、萧封人、吕封人,大概是典守边疆的官。说本方观旭《论语偶记》。
⑵请见、见之——两个"见"字从前都读去声,音现,xiàn。"请见"是请求接见的意思,"见之"是使孔子接见了他的意思。何焯《义门读书记》云:"古者相见必由绍介,逆旅之中无可因缘,故称平日未尝见绝于贤者,见气类之同,致词以代绍介,故从者因而通之。夫子亦不拒其请,与不见孺悲异也。"
⑶从者——"从"去声,zòng。
⑷丧——去声,sàng,失掉官位。
⑸木铎——铜质木舌的铃子。古代公家有什么事要宣布,便摇这铃,召集大家来听。

3.25 子谓《韶》⁽¹⁾,"尽美⁽²⁾矣,又尽善⁽²⁾也"。谓《武》⁽³⁾,"尽美矣,未尽善也"。

【译文】孔子论到《韶》,说:"美极了,而且好极了。"论到《武》,说:"美极了,却还不够好。"

【注释】

(1)《韶》——舜时的乐曲名。

(2)美、善——"美"可能指声音言,"善"可能指内容言。舜的天子之位是由尧"禅让"而来,故孔子认为"尽善"。周武王的天子之位是由讨伐商纣而来,尽管是正义战,依孔子意,却认为"未尽善"。

(3)《武》——周武王时乐曲名。

3.26 子曰:"居上不宽,为礼不敬,临丧不哀,吾何以观之哉?"

【译文】孔子说:"居于统治地位不宽宏大量,行礼的时候不严肃认真,参加丧礼的时候不悲哀,这种样子我怎么看得下去呢?"

里仁篇第四

共二十六章

里仁篇第四

4.1 子曰:"里⁽¹⁾仁为美。择不处⁽²⁾仁,焉得知⁽³⁾?"

【译文】孔子说:"住的地方,要有仁德这才好。选择住处,没有仁德,怎么能是聪明呢?"

【注释】
(1)里——这里可以看为动词。居住也。
(2)处——上声,音杵,chǔ,居住也。
(3)知——《论语》的"智"字都如此写。这一段话,究竟孔子是单纯地指"择居"而言呢,还是泛指,"择邻""择业""择友"等等都包括在内呢?我们已经不敢肯定。《孟子·公孙丑上》云:"孟子曰:'矢人岂不仁于函人哉?矢人惟恐不伤人,函人惟恐伤人。巫、匠亦然。故术不可不慎也。孔子曰,里仁为美。择不处仁,焉得智?'"便是指择业。因此译文于"仁"字仅照字面翻译,不实指为仁人。

4.2 子曰:"不仁者不可以久处约,不可以长处乐。仁者安仁,知者利仁。"

【译文】孔子说:"不仁的人不可以长久地居于穷困中,也不可以长久地居于安乐中。有仁德的人安于仁〔实行仁德便心安,不实行仁德心便不安〕;聪明人利用仁〔他认识到仁德对他长远而巨大的利益,他便实行仁德〕。"

4.3 子曰:"唯仁者能好人,能恶人⑴。"

【译文】孔子说:"只有仁人才能够喜爱某人,厌恶某人。"

【注释】

⑴唯仁者能好人,能恶人——《后汉书•孝明八王传注》引《东观汉记》说:和帝赐彭城王恭诏曰:"孔子曰,'惟仁者能好人,能恶人'。——贵仁者所好恶得其中也。"我认为"贵仁者所好恶得其中",正可说明这句。

4.4 子曰:"苟志于仁矣,无恶也。"

【译文】孔子说:"假如立定志向实行仁德,总没有坏处。"

4.5 子曰:"富与贵,是人之所欲也;不以其道得之,不处也。贫与贱,是人之所恶也;不以其道得之⑴,不去也。君子去仁,恶乎⑵成名?君子无终食之间违⑶仁,造次必于是,颠沛必于是。"

【译文】孔子说:"发大财,做大官,这是人人所盼望的;不用正当的方法去得到它,君子不接受。穷困和下贱,这是人人所厌恶的;不用正当的方法去抛掉它,君子不摆脱。君子抛弃了仁德,怎样去成就他的声名呢?君子没有吃完一餐饭的时间离开仁德,就是在仓猝匆忙的时候一定和仁德同在,就是在颠沛流离的时候一定和仁德同在。"

【注释】

(1)贫与贱……不以其道得之——"富与贵"可以说"得之","贫与贱"却不是人人想"得之"。这里也讲"不以其道得之","得之"应该改为"去之"。译文只就这一整段的精神加以诠释,这里为什么也讲"得之",可能是古人的不经意处,我们不必再在这上面做文章了。

(2)恶乎——恶音乌,wū,何处。"恶乎"即"于何处",译文意译为"怎样"。

(3)违——离开,和《公冶长篇第五》的"弃而违之"的"违"同义。

4.6 子曰:"我未见好仁者,恶不仁者。好仁者,无以尚[1]之;恶不仁者,其为仁矣[2],不使不仁者加乎其身。有能一日用其力于仁矣乎?我未见力不足者。盖[3]有之矣,我未之见也。"

【译文】孔子说:"我不曾见到过爱好仁德的人和厌恶不仁德的人。爱好仁德的人,那是再好也没有的了;厌恶不仁德的人,他行仁德,只是不使不仁德的东西加在自己身上。有谁能在某一天使用他的力量于仁德呢?我没见过力量不够的。大概这样的人还是有的,我不曾见到罢了。"

【注释】

(1)尚——动词,超过之意。

(2)矣——这个"矣"字用法同"也",表示停顿。

(3)盖——副词,大概之意。

4.7 子曰:"人之过也,各于其党。观过,斯知仁[1]矣。"

【译文】孔子说:"[人是各种各样的,人的错误也是各种各样的。]什么样的错误就是由什么样的人犯的。仔细考察某人所犯的错误,就可以知道他是什么样式的人了。"

【注释】

⑴ 仁——同"人"。《后汉书·吴祐传》引此文正作"人"(武英殿本却又改作"仁",不可为据)。

4.8 子曰:"朝闻道,夕死可矣。"

【译文】孔子说:"早晨得知真理,要我当晚死去,都可以。"

4.9 子曰:"士志于道,而耻恶衣恶食者,未足与议也。"

【译文】孔子说:"读书人有志于真理,但又以自己吃粗粮穿破衣为耻辱,这种人,不值得同他商议了。"

4.10 子曰:"君子之于天下也,无适⑴也,无莫⑴也,义之与比⑵。"

【译文】孔子说:"君子对于天下的事情,没规定要怎样干,也没规定不要怎样干,只要怎样干合理恰当,便怎样干。"

【注释】

⑴适,莫——这两字讲法很多,有的解为"亲疏厚薄","无适无莫"

便是"情无亲疏厚薄"。有的解为"敌对与羡慕","无适（读为敌）无莫（读为慕）"便是"无所为仇，无所欣羡"。我则用朱熹《集注》的说法。

(2)比——去声，bì，挨着，靠拢，为邻。从孟子和以后的一些儒家看来，孔子"无必无固"（9.4），通权达变，"可以仕则仕，可以止则止，可以久则久，可以速则速"（《孟子·公孙丑上》），唯义是从，叫做"圣之时"，或者可以做这章的解释。

4.11 子曰："君子怀德，小人怀土[1]；君子怀刑[2]，小人怀惠。"

【译文】孔子说："君子怀念道德，小人怀念乡土；君子关心法度，小人关心恩惠。"

【注释】

(1)土——如果解为田土，亦通。

(2)刑——古代法律制度的"刑"作"刑"，刑罚的"刑"作"荆"，从刀井，后来都写作"刑"了。这"刑"字应该解释为法度。

4.12 子曰："放[1]于利而行，多怨。"

【译文】孔子说："依据个人利益而行动，会招致很多的怨恨。"

【注释】

(1)放——旧读上声，音仿，fǎng，依据。

4.13 子曰:"能以礼让为国乎?何有[1]?不能以礼让为国,如礼何[2]?"

【译文】孔子说:"能够用礼让来治理国家吗?这有什么困难呢?如果不能用礼让来治理国家,又怎样来对待礼仪呢?"

【注释】

(1)何有——这是春秋时代的常用语,在这里是"有何困难"的意思。黄式三《论语后案》、刘宝楠《论语正义》都说:"何有,不难之词。"

(2)如礼何——依孔子的意见,国家的礼仪必有其"以礼让为国"的本质,它是内容和形式的统一体。如果舍弃它的内容,徒拘守那些仪节上的形式,孔子说,是没有什么作用的。

4.14 子曰:"不患无位,患所以立[1]。不患莫己知,求为可知也。"

【译文】孔子说:"不发愁没有职位,只发愁没有任职的本领;不怕没有人知道自己,去追求足以使别人知道自己的本领好了。"

【注释】

(1)患所以立——"立"和"位"古通用,这"立"字便是"不患无位"的"位"字。《春秋》桓公二年"公即位",《石经》作"公即立"可以为证。

4.15 子曰:"参乎!吾道一以贯[1]之。"曾子曰:"唯。"子出,门人问曰:"何谓也?"曾子曰:"夫子之道,忠恕[2]而已矣。"

【译文】孔子说:"参呀!我的学说贯穿着一个基本观念。"曾子说:"是。"孔子走出去以后,别的学生便问曾子道:"这是什么意思?"曾子道:"他老人家的学说,只是忠和恕罢了。"

【注释】
(1) 贯——贯穿、统贯。阮元《揅经室集》有《一贯说》,认为《论语》的"贯"字都是"行""事"的意义,未必可信。
(2) 忠恕——"恕",孔子自己下了定义:"己所不欲,勿施于人。""忠"则是"恕"的积极一面,用孔子自己的话,便应该是:"己欲立而立人,己欲达而达人。"

4.16 子曰:"君子[1]喻于义,小人[1]喻于利。"

【译文】孔子说:"君子懂得的是义,小人懂得的是利。"
【注释】
(1) 君子、小人——这里的"君子""小人"是指在位者,还是指有德者,还是两者兼指,孔子原意不得而知。《汉书·杨恽传·报孙会宗书》曾引董仲舒的话说:"明明求仁义常恐不能化民者,卿大夫之意也,明明求财利常恐困乏者,庶人之事也。"只能看作这一语的汉代经师的注解,不必过信。

4.17 子曰:"见贤思齐焉,见不贤而内自省也。"

【译文】孔子说:"看见贤人,便应该想向他看齐;看见不贤的人,便应该自己反省,〔有没有同他类似的毛病。〕"

4.18 子曰:"事父母几⑴谏,见志不从,又敬不违⑵,劳⑶而不怨。"

【译文】孔子说:"侍奉父母,〔如果他们有不对的地方,〕得轻微婉转地劝止,看到自己的心意没有被听从,仍然恭敬地不触犯他们,虽然忧愁,但不怨恨。"
【注释】
⑴几——平声,音机,jī,轻微,婉转。
⑵违——触忤,冒犯。
⑶劳——忧愁。说见王引之《经义述闻》。

4.19 子曰:"父母在,不远游,游必有方。"

【译文】孔子说:"父母在世,不出远门,如果要出远门,必须有一定的去处。"

4.20 子曰:"三年无改于父之道,可谓孝矣⑴。"

【注释】
⑴见《学而篇第一》。

4.21 子曰:"父母之年,不可不知也。一则以喜,一则以惧。"

【译文】孔子说:"父母的年纪不能不时时记在心里:一方面因〔其高寿〕而喜欢,另一方面又因〔其寿高〕而有所恐惧。"

4.22 子曰:"古者言之不出,耻⁽¹⁾躬之不逮⁽²⁾也。"

【译文】孔子说:"古时候言语不轻易出口,就是怕自己的行动赶不上。"
【注释】
(1)耻——动词的意动用法,以为可耻的意思。
(2)逮——音代,dài,及,赶上。

4.23 子曰:"以约⁽¹⁾失之者鲜矣。"

【译文】孔子说:"因为对自己节制、约束而犯过失的,这种事情总不会多。"
【注释】
(1)约——《论语》的"约"字不外两个意义:(甲)穷困,(乙)约束。至于节俭的意义,虽然已见于《荀子》,却未必适用于这里。

4.24 子曰:"君子欲讷⁽¹⁾于言而敏于行⁽²⁾。"

【译文】孔子说:"君子言语要谨慎迟钝,工作要勤劳敏捷。"

【注释】

(1)讷——读nè,语言迟钝。

(2)讷于言而敏于行——这句和《学而篇》的"敏于事而慎于言"意思一样,所以译文加"谨慎"两字,同时也把"行"字译为"工作"。

4.25 子曰:"德不孤,必有邻⁽¹⁾。"

【译文】孔子说:"有道德的人不会孤单,一定会有[志同道合的人来和他做]伙伴。"

【注释】

(1)德不孤,必有邻——《易·系辞上》说:"方以类聚,物以群分。"又《乾·文言》说:"子曰:同声相应,同气相求。"这都可以作为"德不孤"的解释。

4.26 子游曰:"事君数⁽¹⁾,斯辱矣;朋友数⁽¹⁾,斯疏矣。"

【译文】子游说:"对待君主过于烦琐,就会招致侮辱;对待朋友过于烦琐,就会反被疏远。"

【注释】

(1)数——音朔,shuò,密,屡屡。这里依上下文意译为"烦琐"。《颜渊篇第十二》说:"子贡问友。子曰:'忠告而善道之,不可则止,无自辱焉。'"也正是这个意思。

公冶长篇第五

共二十八章

5.1 子谓公冶长⁽¹⁾，"可妻⁽²⁾也。虽在缧绁⁽³⁾之中，非其罪也"。以其子⁽⁴⁾妻之。

【译文】孔子说公冶长，"可以把女儿嫁给他。他虽然曾被关在监狱之中，但不是他的罪过"。便把自己的女儿嫁给他。

【注释】
(1)公冶长——孔子学生，齐人。
(2)妻——动词，去声，qì。
(3)缧绁——缧同"累"，léi；绁音泄，xiè。缧绁，拴罪人的绳索，这里指代监狱。
(4)子——儿女，此处指的是女儿。

5.2 子谓南容⁽¹⁾，"邦有道，不废；邦无道，免于刑戮"。以其兄之子妻之⁽²⁾。

【译文】孔子说南容，"国家政治清明，〔总有官做，〕不被废弃；国家政治黑暗，也不致被刑罚"。于是把自己的侄女嫁给他。

【注释】
(1)南容——孔子学生南宫适，字子容。
(2)兄之子——孔子之兄叫孟皮，见《史记·孔子世家索隐》引《家语》。这时孟皮可能已死，所以孔子替他女儿主婚。

5.3 子谓子贱⑴，"君子哉若人！鲁无君子者，斯焉取斯？"

【译文】孔子评论宓子贱，说："这人是君子呀！假若鲁国没有君子，这种人从哪里取来这种好品德呢？"

【注释】
⑴子贱——孔子学生宓不齐，字子贱，少于孔子三十岁。(公元前521—？)

5.4 子贡问曰："赐也何如？"子曰："女，器也。"曰："何器也？"曰："瑚琏⑴也。"

【译文】子贡问道："我是一个怎样的人？"孔子道："你好比是一个器皿。"子贡道："什么器皿？"孔子道："宗庙里盛黍稷的瑚琏。"

【注释】
⑴瑚琏——音胡连，又音胡hú辇niǎn，即簠簋，古代祭祀时盛粮食的器皿，方形的叫簠，圆形的叫簋，是相当尊贵的。

5.5 或曰："雍⑴也仁而不佞⑵。"子曰："焉用佞？御人以口给⑶，屡憎于人。不知其仁⑷，焉用佞？"

【译文】有人说："冉雍这个人有仁德，却没有口才。"孔子道："何必要口才呢？强嘴利舌地同人家辩驳，常常被人讨厌。冉雍未必仁，但为什么要有口才呢？"

【注释】

(1)雍——孔子学生冉雍,字仲弓。

(2)佞——音泞,nìng,能言善说,有口才。

(3)口给——给,足也。"口给"犹如后来所说"言词不穷""辩才无碍"。

(4)不知其仁——孔子说不知,不是真的不知,只是否定的另一方式,实际上说冉雍还不能达到"仁"的水平。下文第八章"孟武伯问子路仁乎,子曰,不知也",这"不知"也是如此。

5.7 子使漆雕开⁽¹⁾仕。对曰:"吾斯之未能信⁽²⁾。"子说。

【译文】孔子叫漆雕开去做官。他答道:"我对这个还没有信心。"孔子听了很欢喜。

【注释】

(1)漆雕开——"漆雕"是姓,"开"是名,孔子学生,字子开。

(2)吾斯之未能信——这句是"吾未能信斯"的倒装形式,"之"是用来倒装的词。

5.7 子曰:"道不行,乘桴⁽¹⁾浮于海。从⁽²⁾我者,其由与?"子路闻之喜。子曰:"由也好勇过我,无所取材⁽³⁾。"

【译文】孔子道:"主张行不通了,我想坐个木簰到海外去,跟随我的恐怕只有仲由吧!"子路听到这话,高兴得很。孔子说:"仲由这个人太好勇敢了,好勇的精神大大超过了我,这就没有什么可取的呀!"

【注释】

(1)桴——音孚，fú，古代把竹子或者木头编成簰，以当船用，大的叫筏，小的叫桴，也就是现在的木簰。

(2)从——动词，旧读去声，跟随。

(3)材——同"哉"，古字有时通用。有人解作木材，说是孔子以为子路真要到海外去，便说，"没地方去取得木材"。这种解释一定不符合孔子原意。也有人把"材"看做"剪裁"的"裁"，说是"子路太好勇了，不知道节制、检点"，这种解释不知把"取"字置于何地，因之也不采用。

5.8 孟武伯问子路仁乎？子曰："不知也。"又问。子曰："由也，千乘之国，可使治其赋(1)也，不知其仁也。""求也何如？"子曰："求也，千室之邑(2)，百乘之家(3)，可使为之(4)宰(5)也，不知其仁也。""赤也何如？"子曰："赤也，束带立于朝，可使与宾客(6)言也，不知其仁也。"

【译文】孟武伯向孔子问子路有没有仁德。孔子道："不晓得。"他又问。孔子道："仲由啦，如果有一千辆兵车的国家，可以叫他负责兵役和军政的工作。至于他有没有仁德，我不晓得。"孟武伯继续问："冉求又怎么样呢？"孔子道："求啦，千户人口的私邑，可以叫他当县长；百辆兵车的大夫封地，可以叫他当总管。至于他有没有仁德，我不晓得。""公西赤又怎么样呢？"孔子道："赤啦，穿着礼服，立于朝廷之中，可以叫他接待外宾，办理交涉。至于他有没有仁德，我不晓得。"

【注释】

(1)赋——兵赋,古代的兵役制度。这里自也包括军政工作而言。

(2)邑——《左传》庄公二十八年云:"凡邑,有宗庙先王之主曰都,无曰邑。"又《公羊传》桓公元年云:"田多邑少称田,邑多田少称邑。"可见"邑"就是古代庶民聚居之所,不过有一些田地罢了。

(3)家——古代的卿大夫由国家封以一定的地方,由他派人治理,并且收用当地的租税,这地方便叫采地或者采邑。"家"便是指这种采邑而言。

(4)之——用法同"其",他的。

(5)宰——古代一县的县长叫做"宰",大夫家的总管也叫做"宰"。所以"原思为之宰"(6.5)的宰为"总管",而"季氏使闵子骞为费宰"(6.9)的"宰"是"县长"。

(6)宾客——"宾""客"两字散文则通,对文有异。一般是贵客叫宾,因之天子诸侯的客人叫宾;一般客人叫客,《易经·需卦·爻辞》"有不速之客三人来"的"客"正是此意。这里则把"宾客"合为一词了。

5.9 子谓子贡曰:"女与回也孰愈?"对曰:"赐也何敢望回?回也闻一以知十,赐也闻一以知二。"子曰:"弗如也;吾与⁽¹⁾女弗如也。"

【译文】孔子对子贡道:"你和颜回,哪一个强些?"子贡答道:"我么,怎敢和回相比?他啦,听到一件事,可以推演知道十件事;我唎,听到一件事,只能推知两件事。"孔子道:"赶不上他;我同意你的话,是赶不上他。"

【注释】

(1) 与——动词,同意,赞同。这里不应该看作连词。

5.10 宰予昼寝。子曰："朽木不可雕也，粪土之墙不可杇[1]也；于予与何诛[2]？"子曰[3]："始吾于人也，听其言而信其行；今吾于人也，听其言而观其行。于予与改是。"

【译文】宰予在白天睡觉。孔子说："腐烂了的木头雕刻不得，粪土似的墙壁粉刷不得；对于宰予么，不值得责备呀。"又说："最初，我对人家，听到他的话，便相信他的行为；今天，我对人家，听到他的话，却要考察他的行为。从宰予的事件以后，我改变了态度。"

【注释】
(1)杇——音乌，wū，泥工抹墙的工具叫杇，把墙壁抹平也叫杇。这里依上文的意思译为"粉刷"。
(2)何诛——机械地翻译是"责备什么呢"，这里是意译。
(3)子曰——以下的话虽然也是针对"宰予昼寝"而发出，却是孔子另一个时候的言语，所以又加"子曰"两字以示区别。古人有这种修辞条例，俞樾《古书疑义举例》卷二"一人之辞而加曰字例"曾有所阐述（但未引证此条），可参阅。

5.11 子曰："吾未见刚者。"或对曰："申枨[1]。"子曰："枨也欲，焉得刚？"

【译文】孔子道："我没见过刚毅不屈的人。"有人答道："申枨是这样的人。"孔子道："申枨啦，他欲望太多，哪里能够刚毅不屈？"

【注释】
(1)申枨——枨音橙，chéng。《史记·仲尼弟子列传》有申党，古音

"党"和"枨"相近,那么"申枨"就是"申党"。

5.12 子贡曰:"我不欲人之加⑴诸我也,吾亦欲无加诸人。"子曰:"赐也,非尔所及也。"

【译文】子贡道:"我不想别人欺侮我,我也不想欺侮别人。"孔子说:"赐,这不是你能做到的。"

【注释】
⑴ 加——驾凌,凌辱。

5.13 子贡曰:"夫子之文章⑴,可得而闻也;夫子之言性⑵与天道⑶,不可得而闻也。"

【译文】子贡说:"老师关于文献方面的学问,我们听得到;老师关于天性和天道的言论,我们听不到。"

【注释】
⑴文章——孔子是古代文化的整理者和传播者,这里的"文章"该是指有关古代文献的学问而言。在《论语》中可以考见的有诗、书、史、礼等等。
⑵性——人的本性。古代不可能有阶级观点,因之不知道人的阶级性。而对人的自然的性,孟子、荀子都有所主张,孔子却只说过"性相近也,习相远也"(17.2)一句话。
⑶天道——古代所讲的天道一般是指自然和人类社会吉凶祸福的关系。但《左传》昭公十八年郑国子产的话说:"天道远,人道迩,非所及也。"却是对自然和人类社会的吉凶有必然关系的否认。《左传》昭

公二十六年又有晏婴的话:"天道不谄。"虽然是用人类的美德来衡量自然之神,反对禳灾,也是对当时迷信习惯的破除。这两人都与孔子同时而年龄较大,而且为孔子所称道。孔子不讲天道,对自然和人类社会的关系取存而不论的态度,不知道是否受这种思想的影响。

5.14 子路有闻,未之能行,唯恐有⑴闻。

【译文】子路有所闻,还没有能够去做,只怕又有所闻。

【注释】

⑴有——同"又"。

5.15 子贡问曰:"孔文子⑴何以谓之'文'也?"子曰:"敏而好学,不耻下问,是以谓之'文'也。"

【译文】子贡问道:"孔文子凭什么谥他为'文'?"孔子道:"他聪敏灵活,爱好学问,又谦虚下问,不以为耻,所以用'文'字做他的谥号。"

【注释】

⑴孔文子——卫国的大夫孔圉。考孔文子死于鲁哀公十五年,或者在此稍前;孔子卒于十六年夏四月,那么,这次问答一定在鲁哀公十五年到十六年初的一段时间内。

5.16 子谓子产⑴有君子之道四焉:其行己也恭,其事上也敬,其养民也惠,其使民也义。

【译文】孔子评论子产,说他有四种行为合于君子之道:他自己的容颜态度庄严恭敬,他对待君上负责认真,他教养人民有恩惠,他役使人民合于道理。

【注释】

(1)子产——公孙侨,字子产,郑穆公之孙,为春秋时郑国的贤相,在郑简公、郑定公之时执政二十二年。其时,于晋国当悼公、平公、昭公、顷公、定公五世,于楚国当共王、康王、郏敖、灵王、平王五世,正是两国争强、战争不息的时候。郑国地位冲要,而周旋于这两大强国之间,子产却能不低声下气,也不妄自尊大,使国家得到尊敬和安全,的确是古代中国的一位杰出的政治家和外交家。

5.17 子曰:"晏平仲[1]善与人交,久而敬之[2]。"

【译文】孔子说:"晏平仲善于和别人交朋友,相交越久,别人越发恭敬他。"

【注释】

(1)晏平仲——齐国的贤大夫,名婴。《史记》卷六十二有他的传记。现在所传的《晏子春秋》,当然不是晏婴自己的作品,但亦是西汉以前的书。

(2)久而敬之——《魏著作郎韩显宗墓志》"善与人交,人亦久而敬焉",即本《论语》,义与别本《论语》作"久而人敬之"者相合。故我以"之"字指晏平仲自己。若以为是指相交之人,译文便当这样:"相交越久,越发恭敬别人"。

5.18 子曰:"臧文仲[1]居蔡[2],山节藻棁[3],何如其知[4]也?"

【译文】孔子说:"臧文仲替一种叫蔡的大乌龟盖了一间屋,有雕刻着像山一样的斗栱和画着藻草的梁上短柱,这个人的聪明怎么这样呢?"

【注释】
(1)臧文仲——鲁国的大夫臧孙辰。(?—公元前617年)
(2)居蔡——古代人把大乌龟叫作"蔡"。《淮南子·说山训》说:"大蔡神龟,出于沟壑。"高诱《注》说:"大蔡,元龟之所出地名,因名其龟为大蔡,臧文仲所居蔡是也。"古代人迷信卜筮,卜卦用龟,筮用蓍草。用龟,认为越大越灵。蔡便是这种大龟。臧文仲宝藏着它,使它住在讲究的地方。居,作及物动词用,使动用法,使之居住的意思。
(3)山节藻梲——节,柱上斗栱;"梲"音啄,zhuō,梁上短柱。
(4)知——同"智"。

5.19 子张问曰:"令尹子文[1]三仕[2]为令尹,无喜色;三已[2]之,无愠色。旧令尹之政,必以告新令尹。何如?"子曰:"忠矣。"曰:"仁矣乎?"曰:"未知[3];——焉得仁?""崔子弑齐君[4],陈文子[5]有马十乘,弃而违之。至于他邦,则曰,'犹吾大夫崔子也。'违之。之一邦,则又曰:'犹吾大夫崔子也。'违之。何如?"子曰:"清矣。"曰:"仁矣乎?"曰:"未知[3];——焉得仁?"

【译文】子张问道:"楚国的令尹子文三次做令尹的官,没有高兴的颜色;三次被罢免,没有怨恨的颜色。〔每次交代,〕一定把自己的一切政令全部告诉接位的人。这个人怎么样?"孔子道:"可算尽忠于国家了。"子张道:"算不算仁呢?"孔子道:"不晓得;——这怎么能算是仁呢?"子张又问:"崔杼无理地杀掉齐庄公,陈文子有四十匹马,舍弃不要,离开齐国。到了另一个国家,说道:'这里的执政者同我们的崔子差不多。'又离开。又到了一国,又说道:'这里的执政者同我们的崔子差不多。'于是又离开。这个人怎么样?"孔子道:"清白得很。"子张道:"算不算仁呢?"孔子道:"不晓得;——这怎么能算是仁呢?"

【注释】

(1)令尹子文——楚国的宰相叫做令尹。子文即斗谷(谷音构)於菟(音乌徒)。根据《左传》,子文于鲁庄公三十年开始做令尹,到僖公二十三年让位给子玉,其中相距二十八年。在这二十八年中可能有几次被罢免又被任命,《国语•楚语下》说:"昔子文三舍令尹,无一日之积",也就可以证明。

(2)三仕、三已——"三仕"和"三已"的"三"不一定是实数,可能只是表示那事情的次数之多。

(3)未知——和上文第五章"不知其仁",第八章"不知也"的"不知"相同,不是真的"不知",只是否定的另一方式,孔子停了一下,又说"焉得仁",因此用破折号表示。

(4)崔子弑齐君——崔子,齐国的大夫崔杼;齐君,齐庄公,名光。弑,古代在下的人杀掉在上的人叫做弑。"崔子弑齐君"的事见《左传》襄公二十五年。

(5)陈文子——也是齐国的大夫,名须无。可是《左传》没有记载他离开的事,却记载了他以后在齐国的行为很多,可能是一度离开,终于回到本国了。

5.20 季文子[1]三思[2]而后行。子闻之,曰:"再[3],斯可矣。"

【译文】季文子每件事考虑多次才行动。孔子听到了,说:"想两次也就可以了。"

【注释】

(1)季文子——鲁国的大夫季孙行父,历仕鲁国文公、宣公、成公、襄公诸代。孔子生于襄公二十二年,文子死在襄公五年。(?——公元前568年)孔子说这话的时候,文子死了很久了。

(2)三思——这一"三"字更其不是实实在在的"三"。

(3)再——"再"在古文中一般只当副词用,其下承上文省去了动词"思"字。唐《石经》作"再思","思"字不省。凡事三思,一般总是利多弊少,为什么孔子却不同意季文子这样做呢?宦懋庸《论语稽》说,"文子生平盖祸福利害之计太明,故其美恶两不相掩,皆三思之病也。其思之至三者,特以世故太深,过为谨慎;然其流弊将至利害徇一己之私矣"云云。若以《左传》所载文子先后行事证明,此话不为无理。

5.21 子曰:"宁武子⁽¹⁾,邦有道,则知;邦无道,则愚⁽²⁾。其知可及也,其愚不可及也。"

【译文】孔子说:"宁武子在国家太平时节,便聪明;在国家昏暗时节,便装傻。他那聪明,别人赶得上;那装傻,别人就赶不上了。"

【注释】

(1)宁武子——卫国的大夫,姓宁,名俞。

(2)愚——孔安国以为这"愚"是"佯愚似实",故译为"装傻"。

5.22 子在陈⑴，曰："归与！归与！吾党之小子狂简，斐然成章，不知所以裁之⑵。"

【译文】孔子在陈国，说："回去吧！回去吧！我们那里的学生们志向高大得很，文采又都斐然可观，我不知道怎样去指导他们。"

【注释】
⑴陈——国名，姓妫。周武王灭殷以后，求得舜的后代叫妫满的封于陈。春秋时拥有现在河南开封以东，安徽亳县以北一带地方。都于宛丘，即今天的河南淮阳县。春秋末为楚所灭。
⑵不知所以裁之——《史记·孔子世家》作"吾不知所以裁之"。译文也认为这一句的主语不是承上文"吾党之小子"而省略，而是省略了自称代词。"裁"，剪裁。布要剪裁才能成衣，人要教育才能成才，所以译为"指导"。

5.23 子曰："伯夷、叔齐⑴不念旧恶⑵，怨是用希。"

【译文】孔子说："伯夷、叔齐这两兄弟不记念过去的仇恨，别人对他们的怨恨也就很少。"

【注释】
⑴伯夷、叔齐——孤竹君的两个儿子，父亲死了，互相让位，而都逃到周文王那里。周武王起兵讨伐商纣，他们拦住车马劝阻。周朝统一天下，他们以吃食周朝的粮食为可耻，饿死于首阳山。《史记》卷六十一有传。
⑵恶——嫌隙，仇恨。

5.24 子曰:"孰谓微生高⁽¹⁾直?或乞醯⁽²⁾焉,乞诸其邻而与之。"

【译文】孔子说:"谁说微生高这个人直爽?有人向他讨点醋,[他不说自己没有,]却到邻人那里转讨一点给人。"
【注释】
⑴微生高——《庄子》《战国策》诸书载有尾生高守信的故事,说这人和一位女子相约,在桥梁之下见面。到时候,女子不来,他却老等,水涨了都不走,终于淹死。"微""尾"古音相近,字通,因此很多人认为微生高就是尾生高。
⑵醯——音西,xī,醋。

5.25 子曰:"巧言、令色、足⁽¹⁾恭,左丘明⁽²⁾耻之,丘亦耻之。匿怨而友其人,左丘明耻之,丘亦耻之。"

【译义】孔子说:"花言巧语,伪善的容貌,十足的恭顺,这种态度,左丘明认为可耻,我也认为可耻。内心藏着怨恨,表面上却同他要好,这种行为,左丘明认为可耻,我也认为可耻。"
【注释】
⑴足——"足"字旧读去声,zù。
⑵左丘明——历来相传左丘明为《左传》的作者,又因为司马迁在《报任安书》中说过:"左丘失明,厥有《国语》。"又说他是《国语》的作者。这一问题,经过很多人的研究,我则以为下面的两点结论是可以肯定的:(甲)《国语》和《左传》的作者不是一人;(乙)两书都不可能是和孔子同时甚或较早于孔子(因为孔子这段言语把左丘明放在自己之前,而且引以自重)的左丘明所作。

5.26 颜渊季路侍[1]。子曰:"盍[2]各言尔志?"子路曰:"愿车马衣轻轻字当删裘与朋友共敝之而无憾[3]。"颜渊曰:"愿无伐善,无施[4]劳。"子路曰:"愿闻子之志。"子曰:"老者安之,朋友信之,少者怀之[5]。"

【译文】孔子坐着,颜渊、季路两人站在孔子身边。孔子道:"何不各人说说自己的志向?"子路道:"愿意把我的车马衣服同朋友共同使用坏了也没有什么不满。"颜渊道:"愿意不夸耀自己的好处,不表白自己的功劳。"子路向孔子道:"希望听到您的志向。"孔子道:"〔我的志向是,〕老者使他安逸,朋友使他信任我,年青人使他怀念我。"

【注释】

(1)侍——《论语》有时用一"侍"字,有时用"侍侧"两字,有时用"侍坐"两字。若单用"侍"字,便是孔子坐着,弟子站着。若用"侍坐",便是孔子和弟子都坐着。至于"侍侧",则或坐或立,不加肯定。

(2)盍——"何不"的合音字。

(3)愿车马衣轻裘与朋友共敝之而无憾——这句的"轻"字是后人加上去的,有很多证据可以证明唐以前的本子并没有这一"轻"字。详见刘宝楠《论语正义》。这一句有两种读法。一种从"共"字断句,把"共"字作谓词。一种作一句读,"共"字看作副词,修饰"敝"字。这两种读法所表现的意义并无显明的区别。

(4)施——《淮南子•诠言训》:"功盖天下,不施其美。"这两个"施"字意义相同,《礼记•祭统注》云:"施犹著也。"即表白的意思。

(5)信之、怀之——译文把"信"和"怀"同"安"一样看做动词的使动用法。如果把它看做一般用法,那这两句便应该如此翻译:对"朋友有信任,年轻人便关心他"。

5.27 子曰:"已矣乎,吾未见能见其过而内自讼者也。"

【译文】孔子说:"算了吧!我没有看见过能够看到自己的错误便自我责备的哩。"

5.28 子曰:"十室之邑,必有忠信如丘者焉,不如丘之好学也。"

【译文】孔子说:"就是十户人家的地方,一定有像我这样又忠心又信实的人,只是赶不上我的喜欢学问罢了。"

雍也篇第六

共三十章

6.1 子曰:"雍也可使南面⑴。"

【译文】孔子说:"冉雍这个人,可以让他做一部门或一地方的长官。"

【注释】

⑴南面——古代早就知道坐北朝南的方向是最好的,因此也以这个方向的位置最为尊贵,无论天子、诸侯、卿大夫,当他作为长官出现的时候,总是南面而坐。说见王引之《经义述闻》和凌廷堪《礼经释义》。

6.2 仲弓问子桑伯子⑴。子曰:"可也简⑵。"仲弓曰:"居敬而行简,以临其民,不亦可乎?居简而行简,无乃⑶大⑷简乎?"子曰:"雍之言然。"

【译文】仲弓问到子桑伯子这个人。孔子道:"他简单得好。"仲弓道:"若存心严肃认真,而以简单行之,[抓大体,不烦琐,]来治理百姓,不也可以吗?若存心简单,又以简单行之,不是太简单了吗?"孔子道:"你这番话正确。"

【注释】

⑴子桑伯子——此人已经无可考。有人以为就是《庄子》的子桑户,又有人以为就是秦穆公时的子桑(公孙枝),都未必可靠。既然称"伯

子",很大可能是卿大夫。仲弓说"以临其民",也要是卿大夫才能临民。

(2) 简——《说苑》有子桑伯子的一段故事,说他"不衣冠而处",孔子却认为他"质美而无文",因之有人认为这一"简"字是指其"无文"而言。但此处明明说他"可也简",而《说苑》孔子却说,"吾将说而文之",似乎不能如此解释。朱熹以为"简"之所以"可",在于"事不烦而民不扰",颇有道理,故译文加了两句。

(3) 无乃——相当于"不是",但只用于反问句。

(4) 大——同"太"。

6.3 哀公问:"弟子孰为好学?"孔子对曰:"有颜回者好学,不迁怒,不贰过。不幸短命[1]死矣,今也则亡,未闻好学者也。"

【译文】鲁哀公问:"你的学生中,哪个好学?"孔子答道:"有一个叫颜回的人好学,不拿别人出气;也不再犯同样的过失。不幸短命死了,现在再没有这样的人了,再也没听过好学的人了。"

【注释】

(1) 短命——《公羊传》把颜渊的死列在鲁哀公十四年(公元前481年),其时孔子年七十一,依《史记·仲尼弟子列传》,颜渊少于孔子三十岁,则死时年四十一。但据《孔子家语》等书,颜回卒时年仅三十一,因此毛奇龄(《论语稽求篇》)谓《史记》"少孔子三十岁,原是四十之误"。

6.4 子华[1]使[2]于齐,冉子[3]为其母请粟[4]。子曰:"与之釜[5]。"

请益。曰:"与之庾⁽⁶⁾。"冉子与之粟五秉⁽⁷⁾。子曰:"赤之适齐也,乘肥马⁽⁸⁾,衣⁽⁹⁾轻裘。吾闻之也:君子周⑽急不继富。"

【译文】公西华被派到齐国去作使者,冉有替他母亲向孔子请求小米。孔子道:"给他六斗四升。"冉有请求增加。孔子道:"再给他二斗四升。"冉有却给了他八十石。孔子道:"公西赤到齐国去,坐着由肥马驾的车辆,穿着又轻又暖的皮袍。我听说过:君子只是雪里送炭,不去锦上添花。"

【注释】
(1)子华——孔子学生,姓公西,名赤,字子华,比孔子小四十二岁。
(2)使——旧读去声,出使。
(3)冉子——《论语》中,孔子弟子称"子"的不过曾参、有若、闵子骞和冉有几个人,因之这冉子当然就是冉有。
(4)粟——小米(详《新建设》杂志1954年12月号胡静《我国古代农艺史上的几个问题》)。一般的说法,粟是指未去壳的谷粒,去了壳就叫做米。但在古书中也有把米唤做粟的。见沈彤《周官禄田考》。
(5)釜——音府,fǔ,古代量名,容当时的量器六斗四升,约合今天的容量一斗二升八合。
(6)庾——音羽,yǔ,古代量名,容当日的二斗四升,约合今日的四升八合。
(7)秉——音丙,bǐng,古代量名,十六斛。五秉则是八十斛。古代以十斗为斛,所以译为八十石。南宋的贾似道才改为五斗一斛,一石两斛,沿用到民国初年,现今已经废除这一量名了。周秦的八十斛合今天的十六石。
(8)乘肥马——不能解释为"骑肥马",因为孔子时穿着大袖子宽腰身的衣裳,是不便于骑马的。直到战国时的赵武灵王才改穿少数民族服装,学习少数民族的骑着马射箭,以便利于作战。在所有"经书"中找不到骑马的文字,只有《曲礼》有"前有车骑"一语,但《曲礼》的成书在战国以后。

(9)衣——去声,动词,当"穿"字解。

(10)周——后人写作"赒",救济。

6.5 原思⁽¹⁾为之⁽²⁾宰,与之粟九百⁽³⁾,辞。子曰:"毋!以与尔邻里乡党⁽⁴⁾乎!"

【译文】原思任孔子家的总管,孔子给他小米九百,他不肯受。孔子道:"别辞!有多的,给你地方上[的穷人]吧!"

【注释】

(1)原思——孔子弟子原宪,字子思。

(2)之——用法同"其",他的,指孔子而言。

(3)九百——下无量名,不知是斛是斗,还是别的。习惯上常把最通用的度、量、衡的单位省略不说,古今大致相同。不过这一省略,可把我们迷糊了。

(4)邻里乡党——都是古代地方单位的名称,五家为邻,二十五家为里,万二千五百家为乡,五百家为党。

6.6 子谓仲弓,曰:"犁牛⁽¹⁾之子骍⁽²⁾且角⁽³⁾,虽欲勿用⁽⁴⁾,山川其⁽⁵⁾舍诸⁽⁶⁾?"

【译文】孔子谈到冉雍,说:"耕牛的儿子长着赤色的毛,整齐的角,虽然不想用它作牺牲来祭祀,山川之神难道会舍弃它吗?"

【注释】

⑴犁牛——耕牛。古人的名和字,意义一定互相照应。从孔子学生冉耕字伯牛、司马耕字子牛的现象看来,足以知道生牛犁田的方法当时已经普遍实行。从前人说,耕牛制度开始于汉武帝时的赵过,那是由于误解《汉书·食货志》的缘故。

⑵骍——赤色。周朝以赤色为贵,所以祭祀的时候也用赤色的牲畜。

⑶角——意思是两角长得周正。这是古人用词的简略处。

⑷用——义同《左传》"用牲于社"之"用",杀之以祭也。据《史记·仲尼弟子列传》说,仲弓的父亲是贱人;仲弓却是"可使南面"的人才,因此孔子说了这番话。古代供祭祀的牺牲不用耕牛,而且认为耕牛之子也不配作牺牲。孔子的意思是,耕牛所产之子如果够得上作牺牲的条件,山川之神一定会接受这种祭享。那么,仲弓这样的人才,为什么因为他父亲"下贱"而舍弃不用呢?

⑸其——意义同"岂"。

⑹诸——"之乎"两字的合音字。

6.7 子曰:"回也,其心三月⑴不违仁,其余则日月⑴至焉而已矣。"

【译文】孔子说:"颜回呀,他的心长久地不离开仁德,别的学生么,只是短时期偶然想起一下罢了。"

【注释】

⑴三月、日月——这种词语必须活看,不要被字面所拘束,因此译文用"长久地"译"三月",用"短时期""偶然"来译"日月"。

6.8 季康子问:"仲由可使从政也与?"子曰:"由也果,于从政乎何有？"曰："赐也可使从政也与？"曰："赐也达，于从政乎何有？"曰："求也可使从政也与？"曰："求也艺，于从政乎何有？"

【译文】季康子问孔子："仲由这人，可以使用他治理政事么？"孔子道："仲由果敢决断，让他治理政事有什么困难呢？"又问："端木赐可以使用他治理政事么？"孔子道："端木赐通情达理，让他治理政事有什么困难呢？"又问："冉求可以使用他治理政事么？"孔子道："冉求多才多艺，让他治理政事有什么困难呢？"

6.9 季氏使闵子骞[1]为费[2]宰。闵子骞曰："善为我辞焉！如有复我者，则吾必在汶上[3]矣。"

【译文】季氏叫闵子骞做他采邑费地的县长。闵子骞对来人说道："好好地替我辞掉吧！若是再来找我的话，那我一定会逃到汶水之北去了。"

【注释】
(1) 闵子骞——孔子学生闵损，字子骞，比孔子小十五岁。（公元前536—？）
(2) 费——旧音祕，故城在今山东平邑东南七十里。
(3) 汶上——汶音问，wèn，水名，就是山东的大汶河。桂馥《札朴》云："水以阳为北，凡言某水上者，皆谓水北。""汶上"暗指齐国之地。

6.10 伯牛⁽¹⁾有疾，子问之，自牖执其手，曰："亡之⁽²⁾，命矣夫！斯人也而有斯疾也！斯人也而有斯疾也！"

【译文】伯牛生了病，孔子去探问他，从窗户里握着他的手，道："难得活了，这是命呀！这样的人竟有这样的病！这样的人竟有这样的病！"

【注释】
(1)伯牛——孔子学生冉耕字伯牛。
(2)亡之——这"之"字不是代词，不是"亡"（死亡之意）的宾语，因为"亡"字在这里不应该有宾语，只是凑成一个音节罢了。古代常有这种形似宾语而实非宾语的"之"字，详拙著《文言语法》。

6.11 子曰："贤哉，回也！一箪⁽¹⁾食，一瓢饮，在陋巷，人不堪其忧，回也不改其乐。贤哉，回也！"

【译文】孔子说："颜回多么有修养呀！一竹筐饭，一瓜瓢水，住在小巷子里，别人都受不了那穷苦的忧愁，颜回却不改变他自有的快乐。颜回多么有修养呀！"

【注释】
(1)箪——音单，dān，古代盛饭的竹器，圆形。

6.12 冉求曰："非不说子之道，力不足也。"子曰："力不足者⁽¹⁾，中道而废。今女画⁽²⁾。"

【译文】冉求道："不是我不喜欢您的学说，是我力量不够。"孔子道:"如果真是力量不够,走到半道会再走不动了。现在你却没有开步走。"

【注释】

(1)力不足者——"者"这一表示停顿的语气词,有时兼表假设语气,详《文言语法》。

(2)画——停止。

6.13 子谓子夏曰:"女为君子儒!无为小人儒!"

【译文】孔子对子夏道:"你要去做个君子式的儒者,不要去做那小人式的儒者!"

6.14 子游为武城⑴宰。子曰:"女得人焉耳⑵乎?"曰:"有澹台灭明者⑶,行不由径,非公事,未尝至于偃之室也。"

【译文】子游做武城县县长。孔子道:"你在这儿得到什么人才没有?"他道:"有一个叫澹台灭明的人,走路不抄小道,不是公事,从不到我屋里来。"

【注释】

(1)武城——鲁国的城邑,在今山东费县西南。

(2)耳——通行本作"尔",兹依唐《石经》、宋《石经》、皇侃《义疏》本作"耳"。

(3)有澹台灭明者——澹台灭明字子羽,《史记·仲尼弟子列传》也把他列入弟子。但从这里子游的答话语气来看,说这话时还没有向孔子受业。因为"有……者"的提法,是表示这人是听者以前所不知道的。

若果如《史记》所记，澹台灭明在此以前便已经是孔子学生，那子游这时的语气应该与此不同。

6.15 子曰："孟之反⁽¹⁾不伐，奔而殿，将入门，策其马，曰：'非敢后也，马不进也。'"

【译文】孔子说："孟之反不夸耀自己，[在抵御齐国的战役中，右翼的军队溃退了，]他走在最后，掩护全军，将进城门，便鞭打着马匹，一面说道：'不是我敢于殿后，是马匹不肯快走的缘故。'"

【注释】
⑴孟之反——《左传》哀公十一年作"孟之侧"，译文参照《左传》所叙述的事实有所增加。

6.16 子曰："不有⁽¹⁾祝鮀⁽²⁾之佞，而⁽³⁾有宋朝⁽⁴⁾之美，难乎免于今之世矣。"

【译义】孔子说："假使没有祝鮀的口才，而仅有宋朝的美丽，在今天的社会里怕不易避免祸害了。"

【注释】
⑴不有——这里用以表示假设语气，"假若没有"的意思。
⑵祝鮀——卫国的大夫，字子鱼，《左传》定公四年曾记载着他的外交辞令。
⑶而——王引之《经义述闻》云："而犹与也，言有祝鮀之佞与有宋朝之美也。"很多人同意这种讲法，但我终嫌"不有祝鮀之佞，与有宋

朝之美"为语句不顺，王氏此说恐非原意。

(4)宋朝——宋国的公子朝，《左传》昭公二十年和定公十四年都曾记载着他因为美丽而惹起乱子的事情。

6.17 子曰："谁能出不由户？何莫由斯道也？"

【译文】孔子说："谁能够走出屋外不从房门经过？为什么没有人从我这条路行走呢？"

6.18 子曰："质胜文则野，文胜质则史。文质彬彬(1)，然后君子。"

【译文】孔子说："朴实多于文采，就未免粗野；文采多于朴实，又未免虚浮。文采和朴实，配合适当，这才是个君子。"

【注释】

(1)文质彬彬——此处形容人既文雅又朴实，后来多用来指人文雅有礼貌。

6.19 子曰："人之生也(1)直，罔(2)之生也幸而免。"

【译文】孔子说："人的生存由于正直，不正直的人也可以生存，那是他侥幸地免于祸害。"

【注释】

(1)也——语气词，表"人之生"是一词组作主语，这里无妨作一停顿，下文"直"是谓语。

(2)罔——诬罔的人，不直的人。

6.20 子曰："知之者不如好之者，好之者不如乐之者。"

【译文】孔子说："〔对于任何学问和事业，〕懂得它的人不如喜爱它的人，喜爱它的人又不如以它为乐的人。"

6.21 子曰："中人以上，可以语上也；中人以下，不可以语上也。"

【译文】孔子说："中等水平以上的人，可以告诉他高深学问；中等水平以下的人，不可以告诉他高深学问。"

6.22 樊迟问知。子曰："务民之义，敬鬼神而远之⁽¹⁾，可谓知矣。"问仁。曰："仁者先难⁽²⁾而后获，可谓仁矣。"

【译文】樊迟问怎么样才算聪明。孔子道："把心力专一地放在使人民走向'义'上，严肃地对待鬼神，但并不打算接近他，可以说是聪明了。"又问怎么样才叫做有仁德。孔子道："仁德的人付出一定的力量，然后收获果实，可以说是仁德了。"

【注释】

(1)远之——远作及物动词,去声,yuàn。疏远,不去接近的意思。譬如祈祷、淫祀,在孔子看来都不是"远之"。

(2)先难——《颜渊篇第十二》又有一段答樊迟的话,其中有两句道:"先事后得,非崇德与?"和这里"先难后获可谓仁矣"是一个意思,所以我把"难"字译为"付出一定的力量"。孔子对樊迟两次说这样的话,是不是樊迟有坐享其成的想法,那就不得而知了。

6.23 子曰:"知者乐水,仁者乐山。知者动,仁者静。知者乐,仁者寿。"

【译文】孔子说:"聪明人乐于水,仁人乐于山。聪明人活动,仁人沉静。聪明人快乐,仁人长寿。"

6.24 子曰:"齐一变,至于鲁;鲁一变,至于道。"

【译文】孔子说:"齐国[的政治和教育]一有改革,便达到鲁国的样子;鲁国[的政治和教育]一有改革,便进而合于大道了。"

6.25 子曰:"觚(1)不觚,觚哉!觚哉!"

【译文】孔子说:"觚不像个觚,这是觚吗!这是觚吗!"

【注释】

(1)觚——音孤，gū，古代盛酒的器皿，腹部作四条棱角，足部也作四条棱角。每器容当时容量二升（或曰三升）。孔子为什么说这话，后人有两种较为近于情理的猜想：（甲）觚有棱角，才能叫做觚。可是做出棱角比做圆的难，孔子所见的觚可能只是一个圆形的酒器，而不是上圆下方（有四条棱角）的了。但也名为觚，因之孔子慨叹当日事物名实不符，如"君不君，臣不臣，父不父，子不子"之类。（乙）觚和孤同音，寡少的意思。只能容酒两升（或者三升）的叫觚，是叫人少饮不要沉湎之意。可能当时的觚实际容量已经大大不止此数，由此孔子发出感慨。（古代酿酒，不懂得蒸酒的技术，因之酒精成分很低，而升又小，两三升酒是微不足道的。《史记·滑稽列传》载淳于髡的话，最多能够饮一石，可以想见了。）

6.26 宰我问曰："仁者，虽告之曰，'井有仁(1)焉。'其从之也？"子曰："何为其然也？君子可逝(2)也，不可陷也；可欺(3)也，不可罔(3)也。"

【译文】宰我问道："有仁德的人，就是告诉他：'井里掉下一位仁人啦。'他是不是会跟着下去呢？"孔子道："为什么你要这样做呢？君子可以叫他远远走开不再回来，却不可以陷害他；可以欺骗他，却不可以愚弄他。"

【注释】

(1)仁——即"仁人"的意思，和《学而篇第一》"泛爱众而亲仁"的"仁"用法相同。
(2)逝——古代"逝"字的意义和"往"字有所不同，"往"而不复返才用"逝"字。译文即用此义。俞樾《群经平议》读"逝"为"折"说："逝与折古通用。君子杀身成仁则有之矣，故可得而摧折，然不

237

可以非理陷害之，故可折而不可陷。"亦通。

(3)欺、罔——《孟子·万章上》有这样一段话，和这一段结合，正好说明"欺"和"罔"的区别。那段的原文是："昔者有馈生鱼于郑子产，子产使校人畜之池。校人烹之，反命曰：'始舍之，圉圉焉；少则洋洋焉；攸然而逝。'子产曰：'得其所哉！得其所哉！'校人出，曰：'孰谓子产知？予既烹而食之，曰，得其所哉，得其所哉。'故君子可欺以其方，难罔以非其道。"那么，校人的欺骗子产，是"欺以其方"，而宰我的假设便是"罔以非其道"了。

6.27 子曰："君子博学于文，约之以礼[1]，亦可以弗畔[2]矣夫！"

【译文】孔子说："君子广泛地学习文献，再用礼节来加以约束，也就可以不至于离经叛道了。"

【注释】

(1)博学于文，约之以礼——《子罕篇第九》云："颜渊喟然叹曰：'夫子循循然善诱人，博我以文，约我以礼。'"这里的"博学于文，约之以礼"和《子罕篇》的"博我以文，约我以礼"是不是完全相同呢？如果完全相同，则"约之以礼"的"之"是指代"君子"而言。这是一般人的说法。但毛奇龄的《论语稽求篇》却说："博约是两事，文礼是两物，然与'博我以文，约我以礼'不同。何也？彼之博约是以文礼博约回；此之博约是以礼约文，以约约博也。博在文，约文又在礼也。"毛氏认为"约之以礼"的"之"是指代"文"，正是我们平常所说的"由博返约"的意思。

(2)畔——同"叛"。

6.28 子见南子[1],子路不说。夫子矢之曰:"予所[2]否者,天厌之!天厌之!"

【译文】孔子去和南子相见,子路不高兴。孔子发誓道:"我假若不对的话,天厌弃我罢!天厌弃我罢!"

【注释】
(1)南子——卫灵公夫人,把持着当日卫国的政治,而且有不正当的行为,名声不好。《史记·孔子世家》对"子见南子"的情况有生动的描述。
(2)所——如果,假若。假设连词,但只用于誓词中。详阎若璩《四书释地》。

6.29 子曰:"中庸[1]之为德也,其至矣乎!民[2]鲜久矣。"

【译文】孔子说:"中庸这种道德,该是最高的了,大家已经是长久地缺乏它了。"

【注释】
(1)中庸——这是孔子的最高道德标准。"中",折中,无过,也无不及,调和;"庸",平常。孔子拈出这两个字,就表示他的最高道德标准,其实就是折中的和平常的东西。后代的儒家又根据这两个字作了一篇题为"中庸"的文章,西汉人戴圣收入《礼记》,南宋人朱熹又取入《四书》。司马迁说是子思所作,未必可靠。从其文字和内容看,可能是战国至秦的作品,难免不和孔子的"中庸"有相当距离。
(2)民——这"民"字不完全指老百姓,因以"大家"译之。

6.30 子贡曰:"如有博施⑴于民而能济众,何如?可谓仁乎?"子曰:"何事于仁!必也圣乎!尧舜⑵其犹病诸!夫⑶仁者,己欲立而立人,己欲达而达人。能近取譬,可谓仁之方也已。"

【译文】子贡道:"假若有这么一个人,广泛地给人民以好处,又能帮助大家生活得很好,怎么样?可以说是仁道了吗?"孔子道:"哪里仅是仁道!那一定是圣德了!尧舜或者都难以做到哩!仁是什么呢?自己要站得住,同时也使别人站得住;自己要事事行得通,同时也使别人事事行得通。能够就眼下的事实选择例子一步步去做,可以说是实践仁道的方法了。"

【注释】
⑴施——旧读去声。
⑵尧舜——传说中的上古两位帝王,也是孔子心目中的榜样。
⑶夫——音扶,fú,文言中的提挈词。

述而篇第七

共三十八章

7.1 子曰："述而不作,信而好古(1),窃比于我老彭(2)。"

【译文】孔子说:"阐述而不创作,以相信的态度喜爱古代文化,我私自和我那老彭相比。"

【注释】

(1)作,好古——下文第二十八章说:"盖有不知而作之者,我无是也。"这个"作",大概也是"不知而作"的涵义,很难说孔子的学说中没有创造性。又第二十章说,"好古,敏以求之",也可为这个"好古"的证明。

(2)老彭——人名。有人说是老子和彭祖两人,有人说是殷商时代的彭祖一人,又有人说孔子说"我的老彭",其人一定和孔子相当亲密,未必是古人。《大戴礼·虞戴德篇》有"商老彭",不知即此人不。

7.2 子曰:"默而识(1)之,学而不厌,诲人不倦,何有于我哉(2)?"

【译文】孔子说:"[把所见所闻的]默默地记在心里,努力学习而不厌弃,教导别人而不疲倦,这些事情我做到了哪些呢?"

【注释】

(1)识——音志,zhì,记住。

(2)何有于我哉——"何有"在古代是一常用语,在不同场合表示不同意义。像《诗•邶风•谷风》"何有何亡?黾勉求之"的"何有"便是"有什么"的意思,译文就是用的这一意义。也有人说,《论语》的"何有"都是"不难之辞",那么,这句话便该译为"这些事情对我有什么困难呢"。这种译法便不是孔子谦虚之词,而和下文第二十八章的"多闻,择其善者而从之,多见而识之"以及"抑为之不厌,诲人不倦"的态度相同了。

7.3 子曰:"德之不修,学之不讲,闻义不能徙,不善不能改,是吾忧也。"

【译文】孔子说:"品德不培养;学问不讲习;听到义在那里,却不能亲身赴之;有缺点不能改正,这些都是我的忧虑哩!"

7.4 子之燕居,申申(1)如也,夭夭(2)如也。

【译文】孔子在家闲居,很整齐的,很和乐而舒展的。
【注释】
(1)申申——整敕之貌。
(2)夭夭——和舒之貌。

7.5 子曰:"甚矣吾衰也!久矣吾不复梦见周公(1)!"

【译文】孔子说:"我衰老得多么厉害呀!我好长时间没再梦见周公了!"

【注释】

⑴公——姓姬,名旦,周文王的儿子,武王的弟弟,成王的叔父,鲁国的始祖,又是孔子心目中最敬服的古代圣人之一。

7.6 子曰:"志于道,据于德,依于仁,游于艺⑴。"

【译文】孔子说:"目标在'道',根据在'德',依靠在'仁',而游憩于礼、乐、射、御、书、数六艺之中。"

【注释】

⑴游于艺——《礼记•学记》曾说:"不兴其艺,不能乐学。故君子之于学也,藏焉,修焉,息焉,游焉。夫然,故安其学而亲其师,乐其友而信其道,是以虽离师辅而不反也。"可以阐明这里的"游于艺"。

7.7 子曰:"自行束脩⑴以上,吾未尝无诲焉。"

【译文】孔子说:"只要是主动地给我一点见面薄礼,我从没有不教诲的。"

【注释】

⑴束脩——脩是干肉,又叫脯。每条脯叫一脡(挺),十脡为一束。束脩就是十条干肉,古代用来作初次拜见的礼物。但这一礼物是菲薄的。

7.8 子曰:"不愤⁽¹⁾不启,不悱⁽²⁾不发⁽³⁾。举一隅不以三隅反,则不复也。"

【译文】孔子说:"教导学生,不到他想求明白而不得的时候,不去开导他;不到他想说出来却说不出的时候,不去启发他。教给他东方,他却不能由此推知西、南、北三方,便不再教他了。"

【注释】
(1)愤——心求通而未得之意。
(2)悱——音斐,fěi,口欲言而未能之貌。
(3)不启,不发——这是孔子自述其教学方法,必须受教者先发生困难,有求知的动机,然后去启发他。这样,教学效果自然好些。

7.9 子食于有丧者之侧,未尝饱也。

【译文】孔子在死了亲属的人旁边吃饭,不曾吃饱过。

7.10 子于是日哭,则不歌。

【译文】孔子在这一天哭泣过,就不再唱歌。

7.11 子谓颜渊曰:"用之则行,舍之则藏,惟我与尔有是夫!"子路曰:"子行三军,则谁与⁽¹⁾?"子曰:"暴虎冯河⁽²⁾,死而无悔者,吾不与也。必也临事而惧,好谋而成者也。"

【译文】孔子对颜渊道:"用我呢,就干起来;不用呢,就藏起来。只有我和你才能这样吧!"子路道:"您若率领军队,找谁共事?"孔子道:"赤手空拳和老虎搏斗,不用船只去渡河,这样死了都不后悔的人,我是不和他共事的。〔我所找他共事的,〕一定是面临任务便恐惧谨慎,善于谋略而能成的人哩!"

【注释】

(1)子行三军,则谁与——"行"字古人用得很活,行军犹言行师。《易经•谦卦•上六》云:"利用行师征邑国",又《复卦•上六》:"用行师终有大败",行师似有出兵之意。这种活用,一直到中古都如此。如"子夜歌"的"欢行白日心,朝东暮还西"。"与",动词,偕同的意思。子路好勇,看见孔子夸奖颜渊,便发此问。

(2)暴虎冯河——冯音凭,píng。徒手搏虎曰暴虎,徒足涉河曰冯河。"冯河"两字最初见于《易•泰卦》爻辞,又见于《诗•小雅•小旻》。"暴虎"也见于《诗经•郑风•大叔于田》和《小雅•小旻》,可见都是很早就有的俗语。"河"不一定是专指黄河,古代也有用作通名,泛指江河的。

7.12 子曰:"富而(1)可求也,虽执鞭之士(2),吾亦为之。如不可求,从吾所好。"

【译文】孔子说:"财富如果可以求得的话,就是做市场的守门卒我也干。如果求它不到,还是我干我的罢。"

【注释】

(1)而——用法同"如",假设连词。但是用在句中的多,即有用在句首的,那句也多半和上一句有密切的关连,独立地用在句首的极少见。

(2)执鞭之士——根据《周礼》,有两种人拿着皮鞭,一种是古代天子以及诸侯出入之时,有二至八人拿着皮鞭使行路之人让道。一种是市场的守门人,手执皮鞭来维持秩序。这里讲的是求财,市场是财富所聚集之处,因此译为"市场的守门卒"。

7.13 子之所慎:齐⑴,战,疾⑵。

【译文】孔子所小心慎重的事有三样:斋戒,战争,疾病。
【注释】
⑴齐——同"斋"。古代于祭祀之前,一定先要做一番身心的整洁工作,这一工作便叫做'斋'或者"斋戒"。《乡党篇第十》说孔子"齐必变食,居必迁坐"。
⑵战,疾——上文说到孔子作战必求"临事而惧,好谋而成"的人,因为它关系国家的存亡安危;《乡党篇》又描写孔子病了,不敢随便吃药,因为它关系个人的生死。这都是孔子不能不谨慎的地方。

7.14 子在齐闻《韶》,三月不知肉味,曰:"不图为乐之至于斯也。"

【译文】孔子在齐国听到《韶》的乐章,很长时间尝不出肉味,于是道:"想不到欣赏音乐竟到了这种境界。"

7.15 冉有曰:"夫子为⑴卫君⑵乎?"子贡曰:"诺;吾将问之。"入,曰:"伯夷、叔齐何人也?"曰:"古之贤人也。"曰:"怨乎?"曰:"求仁而得仁,又何怨?"出,曰:"夫子不为也。"

【译文】冉有道:"老师赞成卫君吗?"子贡道:"好罢,我去问问他。"子贡进到孔子屋里,道:"伯夷、叔齐是什么样的人?"孔子道:"是古代的贤人。"子贡道:"〔他们两人互相推让,都不肯做孤竹国的国君,结果都跑到国外,〕是不是后来又怨悔呢?"孔子道:"他们求仁德,便得到了仁德,又怨悔什么呢?"子贡走出,答复冉有道:"老师不赞成卫君。"

【注释】
(1)为——动词,去声,本意是帮助,这里译为"赞成",似乎更合原意。
(2)卫君——指卫出公辄。辄是卫灵公之孙,太子蒯聩之子。太子蒯聩得罪了卫灵公的夫人南子,逃在晋国。灵公死,立辄为君。晋国的赵简子又把蒯聩送回,借以侵略卫国。卫国抵御晋兵,自然也拒绝了蒯聩的回国。从蒯聩和辄是父子关系的一点看来,似乎是两父子争夺卫君的位置,和伯夷、叔齐两兄弟的互相推让,终于都抛弃了君位相比,恰恰成一对照。因之下文子贡引以发问,借以试探孔子对出公辄的态度。孔子赞美伯夷、叔齐,自然就是不赞成出公辄了。

7.16 子曰:"饭疏食(1)饮水(2),曲肱(3)而枕(4)之,乐亦在其中矣。不义而富且贵,于我如浮云。"

【译文】孔子说:"吃粗粮,喝冷水,弯着胳膊做枕头,也有着乐趣。干不正当的事而得来的富贵,我看来好像浮云。"

【注释】

(1)疏食——有两个解释：（甲）粗粮。古代以稻粱为细粮，以稷为粗粮。见程瑶田《通艺录·九谷考》。（乙）糙米。

(2)水——古代常以"汤"和"水"对言，"汤"的意义是热水，"水"就是冷水。

(3)肱——音宫，gōng，胳膊。

(4)枕——这里用作动词，旧读去声。

7.17 子曰："加我数年，五十以学《易》(1)，可以无大过矣。"

【译文】孔子说："让我多活几年，到五十岁的时候去学习《易》，便可以没有大过错了。"

【注释】

(1)《易》——古代一部用以占筮的书，其中的《卦辞》和《爻辞》是孔子以前的作品。

7.18 子所雅言(1)，《诗》、《书》、执礼，皆雅言也。

【译文】孔子有用普通话的时候，读《诗》，读《书》，行礼，都用普通话。

【注释】

(1)雅言——当时中国所通行的语言。春秋时代各国语言不能统一，不但可以想象得到，即从古书中也可以找到证明。当时较为通行的语言便是"雅言"。

7.19 叶公⁽¹⁾问孔子于子路,子路不对。子曰:"女奚不曰,其为人也,发愤忘食,乐以忘忧,不知老之将至云尔⁽²⁾。"

【译文】叶公向子路问孔子为人怎么样,子路不回答。孔子对子路道:"你为什么不这样说:他的为人,用功便忘记吃饭,快乐便忘记忧愁,不晓得衰老会要到来,如此罢了。"

【注释】
(1)叶——旧音摄,shè,地名,当时属楚,今河南叶县南三十里有古叶城。叶公是叶地方的县长,楚君称王,那县长便称公。此人叫沈诸梁,字子高,《左传》定公、哀公之间有一些关于他的记载,在楚国当时还算是一位贤者。
(2)云尔——云,如此;尔同"耳",而已,罢了。

7.20 子曰:"我非生而知之者,好古,敏以求之者也。"

【译文】孔子说:"我不是生来就有知识的人,而是爱好古代文化,勤奋敏捷去求得来的人。"

7.21 子不语怪,力,乱,神。

【译文】孔子不谈怪异、勇力、叛乱和鬼神。

7.22 子曰:"三人行,必有我师焉:择其善者而从之,其不善者而改之⁽¹⁾。"

【译文】孔子说:"几个人一块走路,其中便一定有可以为我所取法的人:我选取那些优点而学习,看出那些缺点而改正。"

【注释】

(1)子曰……改之——子贡说孔子没有特定的老师(见19.22),意思就是随处都有老师,和这章可以以互相证明。《老子》说:"善人,不善人之师;不善人,善人之资。"未尝不是这个道理。

7.23 子曰:"天生德于予,桓魋(1)其如予何(2)?"

【译文】孔子说:"天在我身上生了这样的品德,那桓魋将把我怎样?"

【注释】

(1)桓魋——魋音颓,tuí。桓魋,宋国的司马向魋,因为是宋桓公的后代,所以又叫桓魋。
(2)桓魋其如予何——《史记·孔子世家》有一段这样的记载:"孔子去曹,适宋,与弟子习礼大树下。宋司马桓魋欲杀孔子,拔其树。孔子去,弟子曰'可以速矣!'孔子曰:'天生德于予,桓魋其如予何?'"

7.24 子曰:"二三子以我为隐乎?吾无隐乎尔。吾无行而不与二三子者,是丘也。"

【译文】孔子说:"你们这些学生以为我有所隐瞒吗?我对你们是没有隐瞒的。我没有一点不向你们公开,这就是我孔丘的为人。"

7.25 子以四教:文,行⑴,忠,信。

【译文】孔子用四种内容教育学生:历代文献,社会生活的实践,对待别人的忠心,与人交际的信实。

【注释】

⑴行——作名词用,旧读去声。

7.26 子曰:"圣人,吾不得而见之矣;得见君子者,斯可矣。"子曰:"善人,吾不得而见之矣;得见有恒⑴者,斯可矣。亡而为有,虚而为盈,约而为泰⑵,难乎有恒矣。"

【译文】孔子说:"圣人,我不能看见了;能看见君子,就可以了。"又说:"善人,我不能看见了,能看见有一定操守的人,就可以了。本来没有,却装做有;本来空虚,却装做充足,本来穷困,却要豪华,这样的人便难于保持一定操守了。"

【注释】

⑴有恒——这个"恒"字和《孟子·梁惠王上》的"无恒产而有恒心"的"恒"是一个意义。

⑵泰——这"泰"字和《国语·晋语》的"恃其富宠,以泰于国"、《荀子·议兵篇》的"用财欲泰"的"泰"同义,用度豪华而不吝惜的意思。

7.27 子钓而不纲⑴,弋⑵不射宿⑶。

【译文】孔子钓鱼,不用大绳横断流水来取鱼,用带生丝的箭射鸟,不射归巢的鸟。

【注释】

(1)纲——网上的大绳叫纲,用它来横断水流,再用生丝系钓,着于纲上来取鱼,这也叫纲。"不纲"的"纲"是动词。

(2)弋——音亦,yì,用带生丝的矢来射。

(3)宿——歇宿了的鸟。

7.28 子曰:"盖有不知而作之者,我无是也。多闻,择其善者而从之;多见而识之;知之次也⁽¹⁾。"

【译文】孔子说:"大概有一种自己不懂却凭空造作的人,我没有这种毛病。多多地听,选择其中好的加以接受;多多地看,全记在心里。这样的知,是仅次于'生而知之'的。"

【注释】

(1)次——《论语》的"次"一共享了八次,都是当"差一等""次一等"讲。《季氏篇第十六》云:"孔子曰:'生而知之者,上也;学而知之者,次也。'"这里的"知之次也"正是"学而知之者,次也"的意思。孔子自己也说他是学而知之(好古,敏以求之)的人,所以译文加了几个字。

7.29 互乡⁽¹⁾难与言,童子见,门人惑。子曰:"与其进也,不与其退也,唯何甚?人洁己以进,与其洁也,不保⁽²⁾其往也。"

【译文】互乡这地方的人难于交谈,一个童子得到孔子的接见,弟子们疑惑。孔子道:"我们赞成他的进步,不赞成他的退步,何必做得太过?别人把自己弄得干干净净而来,便应当赞成他的干净,不要死记住他那过去。"

【注释】
(1)互乡——地名,现在已不详其所在。
(2)保——守也,所以译为"死记住"。

7.30 子曰:"仁远乎哉?我欲仁,斯仁至矣。"

【译文】孔子道:"仁德难道离我们很远吗?我要它,它就来了。"

7.31 陈司败⁽¹⁾问昭公⁽²⁾知礼乎,孔子曰:"知礼。"孔子退,揖巫马期⁽³⁾而进之,曰:"吾闻君子不党,君子亦党乎?君取于吴⁽⁴⁾,为同姓⁽⁵⁾,谓之吴孟子⁽⁶⁾。君而知礼,孰不知礼?"巫马期以告。子曰:"丘也幸,苟有过⁽⁷⁾,人必知之。"

【译文】陈司败向孔子问鲁昭公懂不懂礼,孔子道:"懂礼。"孔子走了出来,陈司败便向巫马期作了个揖,请他走近自己,然后说道:"我听说君子无所偏袒,难道孔子竟偏袒吗?鲁君从吴国娶了位夫人,吴和鲁是同姓国家,〔不便叫她做吴姬,〕于是叫她做吴孟子。鲁君若是懂得礼,谁不懂得礼呢?"巫马期把这话转告给孔子。孔子道:"我真幸运,假若有错误,人家一定给指出来。"

【注释】

(1)陈司败——人名。有人说"司败"是官名,也有人说是人名,究竟是什么样的人,今天已经无法知道。

(2)昭公——鲁昭公,名裯,襄公庶子,继襄公而为君。"昭"是谥号,陈司败之问若在昭公死后,则"昭公知礼乎"可能是原来语言。如果他这次发问尚在昭公生时,那"昭公"字眼当是后人的记述。我们已无从判断,所以这句不加引号。

(3)巫马期——孔子学生,姓巫马,名施,字子期,小于孔子三十岁。

(4)君取于吴——"取"这里用作"娶"字。吴,当时的国名,拥有今天淮水、泗水以南以及浙江的嘉兴、湖州等地。哀公时,为越王勾践所灭。

(5)为同姓——鲁为周公之后,姬姓;吴为太伯之后,也是姬姓。

(6)吴孟子——春秋时代,国君夫人的称号一般是所生长之国名加她的本姓。鲁娶于吴,这位夫人便应该称为吴姬。但"同姓不婚"是周朝的礼法,鲁君夫人的称号而把"姬"字标明出来,便是很显明地表示出鲁君的违背了"同姓不婚"的礼制,因之改称为"吴孟子"。"孟子"可能是这位夫人的字。《左传》哀公十二年亦书曰:"昭夫人孟子卒。"

(7)苟有过——根据《荀子•子道篇》关于孔子的另一段故事,和《史记•仲尼弟子列传》对这一事"臣不可言君亲之恶,为讳者礼也"的解释,则孔子对鲁昭公所谓不合礼的行为不是不知,而是不说,最后只得归过于自己。

7.32 子与人歌而善,必使反之,而后和之。

【译文】孔子同别人一道唱歌,如果唱得好,一定请他再唱一遍,然后自己又和他。

7.33 子曰:"文,莫⁽¹⁾吾犹人也。躬行君子,则吾未之有得。"

【译文】孔子说:"书本上的学问,大约我同别人差不多。在生活实践中做一个君子,那我还没有成功。"

【注释】

⑴文莫——以前人都把"文莫"两字连读,看成一个双音词,但又不能得出恰当的解释。吴检斋(承仕)先生在《亡莫无虑同词说》(载于前北京中国大学《国学丛编》第一期第一册)中以为"文"是一词,指孔子所谓的"文章";"莫"是一词,"大约"的意思。关于"莫"字的说法在先秦古籍中虽然缺乏坚强的论证,但解释本文却比所有各家来得较为满意,因之为译者所采用。朱熹《集注》亦云,"莫,疑辞",或为吴说所本。

7.34 子曰:"若圣⁽¹⁾与仁,则吾岂敢?抑为之不厌,诲人不倦,则可谓云尔已矣。"公西华曰:"正唯弟子不能学也。"

【译文】孔子说道:"讲到圣和仁,我怎么敢当?不过是学习和工作总不厌倦,教导别人总不疲劳,就是如此如此罢了。"公西华道:"这正是我们学不到的。"

【注释】

⑴圣——《孟子·公孙丑上》载子贡对这事的看法说:"学不厌,智也;教不倦,仁也。仁且智,夫子既圣矣。"可见当时的学生就已把孔子看成圣人。

7.35 子疾病⁽¹⁾，子路请祷。子曰："有诸？"子路对曰："有之；《诔》⁽²⁾曰：'祷尔于上下神祇⁽³⁾。'"子曰："丘之祷久矣。"

【译文】孔子病重，子路请求祈祷。孔子道："有这回事吗？"子路答道："有的；《诔文》说过：'替你向天神地祇祈祷。'"孔子道："我早就祈祷过了。"

【注释】
(1)疾病——"疾病"连言，是重病。
(2)诔——音耒，lěi，本应作讄，祈祷文。和哀悼死者的"诔"不同。
(3)祇——音祁，qí，地神。

7.36 子曰："奢则不孙⁽¹⁾，俭则固⁽²⁾。与其不孙也，宁固。"

【译文】孔子说："奢侈豪华就显得骄傲，省俭朴素就显得寒伧。与其骄傲，宁可寒伧。"

【注释】
(1)孙——同"逊"。
(2)固——固陋，寒伧。

7.37 子曰："君子坦荡荡，小人长戚戚。"

【译文】孔子说："君子心地平坦宽广，小人却经常局促忧愁。"

7.38 子温而厉,威而不猛,恭而安。

【译文】孔子温和而严厉,有威仪而不凶猛,庄严而安详。

泰伯篇第八

共二十一章

8.1 子曰:"泰伯⁽¹⁾,其可谓至德也已矣。三以天下⁽²⁾让,民无得而称焉。"

【译文】孔子说:"泰伯,那可以说是品德极崇高了。屡次地把天下让给季历,老百姓简直找不出恰当的词语来称赞他。"

【注释】

(1)泰伯——亦作"太伯",周朝祖先古公亶父的长子。古公有三子,太伯、仲雍、季历。季历的儿子就是姬昌(周文王)。据传说,古公预见到昌的圣德,因此想打破惯例,把君位不传长子太伯,而传给幼子季历,从而传给昌。太伯为着实现他父亲的意愿,便偕同仲雍出走至勾吴(为吴国的始祖),终于把君位传给季历和昌。昌后来扩张国势,竟有天下的三分之二,到他儿子姬发(周武王),便灭了殷商,统一天下。

(2)天下——当古公、泰伯之时,周室仅是一个小的部落,谈不上"天下"。这"天下"两字可能即指其当时的部落而言。也有人说,是预指以后的周部落统一了中原的天下而言。

8.2 子曰:"恭而无礼⁽¹⁾则劳,慎而无礼则葸⁽²⁾,勇而无礼则乱,直而无礼则绞⁽³⁾。君子笃于亲,则民兴于仁;故旧不遗,则民不偷⁽⁴⁾。"

【译文】孔子说:"注重容貌态度的端庄,却不知礼,就未免劳倦;只知谨慎,却不知礼,就流于畏葸懦弱;专凭敢作敢为的胆量,却不知礼,就会盲动闯祸;心直口快,却不知礼,就会尖刻刺人。在上位的人能用深厚感情对待亲族,那老百姓就会走向仁德;在上位的人不遗弃他的老同事、老朋友,那老百姓就不致对人冷淡无情。"

【注释】
(1)礼——这里指的是礼的本质。
(2)葸——音喜,xǐ,胆怯,害怕。
(3)绞——尖刻刺人。
(4)偷——淡薄,这里指人与人的感情而言。

8.3 曾子有疾,召门弟子曰:"启⁽¹⁾予足!启予手!《诗》云⁽²⁾,'战战兢兢,如临深渊,如履⁽³⁾薄冰。'而今而后,吾知免夫!小子!"

【译文】曾参病了,把他的学生召集拢来,说道:"看看我的脚!看看我的手!《诗经》上说:'小心呀!谨慎呀!好像面临深深水坑之旁,好像行走薄薄冰层之上。'从今以后,我才晓得自己是可以免于祸害刑戮的了!学生们!"

【注释】
(1)启——《说文》有"瞽"字,云:"视也。"王念孙《广雅疏证》(《释诂》)说,《论语》的这"启"字就是《说文》的"瞽"字。
(2)《诗》云——三句诗见《诗经•小雅•小旻篇》。
(3)履——《易•履卦•爻辞》:"眇能视,跛能履。"履,步行也。

8.4 曾子有疾,孟敬子⁽¹⁾问之。曾子言曰:"鸟之将死,其鸣也哀;人之将死,其言也善。君子所贵乎道者三:动容貌,斯远暴慢⁽²⁾矣;正颜色,斯近信矣;出辞气,斯远鄙倍⁽³⁾矣。笾豆之事⁽⁴⁾,则有司⁽⁵⁾存。"

【译文】曾参病了,孟敬子探问他。曾子说:"鸟要死了,鸣声是悲哀的;人要死了,说出的话是善意的。在上位的人待人接物有三方面应该注重:严肃自己的容貌,就可以避免别人的粗暴和懈怠;端正自己的脸色,就容易使人相信;说话的时候,多考虑言辞和声调,就可以避免鄙陋粗野和错误。至于礼仪的细节,自有主管人员。"

【注释】
(1)孟敬子——鲁国大夫仲孙捷。
(2)暴慢——暴是粗暴无礼,慢是懈怠不敬。
(3)鄙倍——鄙是粗野鄙陋;倍同"背",不合理,错误。
(4)笾豆之事——笾音边,biān,古代的一种竹器,高脚,上面圆口,有些像碗,祭祀时用以盛果实等食品。豆也是古代一种像笾一般的器皿,木料做的,有盖,用以盛有汁的食物,祭祀时也用它。这里"笾豆之事"系代表礼仪中的一切具体细节。
(5)有司——主管其事的小吏。

8.5 曾子曰:"以能问于不能,以多问于寡;有若无,实若虚;犯而不校——昔者吾友⁽¹⁾尝从事于斯矣。"

【译文】曾子说:"有能力却向无能力的人请教,知识丰富却向知识缺少的人请教;有学问像没学问一样,满腹知识像空无所有一样；纵被欺侮，也不计较——从前我的一位朋友便曾这样做了。"

【注释】
⑴吾友——历来的注释家都以为是指颜回。

8.6 曾子曰："可以托六尺⑴之孤，可以寄百里之命，临大节而不可夺也——君子人与？君子人也。"

【译文】曾子说："可以把幼小的孤儿和国家的命脉都交付给他，面临安危存亡的紧要关头，却不动摇屈服——这种人，是君子人吗？是君子人哩。"

【注释】
⑴六尺——古代尺短，六尺约合今日一百三十八厘米，市尺四尺一寸四分。身长六尺的人还是小孩，一般指十五岁以下的人。

8.7 曾子曰："士不可以不弘毅⑴，任重而道远。仁以为己任，不亦重乎？死而后已，不亦远乎？"

【译文】曾子说："读书人不可以不刚强而有毅力，因为他负担沉重，路程遥远。以实现仁德于天下为己任，不也沉重吗？到死方休，不也遥远吗？"

【注释】
⑴弘毅——就是"强毅"。章太炎（炳麟）先生《广论语骈枝》说："《说文》：'弘，弓声也。'后人借'强'为之，用为'彊'义。此'弘'字即今之'强'字也。《说文》：'毅，有决也。'任重须彊，不彊则力绌；致远须决，不决则志渝。"

8.8 子曰:"兴于《诗》,立于礼,成于乐⑴。"

【译文】孔子说:"诗篇使我振奋,礼使我能在社会上站得住,音乐使我的所学得以完成。"

【注释】

⑴成于乐——孔子所谓"乐"的内容和本质都离不开"礼",因此常常"礼乐"连言。他本人也很懂音乐,因此把音乐作为他的教学工作的一个最后阶段。

8.9 子曰:"民可使由之,不可使知之⑴。"

【译文】孔子说:"老百姓,可以使他们照着我们的道路走去,不可以使他们知道那是为什么。"

【注释】

⑴子曰……知之——这两句与"民可以乐成,不可与虑始"(《史记·滑稽列传补》所载西门豹之言,《商君列传》作"民不可与虑始,而可与乐成")意思大致相同,不必深求。后来有些人觉得这种说法不很妥当,于是别生解释,意在为孔子这位"圣人"回护,虽煞费苦心,反失孔子本意。如刘宝楠《正义》以为"上章是夫子教弟子之法,此'民'字亦指弟子"。不知上章"兴于《诗》"三句与此章旨意各别,自古以来亦曾未有以"民"代"弟子"者。宦懋庸《论语稽》则云:"对于民,其可者使其自由之,而所不可者亦使知之。或曰,舆论所可者则使共由之,其不可者亦使共知之。"则原文当读为"民可,使由;不可,使知之"。恐怕古人无此语法。若是古人果是此意,必用"则"字,甚至"使"下再用"之"字以重指"民",作"民可,则使(之)由之;不可,则使(之)知之",方不致晦涩而误解。

8.10 子曰:"好勇疾贫,乱也。人而不仁,疾之已甚,乱也。"

【译文】孔子说:"以勇敢自喜却厌恶贫困,是一种祸害。对于不仁的人,痛恨太甚,也是一种祸害。"

8.11 子曰:"如有周公之才之美,使骄且吝,其余不足观也已。"

【译文】孔子说:"假如才能的美妙真比得上周公,只要骄傲而吝啬,别的方面也就不值得一看了。"

8.12 子曰:"三年学,不至⑴于谷⑵,不易得也。"

【译义】孔子说:"读书三年并不存做官的念头,这是难得的。"
【注释】
⑴至——这"至"字和《雍也篇第六》"回也其心三月不违仁,其余则日月至焉而已矣"的"至"用法相同,指意念之所至。
⑵谷——古代以谷米为俸禄(作用相当于今日的工资),所以"谷"有"禄"的意义。《宪问篇第十四》的"邦有道,谷;邦无道,谷"的"谷"正与此同。

8.13 子曰:"笃信⑴好学,守死善道。危邦不入,乱邦不居⑵。

天下有道则见⁽³⁾，无道则隐。邦有道，贫且贱焉，耻也；邦无道，富且贵焉，耻也。"

【译文】孔子说："坚定地相信我们的道，努力学习它，誓死保全它。不进入危险的国家，不居住祸乱的国家。天下太平，就出来工作；不太平，就隐居。政治清明，自己贫贱，是耻辱；政治黑暗，自己富贵，也是耻辱。"

【注释】

(1)笃信——《子张篇第十九》："执德不弘，信道不笃，焉能为有？焉能为亡？"这一"笃信"应该和"信道不笃"的意思一样。

(2)危邦，乱邦——包咸云"臣弑君，子弑父，乱也；危者，将乱之兆也。"

(3)见——同"现"。

8.14 子曰："不在其位，不谋其政。"

【译文】孔子说："不居于那个职位，便不考虑它的政务。"

8.15 子曰："师挚之始⁽¹⁾，《关雎》之乱⁽²⁾，洋洋乎盈耳哉！"

【译文】孔子说："当太师挚开始演奏的时候，当结尾演奏《关雎》之曲的时候，满耳朵都是音乐呀！"

【注释】

(1)师挚之始——"始"是乐曲的开端，古代奏乐，开始叫做"升歌"，一般由太师演奏。师挚是鲁国的太师,名挚,由他演奏,所以说"师挚之始"。
(2)《关雎》之乱——"始"是乐的开端,"乱"是乐的结束。由"始"到"乱",叫做"一成"。"乱"是"合乐",犹如今日的合唱。当合奏之时,奏《关雎》的乐章,所以说"《关雎》之乱"。

8.16 子曰:"狂而不直,侗而不愿,悾悾而不信,吾不知之矣。"

【译文】孔子说:"狂妄而不直率,幼稚而不老实,无能而不讲信用,这种人我是不知道其所以然的。"

8.17 子曰:"学如不及,犹恐失之。"

【译文】孔子说:"做学问好像〔追逐什么似的,〕生怕赶不上;〔赶上了,〕还生怕丢掉了。"

8.18 子曰:"巍巍乎,舜禹⁽¹⁾之有天下也而不与⁽²⁾焉!"

【译文】孔子说:"舜和禹真是崇高得很呀!贵为天子,富有四海,〔却整年地为百姓勤劳,〕一点也不为自己。"

【注释】
(1)禹——夏朝开国之君。据传说,受虞舜的禅让而即帝位。又是中国主持水利工程最早的有着功勋的人物。

(2)与——音预,yù,参与,关连。这里含着"私有""享受"的意思。

8.19 子曰:"大哉尧之为君也!巍巍乎!唯天为大,唯尧则之。荡荡乎,民无能名焉。巍巍乎其有成功也,焕乎其有文章!"

【译文】孔子说:"尧真是了不得呀!真高大得很呀!只有天最高最大,只有尧能够学习天。他的恩惠真是广博呀!老百姓简直不知道怎样称赞他。他的功绩实在太崇高了,他的礼仪制度也真够美好了!"

8.20 舜有臣五人而天下治。武王曰:"予有乱臣(1)十人。"孔子曰:"才难,不其然乎?唐虞之际,于斯为盛。有妇人焉,九人而已。三分天下有其二(2),以服事殷。周之德,其可谓至德也已矣。"

【译文】舜有五位贤臣,天下便太平。武王也说过,"我有十位能治理天下的臣子。"孔子因此说道:"〔常言道:〕'人才不易得。'不是这样吗?唐尧和虞舜之间以及周武王说那话的时候,人才最兴盛。然而武王十位人才之中还有一位妇女,实际上只是九位罢了。周文王得了天下的三分之二,仍然向商纣称臣,周朝的道德,可以说是最高的了。"

【注释】
(1)乱臣——《说文》:"乱,治也。"《尔雅·释诂》同。《左传》昭公二十四年引《大誓》说:"余有乱臣十人,同心同德。"则"乱臣"就是"治国之臣"。近人周谷城（《古史零证》）认为"乱"有"亲近"的意义，则"乱臣"相当于《孟子·梁惠王下》"王无亲臣矣"的"亲臣"，虽然言之亦能成理，但和下文"才难"之意不吻合，恐非孔子原意。

(2)三分天下有其二——《逸周书·程典篇》说："文王合九州之侯，奉勤于商。"相传当时分九州，文王得六州，是有三分之二。

8.21 子曰："禹，吾无间然矣。菲饮食而致孝乎鬼神，恶衣服而致美乎黻冕⁽¹⁾，卑宫室而尽力乎沟洫⁽²⁾。禹，吾无间然矣。"

【译文】孔子说："禹，我对他没有批评了。他自己吃得很坏，却把祭品办得极丰盛；穿得很坏，却把祭服做得极华美；住得很坏，却把力量完全用于沟渠水利。禹，我对他没有批评了。"

【注释】

(1)黻冕——黻音弗，fú，祭祀时穿的礼服；冕音免，miǎn，古代大夫以上的人的帽子都叫冕，后来只有帝王的帽子才叫冕。这里指祭祀时的礼帽。

(2)沟洫——就是沟渠，这里指农田水利而言。

子罕篇第九

共三十一章

9.1 子罕[(1)]言利与命与仁。

【译文】孔子很少［主动］谈到功利、命运和仁德。

【注释】

(1)罕——副词，少也，只表示动作频率。而《论语》一书，讲"利"的六次，讲"命"的八九次，若以孔子全部语言比较起来，可能还算少的。因之子贡也说过："夫子之言性与天道，不可得而闻也。"（《公冶长篇第五》）至于"仁"，在《论语》中讲得最多，为什么还说"孔子罕言"呢？于是对这一句话便生出别的解释了。金人王若虚（《误谬杂辨》）、清人史绳祖（《学斋占毕》）都以为这句应如此读："子罕言利，与命，与仁。""与"，许也。意思是"孔子很少谈到利，却赞成命，赞成仁"。黄式三（《论语后案》）则认为"罕"读为"轩"，显也。意思是"孔子很明显地谈到利、命和仁"。遇夫先生（《论语疏证》）又以为"所谓罕言仁者，乃不轻许人以仁之意，与罕言利命之义似不同。试以圣人评论仲弓、子路、冉有、公西华、令尹子文、陈文子之为人及克伐怨欲不行之德，皆云不知其仁，更参之以《儒行》之说，可以证明矣"。我则以为《论语》中讲"仁"虽多，但是一方面多半是和别人问答之词，另一方面，"仁"又是孔门的最高道德标准，正因为少谈，孔子偶一谈到，便有记载。不能以记载的多便推论孔子谈得也多。孔子平生所言，自然千万倍于《论语》所记载的，《论语》出现孔子论"仁"之处若用来和所有孔子平生之言相比，可能还是少的。诸家之说未免对于《论语》一书过于拘泥，恐怕不与当时事实相符，所以不取。于省吾读"仁"为"尸"，即"夷狄"之"夷"，未必确。

9.2 达巷党(1)人曰:"大哉孔子!博学而无所成名。"子闻之,谓门弟子曰:"吾何执?执御乎?执射乎?吾执御矣。"

【译文】达街的一个人说:"孔子真伟大!学问广博,可惜没有足以树立名声的专长。"孔子听了这话,就对学生们说:"我干什么呢?赶马车呢?做射击手呢?我赶马车好了。"

【注释】

(1)达巷党——《礼记·杂记》有"余从老聃助葬于巷党"的话,可见"巷党"两字为一词,"里巷"的意思。

9.3 子曰:"麻冕(1),礼也;今也纯(2),俭(3),吾从众。拜下(4),礼也;今拜乎上,泰也。虽违众,吾从下。"

【译文】孔子说:"礼帽用麻料来织,这是合于传统的礼的;今天大家都用丝料,这样省俭些,我同意大家的做法。臣见君,先在堂下磕头,然后升堂又磕头,这是合于传统的礼的。今天大家都免除了堂下的磕头,只升堂后磕头,这是倨傲的表现。虽然违反大家,我仍然主张要先在堂下磕头。"

【注释】

(1)麻冕——一种礼帽,有人说就是缁布冠(古人一到二十岁,便举行加帽子的仪式,叫"冠礼"。第一次加的便是缁布冠),未必可信。

(2)纯——黑色的丝。

(3)俭——绩麻做礼帽,依照规定,要用二千四百缕经线。麻质较粗,必须织得非常细密,这很费工。若用丝,丝质细,容易织成,因而省俭些。

(4)拜下——指臣子对君主的行礼,先在堂下磕头,然后升堂再磕头。《左传》僖公九年和《国语·齐语》都记述齐桓公不听从周襄王的辞让,终于下拜的事。到孔子时,下拜的礼似乎废弃了。

9.4 子绝四——毋意,毋必,毋固,毋我。

【译文】孔子一点也没有四种毛病——不悬空揣测,不绝对肯定,不拘泥固执,不唯我独是。

9.5 子畏于匡[1],曰:"文王既没,文不在兹乎?天之将丧斯文也,后死者[2]不得与[3]于斯文也;天之未丧斯文也,匡人其如予何?"

【译文】孔子被匡地的群众所拘禁,便道:"周文王死了以后,一切文化遗产不都在我这里吗?天若是要消灭这种文化,那我也不会掌握这些文化了;天若是不要消灭这种文化,那匡人将把我怎么样呢?"

【注释】

(1)子畏于匡——《史记•孔子世家》说,孔子离开卫国,准备到陈国去,经过匡。匡人曾经遭受过鲁国阳货的掠夺和残杀,而孔子的相貌很像阳货,便以为孔子就是过去曾经残害过匡地的人,于是囚禁了孔子。"畏"是拘囚的意思,《荀子•赋篇》云:"比干见刳,孔子拘匡。"《史记•孔子世家》作"拘焉五日",可见这一"畏"字和《礼记•檀弓》"死而不吊者三,畏、厌、溺"的"畏"相同,说见俞樾《群经平议》。今河南省长垣县西南十五里有匡城,可能就是当日孔子被囚之地。

(2)后死者——孔子自谓。

(3)与——音预,yù。

9.6 太宰[1]问于子贡曰:"夫子圣者与?何其多能也?"子贡

曰："固天纵之将圣，又多能也。"子闻之，曰："太宰知我乎！吾少也贱，故多能鄙事。君子多乎哉？不多也。"

【译文】太宰向子贡问道："孔老先生是位圣人吗？为什么这样多才多艺呢？"子贡道："这本是上天让他成为圣人，又使他多才多艺。"孔子听到，便道："太宰知道我呀！我小时候穷苦，所以学会了不少鄙贱的技艺。真正的君子会有这样多的技巧吗？是不会的。"

【注释】

⑴太宰——官名。这位太宰已经不知是哪一国人以及姓甚名谁了。

9.7 牢⑴曰："子云，'吾不试⑵，故艺。'"

【译文】牢说："孔子说过，我不曾被国家所用，所以学得一些技艺。"

【注释】

⑴牢——郑玄说是孔子学生，但《史记•仲尼弟子列传》无此人。王肃伪撰之《孔子家语》说"琴张，一名牢，字子开，亦字子张，卫人也"，尤其不可信。说本王引之，详王念孙《读书杂志》卷四之三。

⑵试——《论衡•正说篇》云："尧曰：'我其试哉！'说《尚书》曰：'试者用也。'"这"试"字也应当"用"字解。

9.8 子曰："吾有知乎哉？无知也。有鄙夫问于我，空空如也。我叩其两端而竭焉。"

【译文】孔子说:"我有知识吗?没有哩。有一个庄稼汉问我,我本是一点也不知道的。我从他那个问题的首尾两头去盘问,〔才得到很多意思,〕然后尽量地告诉他。"

9.9 子曰:"凤鸟不至,河不出图⑴,吾已矣夫!"

【译文】孔子说:"凤凰不飞来了,黄河也没有图画出来了,我这一生恐怕是完了吧!"

【注释】

⑴凤鸟、河图——古代传说,凤凰是一种神鸟,祥瑞的象征,出现就是表示天下太平。又说,圣人受命,黄河就出现图画。孔子说这几句话,不过借此比喻当时天下无清明之望罢了。

9.10 子见齐衰⑴者、冕衣裳者⑵与瞽者,见之,虽少,必作;过之,必趋⑶。

【译文】孔子看见穿丧服的人、穿戴着礼帽礼服的人以及瞎了眼睛的人,相见的时候,他们虽然年轻,孔子一定站起来;走过的时候,一定快走几步。

【注释】

⑴齐衰——齐音咨,zī;衰音崔,cuī。齐衰,古代丧服,用熟麻布做的,其下边缝齐(斩衰则用粗而生的麻布,左右及下边也都不缝)。齐衰又有齐衰三年、齐衰期(一年)、齐衰五月、齐衰三月几等;看死了什么人,便服多长日子的孝。这里讲齐衰,自然也包括斩衰而言。斩衰是最重的孝服,儿子对父亲,臣下对君上才斩衰三年。

⑵冕衣裳者——即衣冠整齐的贵族。冕是高等贵族所戴的礼帽,后来只

有皇帝所戴才称冕。衣是上衣,裳是下衣,相当现代的裙。古代男子上穿衣,下着裙。

(3)作,趋——作,起;趋,疾行。这都是一种敬意的表示。

9.11 颜渊喟然叹曰:"仰之弥高,钻之弥坚。瞻之在前,忽焉在后。夫子循循然善诱人,博我以文,约我以礼,欲罢不能。既竭吾才,如有所立卓尔。虽欲从之,末由也已。"

【译文】颜渊感叹着说:"老师之道,越抬头看,越觉得高;越用力钻研,越觉得深。看看,似乎在前面,忽然又到后面去了。〔虽然这样高深和不容易捉摸,可是〕老师善于有步骤地诱导我们,用各种文献来丰富我的知识,又用一定的礼节来约束我的行为,使我想停止学习都不可能。我已经用尽我的才力,似乎能够独立地工作。要想再向前迈进一步,又不知怎样着手了。"

9.12 子疾病,子路使门人为臣(1)。病间,曰:"久矣哉,由之行诈也!无臣而为有臣。吾谁欺?欺天乎!且予与其死于臣之手也,无宁(2)死于二三子之手乎!且予纵不得大葬,予死于道路乎?"

【译文】孔子病得厉害,子路便命孔子的学生组织治丧处。很久以后,孔子的病渐渐好了,就道:"仲由干这种欺假的勾当竟太长久了呀!我本不该有治丧的组织,却一定要使人组织治丧处。我欺哄谁呢?欺哄上天吗?我与其死在治丧的人的手里,宁肯死在你们学生们的手里,不还好些吗?即使不能热热闹闹地办理丧葬,我会死在路上吗?"

【注释】

⑴为臣——和今天的组织治丧处有相似之处,所以译文用来比傅。但也有不同之处。相似之处是死者有一定的社会地位才给他组织治丧处。古代,诸侯之死才能有"臣";孔子当时,可能有许多卿大夫也"僭"行此礼。不同之处是治丧处人死以后才组织,才开始工作。"臣"却不然,死前便工作,死者的衣衾手足的安排以及剪须诸事都由"臣"去处理。所以孔子这里也说"死于臣之手"的话。

⑵无宁——"无"为发语词,无义。《左传》隐公十一年云:"无宁兹许公复奉其社稷。"杜预的《注》说:"无宁,宁也。"

9.13 子贡曰:"有美玉于斯,韫椟而藏诸?求善贾⑴而沽诸?"子曰:"沽之哉!沽之哉!我待贾者也。"

【译文】子贡道:"这里有一块美玉,把它放在柜子里藏起来呢?还是找一个识货的商人卖掉呢?"孔子道:"卖掉,卖掉,我是在等待识货者哩。"

【注释】

⑴贾——音古,gǔ,商人。又同"价",价钱。如果取后一义,"善贾"便是"好价钱","待贾"便是"等好价钱"。不过与其说孔子是等价钱的人,不如说他是等识货者的人。

9.14 子欲居九夷⑴。或曰:"陋,如之何?"子曰:"君子居之,何陋之有⑵?"

【译文】孔子想搬到九夷去住。有人说:"那地方非常简陋,怎么好住?"孔子道:"有君子去住,就不简陋了。"

【注释】

(1)九夷——九夷就是淮夷。《韩非子•说林上篇》云:"周公旦攻九夷而商盖伏。"商盖就是商奄,则九夷本居鲁国之地,周公曾用武力降服他们。春秋以后,盖臣属楚、吴、越三国,战国时又专属楚。以《说苑•君道篇》、《淮南子•齐俗训》、《战国策•秦策》与《魏策》、李斯《上秦始皇书》诸说九夷者考之,九夷实散居于淮、泗之间,北与齐、鲁接壤(说本孙诒让《墨子间诂•非攻篇》)。

(2)何陋之有——直译是"有什么简陋呢",此用意译。

9.15 子曰:"吾自卫反鲁(1),然后乐正,《雅》《颂》各得其所(2)。"

【译文】孔子说:"我从卫国回到鲁国,才把音乐[的篇章]整理出来,使《雅》归《雅》,《颂》归《颂》,各有适当的安置。"

【注释】

(1)自卫反鲁——根据《左传》,事在鲁哀公十一年冬。
(2)《雅》《颂》各得其所——"雅"和"颂"一方面是《诗经》内容分类的类名,一方面也是乐曲分类的类名。篇章内容的分类,可以由今日的《诗经》考见,乐曲的分类,因为古乐早已失传,便无可考证了。孔子的正《雅》《颂》,究竟是正其篇章呢?还是正其乐曲呢?或者两者都正呢?《史记•孔子世家》和《汉书•礼乐志》则以为主要的是正其篇章,因为我们已经得不到别的材料,只得依从此说。孔子只"正乐",调整《诗经》篇章的次序,太史公在《孔子世家》中因而说孔子曾把三千余篇的古诗删为三百余篇,是不可信的。

9.16 子曰:"出则事公卿,入则事父兄⁽¹⁾,丧事不敢不勉,不为酒困,何有于我哉⁽²⁾?"

【译文】孔子说:"出外便服事公卿,入门便服事父兄,有丧事不敢不尽礼,不被酒所困扰,这些事我做到了哪些呢?"

【注释】
(1)父兄——孔子父亲早死,说这话时候,或者他哥孟皮还在,"父兄"二字,只"兄"字有义,古人常有这用法。"父兄"或者在此引申为长者之义。
(2)何有于我哉——如果把"何有"看为"不难之词",那这一句便当译为"这些事对我有什么困难呢"。全文由自谦之词变为自述之词了。

9.17 子在川上,曰:"逝者如斯夫!不舍⁽¹⁾昼夜。"

【译文】孔子在河边,叹道:"消逝的时光像河水一样呀!日夜不停地流去。"

【注释】
(1)舍——上、去两声都可以读。这里读去声,作动词,居住,停留。孔子这话不过感叹光阴之奔驶而不复返罢了,未必有其他深刻的意义。《孟子·离娄下》《荀子·宥坐篇》《春秋繁露·山川颂》对此都各有阐发,很难说是孔子本意。

9.18 子曰:"吾未见好德如好色者也。"

【译文】孔子说:"我没有看见过这样的人,喜爱道德赛过喜爱美貌。"

9.19 子曰:"譬如为山,未成一篑,止,吾止也。譬如平地,虽覆一篑,进,吾往也⑴。"

【译文】孔子说:"好比堆土成山,只要再加一筐土便成山了,如果懒得做下去,这是我自己停止的。又好比在平地上堆土成山,纵是刚刚倒下一筐土,如果决心努力前进,还是要自己坚持啊!"

【注释】

⑴子曰……往也——这一章也可以这样讲解:"好比堆土成山,只差一筐土了,如果[应该]停止,我便停止。好比平地堆土成山,纵是刚刚倒下一筐土,如果[应该]前进,我便前进。"依照前一讲解,便是"为仁由己"的意思;依照后一讲解,便是"唯义与比"的意思。

9.20 子曰:"语之而不惰者,其回也与!"

【译文】孔子说:"听我说话始终不懈怠的,大概只有颜回一个人吧!"

9.21 子谓颜渊,曰:"惜乎!吾见其进也,未见其止也。"

【译文】孔子谈到颜渊,说道:"可惜呀[他死了]!我只看见他不断地进步,从没看见他停留。"

9.22 子曰:"苗而不秀⑴者有矣夫!秀而不实者有矣夫!"

【译文】孔子说:"庄稼生长了,却不吐穗开花的,有过的罢!吐穗开花了,却不凝浆结实的,有过的罢!"

【注释】
⑴秀——"秀"字从禾,则只是指禾黍的吐花。《诗经·大雅·生民》云:"实发实秀,实坚实好。""发"和"秀"是指庄稼的生长和吐穗开花;"坚"和"好"是指谷粒的坚实和壮大。这都是"秀"的本义。现在还把庄稼的吐穗开花叫做"秀穗"。因此译文点明是指庄稼而言。汉人唐人多以为孔子这话是为颜回短命而发。但颜回只是"秀而不实"(祢衡《颜子碑》如此说),则"苗而不秀"又指谁呢?孔子此言必有为而发,但究竟何所指,则不必妄测。

9.23 子曰:"后生可畏,焉知来者之不如今也?四十、五十而无闻焉,斯亦不足畏也已。"

【译文】孔子说:"年少的人是可怕的,怎能断定他的将来赶不上现在的人呢?一个人到了四五十岁还没有什么名望,也就值不得惧怕了。"

9.24 子曰:"法语之言,能无从乎?改之为贵。巽与之言,能无说乎?绎之为贵。说而不绎,从而不改,吾末如之何也已矣。"

【译文】孔子说:"严肃而合乎原则的话,能够不接受吗?改正错误才可贵。顺从己意的话,能够不高兴吗?分析一下才可贵。盲目高兴,不加分析;表面接受,实际不改,这种人我是没有办法对付他的了。"

9.25 子曰:"主忠信,毋友不如己者,过则勿惮改⑴。"

【注释】
⑴见《学而篇第一》。

9.26 子曰:"三军⑴可夺帅也,匹夫不可夺志也。"

【译文】孔子说:"一国军队,可以使它丧失主帅;一个男子汉,却不能强迫他放弃主张。"
【注释】
⑴三军——周朝的制度,诸侯中的大国可以拥有军队三军。因此便用"三军"作军队的通称。

9.27 子曰:"衣⑴敝缊⑵袍,与衣⑴狐貉者立,而不耻者,其由也与?'不忮不求,何用不臧⑶?'"子路终身诵之。子曰:"是道也,何足以臧?"

【译文】孔子说道:"穿着破烂的旧丝绵袍子和穿着狐貉裘的人一道站着,不觉得惭愧的,恐怕只有仲由罢!《诗经》上说:'不嫉妒,不贪求,为什么不会好?'"子路听了,便老念着这两句诗。孔子又道:"仅仅这个样子,怎样能够好得起来?"

【注释】

⑴衣——去声,动词,当"穿"字解。

⑵缊——音运,yùn,旧絮。古代没有草棉,所有"絮"字是指丝绵。一曰,乱麻也。

⑶不忮不求,何用不臧——两句见于《诗经•邶风•雄雉篇》。

9.28 子曰:"岁寒,然后知松柏之后凋⑴也。"

【译文】孔子说:"天冷了,才晓得松柏树是最后落叶的。"

【注释】

⑴凋——凋零,零落。

9.29 子曰:"知者不惑,仁者不忧,勇者不惧。"

【译文】孔子说:"聪明的人不致疑惑,仁德的人经常乐观,勇敢的人无所畏惧。"

9.30 子曰:"可与共学,未可与适道;可与适道,未可与立⑴;可与立,未可与权。"

【译文】孔子说:"可以同他一道学习的人,未必可以同他一道取得某种成就；可以同他一道取得某种成就的人，未必可以同他一道事事依礼而行；可以同他一道事事依礼而行的人，未必可以同他一道通权达变。"

【注释】

(1)立——《论语》的"立"经常包含着"立于礼"的意思，所以这里译为"事事依礼而行"。

9.31 "唐棣之华，偏其反而。岂不尔思？室是远而。"子曰："未之思也，夫何远之有⁽¹⁾？"

【译文】古代有几句这样的诗："唐棣树的花，翩翩地摇摆。难道我不想念你？因为家住得太遥远。"孔子道："他是不去想念哩，真的想念，有什么遥远呢？"

【注释】

(1)唐棣……何远之有——唐棣，一种植物，陆玑《毛诗草木鸟兽虫鱼疏》以为就是郁李（蔷薇科，落叶灌木），李时珍《本草纲目》却以为是枎栘（蔷薇科，落叶乔木）。"唐棣之华，偏其反而"似是捉摸不定的意思，或者和颜回讲孔子之道"瞻之在前，忽焉在后"（9.11）意思差不多。"夫何远之有"可能是"仁远乎哉？我欲仁，斯仁至矣"（7.30）的意思。或者当时有人引此诗（这是"逸诗"，不在今《诗经》中），意在证明道之远而不可捉摸，孔子则说，你不曾努力罢了，其实是一呼即至的。

乡党篇第十

共二十七章

10.1 孔子于乡党，恂恂⑴如也，似不能言者。其在宗庙朝廷，便便⑵言，唯谨尔。

【译文】孔子在本乡的地方上非常恭顺，好像不能说话的样子。他在宗庙里、朝廷上，有话便明白而流畅地说出，只是说得很少。

【注释】
⑴恂恂——音旬，xún，恭顺貌。
⑵便便——旧读骈，pián。

10.2 朝，与下大夫言，侃侃如也；与上大夫言，誾誾⑴如也。君在，踧踖如也，与与如也。

【译文】上朝的时候，[君主还没有到来，]同下大夫说话，温和而快乐的样子；同上大夫说话，正直而恭敬的样子。君主已经来了，恭敬而心中不安的样子，行步安详的样子。

【注释】
⑴誾——音银，yín。

10.3 君召使摈，色勃如也，足躩⑴如也。揖所与立，左右手，衣前后⁽²⁾，襜⁽³⁾如也。趋进⁽⁴⁾，翼如也。宾退，必复命曰："宾不顾矣。"

【译文】鲁君召他去接待外国的贵宾，面色矜持庄重，脚步也快起来。向两旁的人作揖，或者向左拱手，或者向右拱手，衣裳一俯一仰，却很整齐。快步向前，好像鸟儿舒展了翅膀。贵宾辞别后一定向君主回报说："客人已经不回头了。"

【注释】
(1)躩——音矍，jué，皇侃《义疏》引江熙云："不暇闲步，躩，速貌也。"
(2)前后——俯仰的意思。
(3)襜——音幨，chān，整齐之貌。
(4)趋进——在行步时一种表示敬意的行动。

10.4 入公门，鞠躬如⁽¹⁾也，如不容。立不中门，行不履阈。过位⁽²⁾，色勃如也，足躩如也，其言似不足者。摄齐⁽³⁾升堂，鞠躬如也，屏气⁽⁴⁾似不息者。出，降一等，逞颜色，怡怡如也。没阶，趋进⁽⁵⁾，翼如也。复其位，踧踖如也。

【译文】孔子走进朝廷的门，害怕而谨慎的样子，好像没有容身之地。站，不站在门的中间；走，不踩门坎。经过国君的座位，面色便矜庄，脚步也快，言语也好像中气不足。提起下摆向堂上走，恭敬谨慎的样子，憋住气好像不呼吸一般。走出来，降下台阶一级，面色便放松，怡然自得。走完了台阶，快快地向前走几步，好像鸟儿舒展翅膀。回到自己的位置，恭敬而内心不安的样子。

【注释】

(1)鞠躬如——这"鞠躬"两字不能当"曲身"讲。这是双声字,用以形容谨慎恭敬的样子。《论语》所有"□□如"的区别词(区别词是形容词、副词的合称),都不用动词结构。清人卢文弨《龙城札记》说:"……且曲身乃实事,而云曲身如,更无此文法。"

(2)过位——过旧音戈,平声。位是人君的座位,经过之时,人君并不在,座位是空的。

(3)摄齐——齐音咨,zī,衣裳缝了边的下摆;摄,提起。

(4)屏——音丙,bǐng,屏气即屏息,压抑呼吸。

(5)趋进——有些本子无"进"字,不对。自汉以来所有引《论语》此文的都有"进"字,《唐石经》也有"进"字,《太平御览·居处部》、《人事部》引文,《张子正蒙》引文也都有"进"字。

10.5 执圭(1),鞠躬如也,如不胜(2)。上如揖,下如授。勃如战色,足蹜蹜如有循(3)。享礼(4),有容色(5)。私觌(6),愉愉如也。

【译文】 [孔子出使到外国,举行典礼,]拿着圭,恭敬谨慎地,好像举不起来。向上举好像在作揖,向下拿好像在交给别人。面色矜庄好像在作战。脚步也紧凑狭窄,好像在沿着[一条线]走过。献礼物的时候,满脸和气。用私人身份和外国君臣会见,显得轻松愉快。

【注释】

(1)圭——一种玉器,上圆,或者作剑头形,下方,举行典礼的时候,君臣都拿着。

(2)胜——音升,shēng,能担负得了。

(3)足蹜蹜如有循——蹜音缩,suō,"蹜蹜",举脚密而狭的样子。"如有循",所沿循的应当是很窄狭的东西,所以译文加了"一条线"诸字以示意。
(4)享礼——古代出使外国，初到所聘问的国家，便行聘问礼。"执圭"一段所写的正是行聘问礼时孔子的情貌。聘问之后，便行享献之礼。"享礼"就是享献礼，使臣把所带来的各种礼物罗列满庭。
(5)有容色——《仪礼·聘礼》："及享，发气焉盈容。""有容色"就是"发气焉盈容"。
(6)觌——音狄，dí，相见。

10.6 君子不以绀緅饰⁽¹⁾，红紫不以为亵服⁽²⁾。当暑，袗絺绤⁽³⁾，必表而出之。缁衣，羔裘；素衣，麑裘；黄衣，狐裘⁽⁴⁾。亵裘长⁽⁵⁾，短右袂⁽⁶⁾。必有寝衣⁽⁷⁾，长一身有半。狐貉之厚以居。去丧，无所不佩。非帷裳⁽⁸⁾，必杀之⁽⁹⁾。羔裘玄冠不以吊⁽¹⁰⁾。吉月⁽¹¹⁾，必朝服而朝。

【译文】君子不用［近乎黑色的］天青色和铁灰色作镶边，［近乎赤色的］浅红色和紫色不用来作平常居家的衣服。暑天，穿着粗的或者细的葛布单衣，但一定裹着衬衫，使它露在外面。黑色的衣配紫羔，白色的衣配麑裘，黄色的衣配狐裘。居家的皮袄身材较长，可是右边的袖子要做得短些。睡觉一定有小被，长度合本人身长的一又二分之一。用狐貉皮的厚毛作坐垫。丧服满了以后，什么东西都可以佩带。不是［上朝和祭祀穿的］用整幅布做的裙子，一定裁去一些布。紫羔和黑色礼帽都不穿戴着去吊丧。大年初一，一定穿着上朝的礼服去朝贺。

【注释】
(1)绀緅饰——绀音赣，gàn；緅音邹，zōu；都是表示颜色的名称。"绀"是深青中透红的颜色，相当今天的"天青"；"緅"是青多红少，比绀更暗的颜色，这里用"铁灰色"来表明它。"饰"是滚边，镶边，缘边。古代，黑色是正式礼服的颜色，而这两种颜色都近于黑色，所以不用来镶边，为别的颜色作装饰。

(2)红紫不以为亵服——古代大红色叫"朱"，这是很贵重的颜色。"红"和"紫"都属此类，也连带地被重视，不用为平常家居衣服的颜色。

(3)袗絺绤——袗音轸，zhěn，单也。此处用为动词。絺音痴，chī，细葛布；绤音隙，xì，粗葛布。

(4)缁衣羔裘等三句——这三句表示衣服里外的颜色应该相称。古代穿皮衣，毛向外，因之外面一定要用罩衣，这罩衣就叫做裼（音锡）衣。这里"缁衣""素衣""黄衣"的"衣"指的正是裼衣。缁，黑色。古代所谓"羔裘"都是黑色的羊毛，就是今天的紫羔。麑音倪，ní，小鹿，它的毛是白色。

(5)亵裘长——亵裘长为着保暖。古代男子上面穿衣，下面穿裳（裙），衣裳不相连。因之孔子在家的皮袄就做得比较长。

(6)短右袂——袂音妹，mèi，袖子。右袖较短，为着做事方便。有人认为衣袖一长一短，不大好看，孔子不会如此，于是对这一句别生解释，我认为那些解释都不可信。

(7)寝衣——即被。古代大被叫"衾"，小被叫"被"。

(8)帷裳——礼服，上朝和祭祀时穿，用整幅布做，不加剪裁，多余的布作褶叠（褶叠古代叫做襞积），犹如今天的百褶裙。古代男子上衣下裙。

(9)杀——读去声，shài，减少，裁去。"杀之"就是缝制之先裁去多余的布，不用褶叠，省工省料。

(10)羔裘玄冠不以吊——玄冠，一种礼帽。"羔裘玄冠"都是黑色的，古代都用作吉服。丧事是凶事，因之不能穿戴着去吊丧。

(11)吉月——这两个字有各种解释：（甲）每月初一（旧注都如此）；（乙）"吉"字误，应该作"告"。"告月"就是每月月底，司历者以下月初一告之于君（王引之《经义述闻》、俞樾《群经平议》）；

两说都不可信。今从程树德《论语集释》之说。

10.7 齐⁽¹⁾，必有明衣，布⁽²⁾。齐必变食⁽³⁾，居必迁坐⁽⁴⁾。

【译文】斋戒沐浴的时候，一定有浴衣，用布做的。斋戒的时候，一定改变平常的饮食；居住也一定搬移地方〔不和妻妾同房〕。

【注释】
(1)齐——同"斋"。
(2)布——现在的布一般是用草棉（棉花）纺织的，但古代没有草棉，布的质料，王夫之《四书稗疏》说："古之言布者，兼丝麻枲葛而言之。练丝为帛，未练为布，盖今之生丝绢也。《清商曲》有云：'丝布涩难缝'，则晋宋间犹有丝布之名。唯《孔丛子》谓麻苎葛曰布，当亦一隅之论。"赵翼《陔余丛考》说："古时未有棉布，凡布皆麻为之。《记》曰：'治其丝麻，以为布帛'是也。"
(3)变食——变食的内容，古人有三种说法：（甲）《庄子•人间世篇》说："颜回曰：'回之家贫，惟不饮酒不茹荤者数月矣。如此，则可以为齐乎？'曰：'是祭祀之齐，非心齐也。'"有人据此，便把"不饮酒，不茹荤（荤是有浓厚气味的蔬菜，如蒜、韭、葱之属）"来解释"变食"。（乙）《周礼•天官•膳夫》："王日一举……王齐，日三举。"这意思是王每天虽然吃饭三顿，却只在第一顿饭时杀牲，其余两顿，只把第一顿的剩菜回锅罢了。天子如此，其他的人更不会顿顿吃新鲜的。若在斋戒之时那就顿顿吃新鲜的，不吃回锅的剩菜，取其洁净，这便是"变食"。（丙）金鹗《求古录礼说补遗》说，变食不但不饮酒、不食葱蒜等，也不食鱼肉。
(4)迁坐——等于说改变卧室。古代的上层人物平常和妻室居于"燕寝"；斋戒之时则居于"外寝"（也叫"正寝"），和妻室不同房。

唐朝的法律还规定着举行大祭，在斋戒之时官吏不宿于正寝的，每一晚打五十竹板。这或者犹是古代风俗的残余。

10.8 食不厌精，脍不厌细。食饐而餲(1)，鱼馁而肉败(2)，不食。色恶，不食。臭恶，不食。失饪，不食。不时(3)，不食。割不正(4)，不食。不得其酱，不食。肉虽多，不使胜食气(5)。唯酒无量，不及乱(6)。沽酒市脯不食。不撤姜食，不多食。

【译文】粮食不嫌舂得精，鱼和肉不嫌切得细。粮食霉烂发臭，鱼和肉腐烂，都不吃。食物颜色难看，不吃。气味难闻，不吃。烹调不当，不吃。不到该当吃食时候，不吃。不是按一定方法砍割的肉，不吃。没有一定调味的酱醋，不吃。席上肉虽然多，吃它不超过主食。只有酒不限量，却不至醉。买来的酒和肉干不吃。吃完了，姜不撤除，但吃得不多。

【注释】

(1)饐而餲——饐音懿，yì；餲音艾，ài；饮食经久而腐臭。

(2)馁，败——馁音"内"的上声，něi，鱼腐烂叫"馁"，肉腐烂叫"败"。

(3)不时——有两说：（甲）过早的食物，冬天在温室种菜蔬，在《汉书•循吏•召信臣传》和桓宽《盐铁论•散不足篇》里便称为"不时之物"。但在汉朝，也只有"太官园"和其他少数园圃才能供奉，也只有皇上和极为富贵之家才能享受，而在孔子时，不但不必有温室种菜的技术，即有，孔子也未必能够享受。（乙）不是该当吃食的时候。《吕氏春秋•尽数篇》："食能以时，身必无灾。"即此意。

(4)割不正——"割"和"切"不同。"割"指宰杀猪牛羊时肢体的分解。古人有一定的分解方法，不按那方法分解的，便叫"割不正"。说本王夫之《四书稗疏》。

(5) 食气——食音嗣，sì。"气"，《说文》引作"既"。"既""气""饩"三字古书通用。"食气"，饭料。
(6) 乱——高亨《周易古经今注》云："乱者神志昏乱也。《左传》宣公十五年传：'疾病则乱。'《论语•乡党篇》：'唯酒无量不及乱。'《易•象传》曰：'乃乱乃萃，其志乱也。'得其旨矣。"

10.9 祭于公，不宿肉⁽¹⁾。祭肉⁽²⁾不出三日。出三日，不食之矣。

【译文】参与国家祭祀典礼，不把祭肉留到第二天。别的祭肉留存不超过三天。若是存放过了三天，便不吃了。

【注释】
(1) 不宿肉——古代的大夫、士都有助君祭祀之礼。天子诸侯的祭礼，当天清早宰杀牲畜，然后举行祭典。第二天又祭，叫做"绎祭"。绎祭之后才令各人拿自己带来助祭的肉回去，或者又依贵贱等级分别颁赐祭肉。这样，祭于公的肉，在未颁下来以前，至少是放了一两宵了，因之不能再存放一夜。
(2) 祭肉——这一祭肉或者指自己家中的，或者指朋友送来的，都可以。

10.10 食不语，寝不言。

【译文】吃饭的时候不交谈，睡觉的时候不说话。

10.11 虽疏食菜羹，瓜祭⁽¹⁾，必齐如也。

【译文】虽然是糙米饭小菜汤,也一定得先祭一祭,而且祭的时候还一定恭恭敬敬,好像斋戒了的一样。

【注释】

(1)瓜祭——有些本子作"必祭","瓜"恐怕是错字。这是食前将席上各种食品拿出少许,放在食器之间,祭最初发明饮食的人,《左传》叫泛祭。

10.12 席⁽¹⁾不正,不坐。

【译文】坐席摆的方向不合礼制,不坐。

【注释】

(1)席——古代没有椅和凳,都是在地面上铺席子,坐在席子上。席子一般是用蒲苇、剸草、竹篾以至禾穰为质料。现在日本人还保留着席地而坐的习惯。《墨子·非儒篇》说:"哀公迎孔子,席不端,不坐。"以"端"解"正",则"席不正",是坐席不端正之意。然而《汉书·王尊传》说,"[匡]衡与中二千石大鸿胪赏等会坐殿门下,衡南乡,赏等西乡。衡更为赏布东乡席,起立延赏坐……而设不正之席,使下坐上"云云,那么,"席不正"是布席不合礼制之意。

10.13 乡人饮酒⁽¹⁾,杖者出,斯出矣。

【译文】行乡饮酒礼后,要等老年人都出去了,自己这才出去。

【注释】

(1)乡人饮酒——即行乡饮酒礼,据《礼记·乡饮酒义》"少长以齿"。《王制》也说:"习乡尚齿。"既论年龄大小,所以孔子必须让杖者先出。

10.14 乡人傩⑴，朝服而立于阼阶⑵。

【译文】本地方人迎神驱鬼，穿着朝服站在东边的台阶上。

【注释】
(1)傩——音挪，nuó，古代的一种风俗，迎神以驱逐疫鬼。解放前的湖南，如果家中有病人，还有雇请巫师以驱逐疫鬼的迷信，叫做"冲傩"，可能是这种风俗的残余。
(2)阼阶——阼音祚，zuò，东面的台阶，主人所立之地。

10.15 问⑴人于他邦，再拜⑵而送之。

【译文】托人给在外国的朋友问好送礼，便向受托者拜两次送行。

【注释】
(1)问——问讯，问好。不过古代问好，也致送礼物以表示情意，如《诗经·郑风·女曰鸡鸣》"杂佩以问之"，《左传》成公十六年"楚子使工尹襄问之以弓"，哀公十一年"使问弦多以琴"，因此译文加了"送礼"两字。
(2)拜——拱手并弯腰。

10.16 康子馈药，拜而受之。曰："丘未达，不敢尝。"

【译文】季康子给孔子送药，孔子拜而接受，却说道："我对这药性不很了解，不敢试服。"

10.17 厩焚。子退朝,曰:"伤人乎?"不问马。

【译文】孔子的马棚失了火。孔子从朝廷回来,道:"伤了人吗?"不问到马。

10.18 君赐食,必正席先尝之。君赐腥,必熟而荐⁽¹⁾之。君赐生,必畜之。侍食于君,君祭,先饭。

【译文】国君赐以熟食,孔子一定摆正座位先尝一尝。国君赐以生肉,一定煮熟了,先〔给祖宗〕进供。国君赐以活物,一定养着它。同国君一道吃饭,当他举行饭前祭礼的时候,自己先吃饭,〔不吃菜。〕

【注释】
⑴荐——进奉。这里进奉的对象是自己的祖先,但不能看为祭祀。

10.19 疾,君视之,东首⁽¹⁾,加朝服,拖绅⁽²⁾。

【译文】孔子病了,国君来探问,他便脑袋朝东,把上朝的礼服披在身上,拖着大带。

【注释】
⑴东首——指孔子病中仍旧卧床而言。古人卧榻一般设在南窗的西面。国君来,从东边台阶走上来(东阶就是阼阶,原是主人的位向,但国君自以为是全国的主人,就是到其臣下家中,仍从阼阶上下),所以孔子面朝东来迎接他。

(2)加朝服,拖绅——孔子卧病在床,自不能穿朝服,只能盖在身上。绅是束在腰间的大带。束了以后,仍有一节垂下来。

10.20 君命召,不俟驾行矣。

【译文】国君呼唤,孔子不等待车辆驾好马,立即先步行。

10.21 入太庙,每事问[1]。

【注释】
(1)《八佾篇第三》。

10.22 朋友死,无所归,曰:"于我殡[1]。"

【译文】朋友死亡,没有负责收殓的人,孔子便道:"丧葬由我来料理。"

【注释】
(1)殡——停放灵柩叫殡,埋葬也可以叫殡,这里当指一切丧葬事务而言。

10.23 朋友之馈,虽车马,非祭肉,不拜。

【译文】朋友的赠品,即使是车马,只要不是祭肉,孔子在接受的时候,不行礼。

10.24 寝不尸，居不客[1]。

【译文】孔子睡觉不像死尸一样［直躺着］，平日坐着，也不像接见客人或者自己做客人一样，［跪着两膝在席上。］

【注释】

(1)居不客——客本作"容"，今从《释文》和《唐石经》校订作"客"。居，坐；客，宾客。古人的坐法有几种，恭敬的是屈着两膝，膝盖着地，而足跟承着臀部。做客和见客时必须如此。不过这样难以持久，居家不必如此。省力的坐法是脚板着地，两膝耸起，臀部向下而不贴地，和蹲一样。所以《说文》说："居，蹲也。"（这几个字是依从段玉裁的校本。）最不恭敬的坐法是臀部贴地，两腿张开，平放而直伸，像箕一样，叫做"箕踞"。孔子平日的坐式可能像蹲。说见段玉裁《说文解字注》。

10.25 见齐衰者，虽狎，必变。见冕者与瞽者，虽亵，必以貌。凶服者式[1]之。式负版[2]者。有盛馔，必变色而作。迅雷风烈[3]必变。

【译文】孔子看见穿齐衰孝服的人，就是极亲密的，也一定改变态度，［表示同情。］看见戴着礼帽和瞎了眼睛的人，即使常相见，也一定有礼貌。在车中遇着拿了送死人衣物的人，便把身体微微地向前一俯，手伏着车前的横木，［表示同情。］遇见背负国家图籍的人，也手伏车前横木。一有丰富的菜肴，一定神色变动，站立起来。遇见疾雷、大风，一定改变态度。

【注释】

⑴式——同"轼",古代车辆前的横木叫"轼",这里作动词用,用手伏轼的意思。

⑵版——国家图籍。

⑶迅雷风烈——就是"迅雷烈风"的意思。

10.26 升车,必正立,执绥。车中,不内顾,不疾言,不亲指。

【译文】孔子上车,一定先端正地站好,拉着扶手带[登车]。在车中,不向内回顾,不很快地说话,不用手指指画画。

10.27 色斯举矣,翔而后集。曰:"山梁雌雉,时哉时哉!"子路共⑴之,三嗅⑵而作⑶。

【译文】[孔子在山谷中行走,看见几只野鸡。]孔子的脸色一动,野鸡便飞向天空,盘旋一阵,又都停在一处。孔子道:"这些山梁上的雌雉,得其时呀!得其时呀!"子路向它们拱拱手,它们又振一振翅膀飞去了。

【注释】

⑴共——同"拱"。

⑵嗅——当作狊,jù,张两翅之貌。

⑶这段文字很费解,自古以来就没有满意的解释,很多人疑它有脱误,我只能取前人的解释之较为平易者翻译出来。

先进篇第十一

共二十六章

先进篇第十一

11.1 子曰:"先进[1]于礼乐,野人也;后进[1]于礼乐,君子也。如用之,则吾从先进。"

【译文】孔子说:"先学习礼乐而后做官的是未曾有过爵禄的一般人,先有了官位而后学习礼乐的是卿大夫的子弟。如果要我选用人才,我主张选用先学习礼乐的人。"

【注释】
[1]先进,后进——这两个术语的解释很多,都不恰当。译文本刘宝楠《论语正义》之说而略有取舍。孔子是主张"学而优则仕"的人,对于当时的卿大夫子弟,承袭父兄的庇荫,在做官中去学习的情况可能不满意。《孟子•告子下》引葵丘之会盟约说,"士无世官",又说,"取士必得",那么,孔子所谓"先进"一般指"士"。

11.2 子曰:"从我于陈、蔡[1]者,皆不及门[2]也。"

【译文】孔子说:"跟着我在陈国、蔡国之间忍饥受饿的人,都不在我这里了。"

【注释】
[1]从我于陈、蔡——从读去声,zòng。《史记•孔子世家》云:"吴伐陈,楚救陈,军于城父。闻孔子在陈、蔡之间,楚使人聘孔子,孔子将往拜礼。陈、蔡大夫谋曰:'孔子贤者,所刺讥皆中诸侯之疾,

今者久留陈、蔡之间，诸大夫所设行皆非仲尼之意。今楚，大国也，来聘孔子。孔子用于楚，则陈、蔡用事大夫危矣。'乃相与发徒役围孔子于野。不得已，绝粮。从者病，莫能兴。……于是使子贡至楚。楚昭王兴师迎孔子，然后得免。"

(2)不及门——汉唐旧解"不及门"为"不及仕进之门"或"不仕于卿大夫之门"，刘宝楠因而傅会《孟子》的"无上下之交"，解为"孔子弟子无仕陈蔡者"，我则终嫌与文意不甚密合，故不取，而用朱熹之说。郑珍《巢经巢文集》卷二《驳朱竹垞孔子门人考》有云："古之教者家有塾，塾在门堂之左右，施教受业者居焉。所谓'皆不及门'，及此门也。'奚为于丘（原作某，由于避讳故，今改）之门'，于此门也。滕更之'在门'，在此门也，故曰'愿留而受业于门'（按上两句俱见《孟子》）。"亦见朱熹此说之有据。

11.3 德行：颜渊，闵子骞，冉伯牛，仲弓。言语：宰我，子贡。政事：冉有，季路。文学⁽¹⁾：子游，子夏。

【说明】许渊冲英译缺此章。

【译文】[孔子的学生各有所长。]德行好的：颜渊，闵子骞，冉伯牛，仲弓。会说话的：宰我，子贡。能办理政事的：冉有，季路。熟悉古代文献的：子游，子夏。

【注释】

(1)文学——指古代文献，即孔子所传的《诗》《书》《易》等。皇侃《义疏》引范宁说如此。《后汉书·徐防传》说："防上疏云：'经书礼乐，定自孔子；发明章句，始于子夏。'"似亦可为证。又这一章和上一章"从我于陈、蔡者"不相连。朱熹《四书集注》说这十人即当在陈、蔡之时随行的人，是错误的。根据《左传》，冉有其时在鲁国为季氏之臣，未必随行。根据《史记•仲尼弟子列传》，当时随行的还有子张，何以这里不说及？根据各种史料，确知孔子在陈绝粮之时为鲁哀公四年，时孔子六十一岁。又据《史记•仲尼弟子列传》，子游小于孔子四十五岁，子夏小于孔子四十四岁，那么，孔子在陈、蔡受困时，子游不过十六岁，子夏不过十七岁，都不算成人。这么年幼的人即使已经在孔子门下受业，也未必都跟去了。可见这几句话不过是孔子对这十个学生的一时的叙述，由弟子转述下来的记载而已。

11.4 子曰："回也非助我者也，于吾言无所不说。"

【译文】孔子说："颜回不是对我有所帮助的人，他对我的话没有不喜欢的。"

11.5 子曰："孝哉闵子骞！人不间于其父母昆弟之言。"

【译文】孔子说："闵子骞真是孝顺呀！别人对于他爹娘兄弟称赞他的言语并无异议。"

11.6 南容三复白圭⑴，孔子以其兄之子妻之。

【译文】南容把"白圭之玷，尚可磨也；斯言之玷，不可为也"的几句诗读了又读，孔子便把自己的侄女嫁给他。

【注释】

⑴白圭——白圭的诗四句见于《诗经•大雅•抑篇》,意思是白圭的污点还可以磨掉,我们言语中的污点便没有办法去掉。大概南容是一个谨小慎微的人,所以能做到"邦有道,不废;邦无道,免于刑戮"(5.2)。

11.7 季康子问⑴:"弟子孰为好学?"孔子对曰:"有颜回者好学,不幸短命死矣,今也则亡。"

【译文】季康子问道:"你学生中谁用功?"孔子答道:"有一个叫颜回的用功,不幸短命死了,现在就再没有这样的人了。"

【注释】

⑴季康子问——鲁哀公曾经也有此问(6.3),孔子的回答较为详细。有人说,从此可见孔子与鲁君的问答和与季氏的问答有繁简之不同。

11.8 颜渊死,颜路⑴请子之车以为之⑵椁⑶。子曰:"才不才,亦各言其子也。鲤⑷也死,有棺而无椁。吾不徒行以为之椁。以吾从大夫之后⑸,不可徒行也。"

【译文】颜渊死了,他父亲颜路请求孔子卖掉车子来替颜渊办外椁。孔子道:"不管有才能或者没有才能,但总是自己的儿子。我的儿子鲤死了,也只有内棺,没有外椁。我不能〔卖掉车子〕步行来替他买椁。因为我也曾做过大夫,是不可以步行的。"

【注释】

(1)颜路——颜回的父亲,据《史记·仲尼弟子列传》,名无繇,字路,也是孔子学生。

(2)之——用法同"其"。

(3)椁——音果,guǒ。古代大官棺木至少用两重,里面的一重叫棺,外面又一重大的叫椁,平常我们说"内棺外椁"就是这个意思。

(4)鲤也死——鲤,字伯鱼,年五十死,那时孔子年七十。

(5)从大夫之后——孔子在鲁国曾经做过司寇的官,是大夫之位。不过此时孔子已经去位多年。他不说"我曾为大夫",而说"吾从大夫之后"(在大夫行列之后随行的意思)只是一种谦逊的口气罢了。

11.9 颜渊死。子曰:"噫!天丧予⁽¹⁾!天丧予!"

【译文】颜渊死了,孔子道:"咳!天老爷要我的命呀!天老爷要我的命呀!"

【注释】

(1)天丧予——译文只就字面译出。

11.10 颜渊死,子哭之恸⁽¹⁾。从者曰:"子恸矣!"曰:"有恸乎?非夫人之为恸而谁为⁽²⁾?"

【译文】颜渊死了,孔子哭得很伤心。跟着孔子的人道:"您太伤心了!"孔子道:"真的太伤心了吗?我不为这样的人伤心,还为什么人伤心呢!"

【注释】

(1)恸——郑玄《注》:"恸,变动容貌。"马融《注》:"恸,哀过也。"译文从马。

(2)非夫人之为恸而谁为——"非夫人之为恸"是"非为夫人恸"的倒装形式。"夫人"的"夫"读阳平,音扶,fú,指示形容词,"那"的意思。"之为"的"之"是专作帮助倒装用的,无实际意义。这一整句下文的"谁为",依现代汉语的格式说也是倒装,不过在古代,如果介词或者动词的宾语是疑问代词,一般都放在介词或者动词之上。

11.11 颜渊死,门人欲厚葬(1)之。子曰:"不可。"门人厚葬之。子曰:"回也视予犹父也,予不得视犹子也。非我也,夫二三子也。"

【译文】颜渊死了,孔子的学生们想要很丰厚地埋葬他。孔子道:"不可以。"学生们仍然很丰厚地埋葬了他。孔子道:"颜回呀!你看待我好像看待父亲,我却不能够像对待儿子一般地看待你。这不是我的主意呀,是你那班同学干的呀。"

【注释】

(1)厚葬——根据《檀弓》所记载孔子的话,丧葬应该"称家之有亡。有,毋过礼。苟亡矣,敛首足形,还葬,县棺而封"。颜子家中本穷,而用厚葬,从孔子看来,是不应该的。孔子的叹,实是责备那些主持厚葬的学生。

11.12 季路问事鬼神。子曰:"未能事人,焉能事鬼?"曰:"敢(1)问死。"曰:"未知生,焉知死?"

【译文】子路问服事鬼神的方法。孔子道:"活人还不能服事,怎么能去服事死人?"子路又道:"我大胆地请问死是怎么回事。"孔子道:"生的道理还没有弄明白,怎么能够懂得死?"

【注释】

(1)敢——表敬副词,无实际意义。《仪礼·士虞礼》郑玄《注》云:"敢,冒昧之词。"贾公彦《疏》云:"凡言'敢'者,皆是以卑触尊不自明之意。"

11.13 闵子侍侧,訚訚如也;子路,行行⁽¹⁾如也;冉有、子贡,侃侃如也。子乐。"若由也,不得其死然⁽²⁾。"

【译文】闵子骞站在孔子身旁,恭敬而正直的样子;子路很刚强的样子;冉有、子贡温和而快乐的样子。孔子高兴起来了。[不过,又道:]"像仲由吧,怕得不到好死。"

【注释】

(1)行行——旧读去声,hàng。
(2)不得其死然——得死,当时俗语,谓得善终。《左传》僖公十九年"得死为幸";哀公十六年"得死,乃非我"。然,语气词,用法同"焉"。

11.14 鲁人⁽¹⁾为长府。闵子骞曰:"仍旧贯,如之何?何必改作?"子曰:"夫人不言,言必有中。"

【译文】鲁国翻修叫长府的金库。闵子骞道:"照着老样子下

307

去怎么样？为什么一定要翻造呢？"孔子道："这个人平日不大开口，一开口一定中肯。"

【注释】

(1)鲁人——"鲁人"的"人"指其国的执政大臣而言。此"人"和"民"的区别。

11.15 子曰："由之瑟(1)奚为于丘之门？"门人不敬子路。子曰："由也升堂矣，未入于室(2)也。"

【译文】孔子道："仲由弹瑟，为什么在我这里来弹呢？"因此孔子的学生们瞧不起子路。孔子道："由么，学问已经不错了，只是还不够精深罢了。"

【注释】

(1)瑟——音涩，sè，古代的乐器，和琴同类。这里孔子不是不高兴子路弹瑟，而是不高兴他所弹的音调。《说苑·修文篇》对这段文字曾有所发挥。

(2)升堂入室——这是比喻话。"堂"是正厅，"室"是内室。先入门，次升堂，最后入室，表示做学问的几个阶段。"入室"犹如今天的俗语"到家"。我们说"这个人的学问到家了"，正是表示他的学问极好。

11.16 子贡问："师与商也孰贤？"子曰："师也过，商也不及。"曰："然则师愈与？"子曰："过犹不及。"

【译文】子贡问孔子："颛孙师（子张）和卜商（子夏）两个人，谁强一些？"孔子道："师呢，有些过分；商呢，有些赶不上。"子贡道:"那么,师强一些吗?"孔子道:"过分和赶不上同样不好。"

11.17 季氏富于周公⑴,而求也为之聚敛而附益之⑵。子曰:"非吾徒也。小子鸣鼓而攻之,可也。"

【译文】季氏比周公还有钱,冉求却又替他搜括,增加更多的财富。孔子道:"冉求不是我们的人,你们学生很可以大张旗鼓地来攻击他。"

【注释】
⑴周公——有两说:(甲)周公旦;(乙)泛指在周天子左右做卿士的人,如周公黑肩、周公阅之类。
⑵聚敛而附益之——事实可参阅《左传》哀公十一年和十二年文。季氏要用田赋制度,增加赋税,使冉求征求孔子的意见,孔子则主张"施取其厚,事举其中,敛从其薄"。结果冉求仍旧听从季氏,实行田赋制度。聚敛,《礼记·大学》说:"百乘之家,不畜聚敛之臣。与其有聚敛之臣,宁有盗臣。"可见儒家为了维护统治,反对对人民的过分剥削。其思想渊源或者本于此章。

11.18 柴⑴也愚,参也鲁,师也辟⑵,由也喭。

【译文】高柴愚笨,曾参迟钝,颛孙师偏激,仲由卤莽。

【注释】
⑴柴——高柴,字子羔,孔子学生,比孔子小三十岁(公元前521—?)。

(2)辟——音僻，pì。黄式三《论语后案》云："辟读若《左传》'阙西辟'之辟，偏也。以其志过高而流于一偏也。"

11.19 子曰："回也其庶⁽¹⁾乎，屡空⁽²⁾。赐不受命⁽³⁾，而货殖焉，亿则屡中。"

【译文】孔子说："颜回的学问道德差不多了罢，可是常常穷得没有办法。端木赐不安本分，去囤积投机，猜测行情，竟每每猜对了。"

【注释】
(1)庶——庶几，差不多。一般用在称赞的场合。
(2)空——世俗把"空"字读去声，不但无根据，也无此必要。"贫"和"穷"两字在古代有时有些区别，财货的缺少叫贫；生活无着落，前途无出路叫穷。"空"字却兼有这两方面的意思，所以用"穷得没有办法"来译它。
(3)赐不受命——此语古今颇有不同解释，关键在于"命"字的涵义。有把"命"解为"教命"的，则"不受命"为"不率教"，其为错误甚明显。王弼、江熙把"命"解为"爵命""禄命"，则"不受命"为"不做官"，自然很讲得通，可是子贡并不是不曾做官。《史记·仲尼弟子列传》说他"常相鲁卫"，《货殖列传》又说他"既学于仲尼，退而仕于卫，废著鬻财于曹鲁之间"，则子贡的经商和做官是不相先后的。那么，这一说既不合事实，也就不合孔子原意了。又有人把"命"讲为"天命"（《皇疏》引或说，朱熹《集注》），俞樾《群经平议》则以为古之经商皆受命于官，"若夫不受命于官而自以其财市贱鬻贵，逐什一之利，是谓不受命而货殖"。两说皆言之成理，而未知孰是，故译文仅以"不安本分"言之。

11.20 子张问善人[1]之道。子曰:"不践迹,亦不入于室。"

【译文】子张问怎样才是善人。孔子道:"善人不踩着别人的脚印走,学问道德也难以到家。"

【注释】

⑴善人——孔子曾三次论到"善人",这章可和(7.26)、(13.11)两章合看。

11.21 子曰:"论笃是与[1],君子者乎?色庄者乎?"

【译文】孔子说:"总是推许言论笃实的人,这种笃实的人是真正的君子呢?还是神情上伪装庄重的人呢?"

【注释】

⑴论笃是与——这是"与论笃"的倒装形式,"是"是帮助倒装之用的词,和"唯你是问"的"是"用法相同。"与",许也。"论笃"就是"论笃者"的意思。

11.22 子路问:"闻斯行诸?"子曰:"有父兄在,如之何其闻斯行之?"冉有问:"闻斯行诸?"子曰:"闻斯行之。"公西华曰:"由也问闻斯行诸,子曰,'有父兄在';求也问闻斯行诸,子曰,'闻斯行之'。赤也惑,敢问。"子曰:"求也退,故进之;由也兼人[1],故退之。"

【译文】子路问:"听到就干起来吗?"孔子道:"有爸爸哥哥活着,怎么能听到就干起来?"冉有问:"听到就干起来吗?"孔子道:"听到就干起来。"公西华道:"仲由问听到就干起来吗,您说:'有爸爸哥哥活着,〔不能这样做。〕'冉求问听到就干起来吗,您说:'听到就干起来。'〔两个人问题相同,而您的答复相反,〕我有些糊涂,大胆地来问问。"孔子道:"冉求平日做事退缩,所以我给他壮胆;仲由的胆量却有两个人的大,勇于作为,所以我要压压他。"

【注释】

(1)兼人——孔安国和朱熹都把"兼人"解为"胜人",但子路虽勇,未必"务在胜尚人";反不如张敬夫把"兼人"解为"勇为"为适当。

11.23 子畏于匡,颜渊后。子曰:"吾以女为死矣。"曰:"子在,回何敢死?"

【译文】孔子在匡被囚禁了之后,颜渊最后才来。孔子道:"我以为你是死了。"颜渊道:"您还活着,我怎么敢死呢?"

11.24 季子然(1)问:"仲由、冉求可谓大臣与?"子曰:"吾以子为异之问,曾由与求之问。所谓大臣者,以道事君,不可则止。今由与求也,可谓具臣矣(2)。"曰:"然则从之者与?"子曰:"弑父与君,亦不从也。"

【译文】季子然问:"仲由和冉求可以说是大臣吗?"孔子道:"我以为你是问别的人,竟问由和求呀。我们所说的大臣,他用最合于仁义的内容和方式来对待君主,如果这样行不通,宁肯辞职不干。如今由和求这两个人,可以说是具有相当才能的臣属了。"季子然又道:"那么,他们会一切顺从上级吗?"孔子道:"杀父亲、杀君主的事情,他们也不会顺从的。"

【注释】

(1)季子然——当为季氏的同族之人,《史记·仲尼弟子列传》作"季孙问曰:子路可谓大臣与",与《论语》稍异。

(2)这一章可以和孔子不以仁来许他们的一章(5.8)以及季氏旅泰山,冉有不救章(3.6)、季氏伐颛臾,冉有、子路为他解脱章(16.1)合看。

11.25 子路使子羔为费宰。子曰:"贼夫人之子。"子路曰:"有民人焉,有社稷焉,何必读书,然后为学?"子曰:"是故恶夫佞者。"

【译文】子路叫了羔去做费县县长。孔子道:"这是害了别人的儿子!"子路道:"那地方有老百姓,有土地和五谷,为什么定要读书才叫做学问呢?"孔子道:"所以我讨厌强嘴利舌的人。"

11.26 子路、曾皙[1]、冉有、公西华侍坐。子曰:"以吾一日长乎尔,毋吾以也。居[2]则曰:'不吾知也!'如或知尔,则何以哉?"子路率尔而对曰:"千乘之国,摄乎大国之间,加之以师旅,因之以饥馑;由也为之,比[3]及三年,可使有勇,且知方也。"夫子哂之。"求!尔何如?"对曰:

"方六七十[4]，如[5]五六十，求也为之，比[3]及三年，可使足民。如其礼乐，以俟君子。""赤！尔何如？"对曰："非曰能之，愿学焉。宗庙之事，如会同，端章甫[6]，愿为小相[7]焉。""点！尔何如？"鼓瑟希，铿尔，舍瑟而作[8]，对曰："异乎三子者之撰。"子曰："何伤乎？亦各言其志也。"曰："莫[9]春者，春服既成[10]，冠者五六人，童子六七人，浴乎沂[11]，风乎舞雩[12]，咏而归。"夫子喟然叹曰："吾与点也！"三子者出，曾晳后。曾晳曰："夫三子者之言何如？"子曰："亦各言其志也已矣。"曰："夫子何哂由也？"曰："为国以礼，其言不让，是故哂之。""唯[13]求则非邦也与？""安见方六七十如五六十而非邦也者？""唯赤则非邦也与？""宗庙会同，非诸侯而何？赤也为之[14]小，孰能为之[14]大？"

【译文】子路、曾晳、冉有、公西华四个人陪着孔子坐着。孔子说道："因为我比你们年纪都大，〔老了，〕没有人用我了。你们平日说：'人家不了解我呀！'假若有人了解你们，〔打算请你们出去，〕那你们怎么办呢？"子路不加思索地答道："一千辆兵车的国家，局促地处于几个大国的中间，外面有军队侵犯它，国内又加以灾荒。我去治理，等到三年光景，可以使人人有勇气，而且懂得大道理。"孔子微微一笑。又问："冉求，你怎么样？"答道："国土纵横各六七十里或者五六十里的小国家，我去治理，等到三年光景，可以使人人富足。至于修明礼乐，那只有等待贤人君子了。"又问："公西赤！你怎么样？"答道："不是说我已经很有本领了，我愿意这样学习：祭祀的工作或者同外国盟会，我愿意穿着礼服，戴着礼帽，做一个小司仪者。"又问："曾点！你怎么样?"他弹瑟正近尾声,铿的一声把瑟放下,站了起来答道:"我的志向和他们三位所讲的不同。"孔子道:"那有什么妨碍呢?正是要各人说出自己的志向呵!"曾皙便道:"暮春三月,春天衣服都穿定了,我陪同五六位成年人,六七个小孩,在沂水旁边洗洗澡,在舞雩台上吹吹风,一路唱歌,一路走回来。"孔子长叹一声道:"我同意曾点的主张呀!"子路、冉有、公西华三人都出来了,曾皙后走。曾皙问道:"那三位同学的话怎样?"孔子道:"也不过各人说说自己的志向罢了。"曾皙又道:"您为什么对仲由微笑呢?"孔子道:"治理国家应该讲求礼让,可是他的话却一点不谦虚,所以笑笑他。""难道冉求所讲的就不是国家吗?"孔子道:"怎样见得横纵各六七十里或者五六十里的土地就不够是一个国家呢?""公西赤所讲的不是国家吗?"孔子道:"有宗庙,有国际间的盟会,不是国家是什么?〔我笑仲由的不是说他不能治理国家,关键不在是不是国家,而是笑他说话的内容和态度不够谦虚。譬如公西赤,他是个十分懂得礼仪的人,但他只说愿意学着做一个小司仪者。〕如果他只做一小司仪者,又有谁来做大司仪者呢?"

【注释】

(1)曾皙——名点,曾参的父亲,也是孔子的学生。
(2)居——义与唐、宋人口语"平居"同,平日、平常的意思。
(3)比——去声,bì,等到的意思。
(4)方六七十——这是古代的土地面积计算方式,"方六七十"不等于"六七十方里",而是每边长六七十里的意思。
(5)如——或者的意思。
(6)端章甫——端,古代礼服之名;章甫,古代礼帽之名。"端章甫"为修饰句,在古代可以不用动词。

(7)相——去声，xiàng，名词，赞礼之人。

(8)舍瑟而作——作，站起来的意思。曾点答孔子之问站了起来，其他学生也同样站了起来可以推知，不过上文未曾明说罢了。

(9)莫——同"暮"。

(10)成——定也。《国语·吴语》："吴晋争长未成"，就是争为盟主而未定的意思。

(11)沂——水名，但和大沂河以及流入于大沂河的小沂河都不同。这沂水源出山东邹县东北，西流经曲阜与洙水合，入于泗水。也就是《左传》昭公二十五年"季平子请待于沂上"的"沂"。

(12)舞雩——《水经注》："沂水北对稷门，一名高门，一名雩门。南隔水有雩坛，坛高三丈，即曾点所欲风处也。"当在今曲阜县南。

(13)唯——语首词，无义。

(14)之——用法同"其"。

颜渊篇第十二

共二十四章

12.1 颜渊问仁。子曰:"克己复礼为仁[1]。一日克己复礼,天下归仁[2]焉。为仁由己,而由人乎哉?"颜渊曰:"请问其目。"子曰:"非礼勿视,非礼勿听,非礼勿言,非礼勿动。"颜渊曰:"回虽不敏,请事斯语矣。"

【译文】颜渊问仁德。孔子道:"抑制自己,使言语行动都合于礼,就是仁。一旦这样做到了,天下的人都会称许你是仁人。实践仁德,全凭自己,还凭别人吗?"颜渊道:"请问行动的纲领。"孔子道:"不合礼的事不看,不合礼的话不听,不合礼的话不说,不合礼的事不做。"颜渊道:"我虽然迟钝,也要实行您这话。"

【注释】
(1)克己复礼为仁——《左传》昭公十二年说:"仲尼曰:'古也有志:克己复礼,仁也。'"那么,"克己复礼为仁"是孔子用前人的话赋予新的含义。
(2)归仁——"称仁"的意思,说见毛奇龄《论语稽求篇》。朱熹《集注》谓"归犹与也",也是此意。

12.2 仲弓问仁。子曰:"出门如见大宾,使民如承大祭。己所不欲,勿施于人。在邦无怨,在家[1]无怨。"仲弓曰:"雍虽不敏,请事斯语矣。"

【译文】仲弓问仁德。孔子道:"出门[工作]好像去接待贵宾,役使百姓好像去承当大祀典,[都得严肃认真,小心谨慎。]自己所不喜欢的事物,就不强加于别人。在工作岗位上不对工作有怨恨,就是不在工作岗位上也没有怨恨。"

仲弓道:"我虽然迟钝,也要实行您这话。"

【注释】

⑴在家——刘宝楠《论语正义》说:"在邦谓仕于诸侯之邦,在家谓仕于卿大夫之家也。"把"家"字拘泥于"大夫曰家"的一个意义,不妥当。

12.3 司马牛⑴问仁。子曰:"仁者,其言也讱。"曰:"其言也讱,斯谓之仁已乎?"子曰:"为之难,言之得无讱乎?"

【译文】司马牛问仁德。孔子道:"仁人,他的言语迟钝。"司马牛道:"言语迟钝,这就叫做仁了吗?"孔子道:"做起来不容易,说话能够不迟钝吗?"

【注释】

⑴司马牛——《史记·仲尼弟子列传》云:"司马耕,字子牛。牛多言而躁,问仁于孔子。孔子曰:'仁者其言也讱。'"根据司马迁的这一说法,孔子的答语是针对问者"多言而躁"的缺点而说的。

12.4 司马牛问君子。子曰:"君子不忧不惧。"曰:"不忧不惧,斯谓之君子已乎?"子曰:"内省不疚,夫何忧何惧?"

【译文】司马牛问怎样去做一个君子。孔子道:"君子不忧愁,不恐惧。"司马牛道:"不忧愁,不恐惧,这样就可以叫做君子了吗?"孔子道:"自己问心无愧,那有什么可以忧愁和恐惧的呢?"

12.5 司马牛忧曰:"人皆有兄弟,我独亡⑴。"子夏曰:"商闻之矣:死生有命,富贵在天。君子敬而无失,与人恭而有礼。四海之内,皆兄弟也——君子何患乎无兄弟也?"

【译文】司马牛忧愁地说道:"别人都有好兄弟,单单我没有。"子夏道:"我听说过:死生听之命运,富贵由天安排。君子只是对待工作严肃认真,不出差错,对待别人词色恭谨,合乎礼节,天下之大,到处都是好兄弟——君子又何必着急没有好兄弟呢?"

【注释】

⑴人皆有兄弟,我独亡——自来的注释家都说这个司马牛就是宋国桓魋的兄弟。桓魋为人很坏,结果是谋反失败,他的几个兄弟也都跟着失败了。其中只有司马牛不赞同他这些兄弟的行为。但结果也是逃亡在外,死于道路(事见《左传》哀公十四年)。译文姑且根据这种说法。但我却认为,孔子的学生司马牛和宋国桓魋的弟弟司马牛可能是两个不同的人,难于混为一谈。第一,《史记·仲尼弟子列传》既不说这一个司马牛是宋人,更没有把《左传》上司马牛的事情记载上去,太史公如果看到了这类史料而不采取,可见他是把两个司马牛作不同的人看待的。第二,说《论语》的司马牛就是《左传》的司马牛者始于孔安国。孔安国又说司马牛名犁,又和《史记·仲尼弟子列传》说司马牛名耕不同。如果孔安国之言有所本,那么,原本就有两个司马牛,一个名耕,孔子弟子;一个名犁,桓魋之弟。但自孔安国以后的若干人却误把名犁的也当作孔子学生了。姑识于此,以供参考。

12.6 子张问明。子曰:"浸润之谮,肤受之愬,不行焉,可谓明也已矣。浸润之谮,肤受之愬,不行焉,可谓远也已矣。"

【译文】子张问怎样才叫做见事明白。孔子道:"点滴而来,日积月累的谗言和肌肤所受、急迫切身的诬告都在你这里行不通,那你可以说是看得明白的了。点滴而来,日积月累的谗言和肌肤所受、急迫切身的诬告也都在你这里行不通,那你可以说是看得远的了。"

12.7 子贡问政。子曰:"足食,足兵[1],民信之矣。"子贡曰:"必不得已而去,于斯三者何先?"曰:"去兵。"子贡曰:"必不得已而去,于斯二者何先?"曰:"去食。自古皆有死,民无信不立。"

【译文】子贡问怎样去治理政事。孔子道:"充足粮食,充足军备,百姓对政府就有信心了。"子贡道:"如果迫于不得已,在粮食、军备和人民的信心三者之中一定要去掉一项,先去掉哪一项?"孔子道:"去掉军备。"子贡道:"如果迫于不得已,在粮食和人民的信心两者之中一定要去掉一项,先去掉哪一项?"孔子道:"去掉粮食。〔没有粮食,不过死亡,但〕自古以来谁都免不了死亡。如果人民对政府缺乏信心,国家是站不起来的。"

【注释】

[1]兵——在《五经》和《论语》《孟子》中,"兵"字多指兵器而言,但也偶有解作兵士的。如《左传》隐公四年"诸侯之师败郑徒兵",

襄公元年"败其徒兵于洎上"。顾炎武、阎若璩都以为《五经》中的"兵"字无作士兵解者,恐未谛(刘宝楠说)。但此"兵"字仍以解为军器为宜,故以军备译之。

12.8 棘子成⁽¹⁾曰:"君子质而已矣,何以文为?"子贡曰:"惜乎,夫子之说君子也⁽²⁾!驷不及舌。文犹质也,质犹文也。虎豹之鞟犹犬羊之鞟。"

【译文】棘子成道:"君子只要有好的本质便够了,要那些文彩[那些仪节、那些形式]干什么?"子贡道:"先生这样地谈论君子,可惜说错了。一言既出,驷马难追。本质和文彩,是同等重要的。假若把虎豹和犬羊两类兽皮拔去有文彩的毛,那这两类皮革就很少区别了。"

【注释】
(1)棘子成——卫国大夫。古代大夫都可以被尊称为"夫子",所以子贡这样称呼他。
(2)惜乎,夫子之说君子也——朱熹《集注》把它作两句读:"惜乎!夫子之说,君子也。"便应该这样翻译:"先生的话,是出自君子之口,可惜说错了。"我则以为"夫子之说君子也"为主语,"惜乎"为谓语,此为倒装句。

12.9 哀公问于有若曰:"年饥,用不足,如之何?"有若对曰:"盍彻乎?"曰:"二,吾犹不足,如之何其彻也?"对曰:"百姓足,君孰与不足?百姓不足,君孰与足?"

【译文】鲁哀公向有若问道:"年成不好,国家用度不够,应该怎么办?"有若答道:"为什么不实行十分抽一的税率呢?"哀公道:"十分抽二,我还不够,怎么能十分抽一呢?"答道:"如果百姓的用度够,您怎么会不够?如果百姓的用度不够,您又怎么会够?"

12.10 子张问崇德辨惑。子曰:"主忠信,徙义,崇德也。爱之欲其生,恶之欲其死。既欲其生,又欲其死,是惑也。'诚不以富,亦只以异(1)。'"

【译文】子张问如何去提高品德,辨别迷惑。孔子道:"以忠诚信实为主,唯义是从,这就可以提高品德。爱一个人,希望他长寿;厌恶起来,恨不得他马上死去。既要他长寿,又要他短命,这便是迷惑。这样,的确对自己毫无好处,只是使人奇怪罢了。"

【注释】

(1)诚不以富,亦只以异——《诗经·小雅·我行其野篇》诗句,引在这里,很难解释。程颐说是"错简"(别章的文句,因为书页次序错了,误在此处),但无证据。我这里姑且依朱熹《集注》的解释而意译之。

12.11 齐景公问政于孔子。孔子对曰:"君君,臣臣,父父,子子。"公曰:"善哉!信如君不君,臣不臣,父不父,子不子,虽有粟,吾得而食诸?"

【译文】齐景公向孔子问政治。孔子答道:"君要像个君,臣要像个臣,父亲要像父亲,儿子要像儿子。"景公道:"对呀!若是君不像君,臣不像臣,父不像父,子不像子,即使粮食很多,我能吃得着吗?"

12.12 子曰:"片言可以折狱[1]者,其由也与?"子路无宿诺[2]。

【译文】孔子说:"根据一方面的语言就可以判决案件的,大概只有仲由吧!"子路从不拖延诺言。
【注释】
[1]片言折狱——"片言"古人也叫做"单辞"。打官司一定有原告和被告两方面的人,叫做两造。自古迄今从没有只根据一造的言辞来判决案件的(除掉被告缺席裁判)。孔子说子路"片言可以折狱",不过表示他的为人诚实直率,别人不愿欺他罢了。
[2]子路无宿诺——这句话与上文有什么逻辑关系,从来没有人说得明白(焦循《论语补疏》的解释也不可信)。唐陆德明《经典释文》云:"或分此为别章。"

12.13 子曰:"听讼[1],吾犹人也。必也使无讼乎!"

【译文】孔子说:"审理诉讼,我同别人差不多。一定要使诉讼的事件完全消灭才好。"
【注释】
[1]听讼——据《史记·孔子世家》,孔子在鲁定公时,曾为大司寇,司寇为治理刑事的官,孔子这话或许是刚作司寇时所说。

12.14 子张问政。子曰:"居之无倦,行之以忠。"

【译文】子张问政治。孔子道:"在位不要疲倦懈怠,执行政令要忠心。"

12.15 子曰:"博学于文,约之以礼,亦可以弗畔矣夫[1]!"

【注释】
[1]见《雍也篇第六》(6.27)。

12.16 子曰:"君子成人之美,不成人之恶。小人反是。"

【译文】孔子说:"君子成全别人的好事,不促成别人的坏事。小人却和这相反。"

12.17 季康子问政于孔子。孔子对曰:"政者,正也。子帅以正,孰敢不正?"
【译文】季康子向孔子问政治。孔子答道:"政字的意思就是端正。您自己带头端正,谁敢不端正呢?"

12.18 季康子患盗,问于孔子。孔子对曰:"苟子之不欲,虽赏之不窃。"

【译文】季康子苦于盗贼太多,向孔子求教。孔子答道:"假若您不贪求太多的财货,就是奖励偷抢,他们也不会干。"

12.19 季康子[1]问政于孔子曰:"如杀无道,以就有道,何如?"孔子对曰:"子为政,焉用杀?子欲善而民善矣。君子之德风,小人之德草。草上之风,必偃。"

【译文】季康子向孔子请教政治,说道:"假若杀掉坏人来亲近好人,怎么样?"孔子答道:"您治理政治,为什么要杀戮?您想把国家搞好,百姓就会好起来。领导人的作风好比风,老百姓的作风好比草。风向哪边吹,草向哪边倒。"

【注释】

[1]季康子——根据《春秋》以及《左传》,季孙斯(桓子)死于哀公三年秋七月,季孙肥(康子)随即袭位。则以上三章季康子之问,当在鲁哀公三年七月以后。

12.20 子张问:"士何如斯可谓之达矣?"子曰:"何哉,尔所谓达者?"子张对曰:"在邦必闻,在家必闻。"子曰:"是闻也,非达也。夫达也者,质直而好义,察言而观色,虑以下人。在邦必达,在家必达。夫闻也者,色取仁而行违,居之不疑。在邦必闻,在家必闻。"

【译文】子张问:"读书人要怎样做才可以叫达了?"孔子道:"你所说的达是什么意思?"子张答道:"做国家的官时一定有名望,在大夫家工作时一定有名望。"孔子道:"这个叫闻，不叫达。怎样才是达呢？品质正直，遇事讲理，善于分析别人的言语，观察别人的颜色，从思想上愿意对别人退让。这种人，做国家的官时固然事事行得通，在大夫家一定事事行得通。至于闻，表面上似乎爱好仁德，实际行为却不如此，可是自己竟以仁人自居而不加疑惑。这种人，做官的时候一定会骗取名望，居家的时候也一定会骗取名望。"

12.21 樊迟从游于舞雩之下，曰："敢问崇德，修慝，辨惑。"子曰："善哉问！先事后得，非崇德与？攻其恶，无攻人之恶，非修慝与？一朝之忿，忘其身，以及其亲，非惑与？"

【译文】樊迟陪侍孔子在舞雩台下游逛，说道："请问怎样提高自己的品德，怎样消除别人对自己不露面的怨恨，怎样辨别出哪种是糊涂事。"孔子道："问得好！首先付出劳动，然后收获，不是提高品德了吗？批判自己的坏处，不去批判别人的坏处，不就消除无形的怨恨了吗？因为偶然的忿怒，便忘记自己，甚至也忘记了爹娘，不是糊涂吗？"

12.22 樊迟问仁。子曰："爱人。"问知。子曰："知人。"樊迟未达。子曰："举直错诸枉，能使枉者直。"樊迟退，见子夏曰："乡[1]也吾见于夫子而问知，子曰，'举直错诸枉，能使枉者直'，何谓也？"子夏曰："富哉言乎！舜有天下，选于众，举皋陶[2]，不仁者远[3]矣。汤[4]有天下，选于众，举伊尹[5]，不仁者远矣[6]。"

【译文】樊迟问仁。孔子道:"爱人。"又问智。孔子道:"善于鉴别人物。"樊迟还不透彻了解。孔子道:"把正直人提拔出来,位置在邪恶人之上,能够使邪恶人正直。"樊迟退了出来,找着子夏,说道:"刚才我去见老师向他问智,他说,'把正直人提拔出来,位置在邪恶人之上',这是什么意思?"子夏道:"意义多么丰富的话呀!舜有了天下,在众人之中挑选,把皋陶提拔出来,坏人就难以存在了。汤有了天下,在众人之中挑选,把伊尹提拔出来,坏人也就难以存在了。"

【注释】

(1)乡——去声,xiàng,同"向"。

(2)皋陶——音高摇,gāo yáo,舜的臣子。

(3)远——本是"离开""遁逃"之意,但人是可以转变的,何必非逃离不可。译文用"难以存在"来表达,比之拘泥字面或者还符合子夏的本意些。

(4)汤——卜辞作"唐",罗振玉云:"唐殆太乙之谥。"(《增订殷虚书契考释》)商朝开国之君,名履(卜辞作"大乙",而无"履"字),伐夏桀而得天下。

(5)伊尹——汤的辅相。

(6)"举直"而"使枉者直",属于"仁";知道谁是直人而举他,属于"智",所以"举直错诸枉"是仁智之事,而孔子屡言之(参2.19)。

12.23 子贡问友。子曰:"忠告[1]而善道之,不可则止,毋自辱焉。"

【译文】子贡问对待朋友的方法。孔子道:"忠心地劝告他,好好地引导他,他不听从,也就罢了,不要自找侮辱。"

【注释】

⑴告——旧读梏,gù。

12.24 曾子曰:"君子以文会友,以友辅仁。"

【译文】曾子说:"君子用文章学问来聚会朋友,用朋友来帮助我培养仁德。"

子路篇第十三

共三十章

13.1 子路问政。子曰:"先之⁽¹⁾劳之。"请益。曰:"无倦⁽²⁾。"

【译文】子路问政治。孔子道:"自己给百姓带头,然后让他们勤劳地工作。"子路请求多讲一点。孔子又道:"永远不要懈怠。"

【注释】
(1)先之——就是下一章"先有司"之意。
(2)无倦——也就是"居之无倦"(12.14)之意。

13.2 仲弓为季氏宰,问政。子曰:"先有司,赦小过,举贤才。"曰:"焉知贤才而举之?"子曰:"举尔所知;尔所不知,人其舍诸?"

【译文】仲弓做了季氏的总管,向孔子问政治。孔子道:"给工作人员带头,不计较人家的小错误,提拔优秀人才。"仲弓道:"怎样去识别优秀人才把他们提拔出来呢?"孔子道:"提拔你所知道的;那些你所不知道的,别人难道会埋没他吗?"

13.3 子路曰:"卫君⁽¹⁾待子而为政,子将奚先?"子曰:"必也正名⁽²⁾乎!"子路曰:"有是哉,子之迂也!奚其正?"子曰:"野哉,由也!君子于其所不知,盖阙如也。名不正,则言不顺;言不顺,则事不成;事不成,则礼乐不兴;礼乐不兴,则刑罚不中;刑罚不中,则民无所错⁽³⁾手足。故君子名之必可言也,言之必可行也。君子于其言,无所苟而已矣。"

【译文】子路对孔子说:"卫君等着您去治理国政,您准备首先干什么?"孔子道:"那一定是纠正名分上的用词不当罢!"子路道:"您的迂腐竟到如此地步吗!这又何必纠正?"孔子道:"你怎么这样卤莽!君子对于他所不懂的,大概采取保留态度,〔你怎么能乱说呢?〕用词不当,言语就不能顺理成章;言语不顺理成章,工作就不可能搞好;工作搞不好,国家的礼乐制度也就举办不起来;礼乐制度举办不起来,刑罚也就不会得当;刑罚不得当,百姓就会〔惶惶不安,〕连手脚都不晓得摆在哪里才好。所以君子用一个词,一定〔有它一定的理由,〕可以说得出来;而顺理成章的话也一定行得通。君子对于措词说话要没有一点马虎的地方才罢了。"

【注释】

(1)卫君——历来的注释家都说是卫出公辄。

(2)正名——关于这两个字的解释,从汉以来便异说纷纭。皇侃《义疏》引郑玄的《注》云:"正名谓正书字也,古者曰名,今世曰字。"这说恐不合孔子原意。《左传》成公二年曾经载有孔子的话,说:"唯器(礼器)与名(名义、名分)不可以假人。"《论语》这一"名"字应该和《左传》的这一"名"字相同。《论语》中有孔子"觚不觚"之叹。"觚"而不像"觚",有其名,无其实,就是名不正。孔子对齐景公之问,说,"君君,臣臣,父父,子子",也就是正名。《韩诗外传》卷五记载着孔子的一段故事,说，"孔子侍坐于季孙，季孙之宰通曰：'君使人假马，其与之乎？'孔子曰：'吾闻：君取于臣曰取，不曰假。'季孙悟，告宰通曰：'今以往，君有取谓之取，无曰假。'孔子曰：'正假马之言而君臣之义定矣。'"更可以说明孔子正名的实际意义。我这里用"名分上的用词不当"来解释"名不正"，似乎较为接近孔子原意。但孔子所要纠正的，只是有关古代礼制、名分上的用词不当的现象，而不是一般的用词不当的现象。一般的用词不当的现象，是语法修辞范畴中的问题；礼制上、名分上的用词不当的现象，依孔子的意见，是有关伦理和政治的问题，这两点必须区别开来。

(3) 错——同"措"，安置也。

13.4 樊迟请学稼。子曰："吾不如老农。"请学为圃。曰："吾不如老圃。"樊迟出。子曰："小人哉，樊须也！上好礼，则民莫敢不敬；上好义，则民莫敢不服；上好信，则民莫敢不用情。夫如是，则四方之民襁负其子而至矣，焉用稼？"

【译文】樊迟请求学种庄稼。孔子道："我不如老农民。"又请求学种菜蔬。孔子道："我不如老菜农。"樊迟退了出来。孔子道："樊迟真是小人！统治者讲究礼节，百姓就没有人敢不尊敬；统治者行为正当，百姓就没有人敢不服从；统治者诚恳信实，百姓就没有人敢不说真话。做到这样，四方的百姓都会背负着小儿女来投奔，为什么要自己种庄稼呢？"

13.5 子曰："诵《诗》三百，授之以政，不达；使于四方，不能专对[1];虽多,亦奚以为[2]?"

【译文】孔子说:"熟读《诗经》三百篇,交给他以政治任务,却办不通;叫他出使外国,又不能独立地去谈判酬酢;纵是读得多,有什么用处呢?"

【注释】

[1]不能专对——古代的使节,只接受使命,至于如何去交涉应对,只能随机应变,独立行事,更不能事事请示或者早就在国内一切安排好,这便叫做"受命不受辞",也就是这里的"专对"。同时春秋时代的外交酬酢和谈判,多半背诵诗篇来代替语言(《左传》里充满了这种记载),所以《诗》是外交人才的必读书。

[2]亦奚以为——以,动词,用也。为,表疑问的语气词,但只跟"奚"、"何"诸字连用,如"何以文为""何以伐为"。

13.6 子曰:"其身正,不令而行;其身不正,虽令不从。"

【译文】孔子说:"统治者本身行为正当,不发命令,事情也行得通。他本身行为不正当,纵三令五申,百姓也不会信从。"

13.7 子曰:"鲁卫之政,兄弟也。"

【译文】孔子说:"鲁国的政治和卫国的政治,像兄弟一般[地相差不远]。"

13.8 子谓卫公子荆⁽¹⁾,"善居室⁽²⁾。始有,曰:'苟合⁽³⁾矣。'少有,曰:'苟完矣。'富有,曰:'苟美矣。'"

【译文】孔子谈到卫国的公子荆,说:"他善于居家过日子,刚有一点,便说道:'差不多够了。'增加了一点,又说道:'差不多完备了。'多有一点,便说道:'差不多富丽堂皇了。'"

【注释】

(1)卫公子荆——卫国的公子,吴季札曾把他列为卫国的君子,见《左传》襄公二十九年。有人说:"此取荆之善居室以风有位者也。"因为当时的卿大夫,不但贪污,而且奢侈成风,所以孔子"以廉风贪,以俭风侈"。似可备一说。

(2)居室——这一词组意义甚多:(甲)居住房舍,《礼记•曲礼》:"君子将营宫室,宗庙为先,厩库为次,居室为后。"(乙)夫妇同居,《孟子•万章上》:"男女居室,人之大伦也。"(丙)汉代又以为狱名,《史记•卫将军骠骑列传》:"青尝从入至甘泉居室。"(丁)此则为积蓄家业居家度日之义。"居"读为"奇货可居"之"居"。

(3)合——给也,足也。此依俞樾《群经平议》说。

13.9 子适卫,冉有仆⁽¹⁾。子曰:"庶矣哉!"冉有曰:"既庶矣,又何加焉?"曰:"富之。"曰:"既富矣,又何加焉?"曰:"教之⁽²⁾。"

【译文】孔子到卫国,冉有替他驾车子。孔子道:"好稠密的人口!"冉有道:"人口已经众多了,又该怎么办呢?"孔子道:"使他们富裕起来。"冉有道:"已经富裕了,又该怎么办呢?"孔子道:"教育他们。"

【注释】

⑴仆——动词,驾御车马。其人则谓之仆夫,《诗•小雅•出车》"仆夫况瘁"可证。仆亦作名词,驾车者,《诗•小雅•正月》"屡顾尔仆"是也。

⑵既富……教之——孔子主张"先富后教",孟子、荀子也都继续发挥了这一主张。所以孟子说:"乐岁终身苦,凶年不免于死亡。此惟救死而恐不赡,奚暇治礼义哉?"(《孟子•梁惠王上》)也和《管子•治国篇》的"凡治国之道,必先富民"的主张相同。

13.10 子曰:"苟有用我者,期月⑴而已可也,三年有成。"

【译文】孔子说:"假若有用我主持国家政事的,一年便差不多了,三年便会很有成绩。"

【注释】

⑴期月——期同"稘",有些本子即作"稘",音姬,jī。期月,一年。

13.11 子曰:"'善人为邦百年,亦可以胜⑴残去⑵杀矣⑶。'诚哉是言也!"

【译文】孔子说:"'善人治理国政连续到一百年,也可以克服残暴免除虐杀了。'这句话真说得对呀!"

【注释】

⑴胜——旧读平声,shēng。

(2)去——旧读上声,qǔ。

(3)善人……去杀矣——依文意是孔子引别人的话。

13.12 子曰:"如有王者,必世而后仁。"

【译文】孔子说:"假若有王者兴起,一定需要三十年才能使仁政大行。"

13.13 子曰:"苟正其身矣,于从政乎何有?不能正其身,如正人何?"

【译文】孔子说:"假若端正了自己,治理国政有什么困难呢?连本身都不能端正,怎么端正别人呢?"

13.14 冉子退朝。子曰:"何晏也?"对曰:"有政。"子曰:"其事也。如有政,虽不吾以,吾其与闻之[1]。"

【译文】冉有从办公的地方回来。孔子道:"为什么今天回得这样晚呢?"答道:"有政务。"孔子道:"那只是事务罢了。若是有政务,虽然不用我了,我也会知道的。"

【注释】

(1)与闻之——与,去声,yù,参预之意。《左传》哀公十一年曾有记载,季氏以用田赋的事征求孔子意见,并且说:"子为国老,待子而行。"可见孔子"如有政,吾其与闻之"这话是有根据的。只是冉有不明白"政"和"事"的分别，一时用词不当罢了。依我看，这章并无其他意义，前人有故求深解的，未必对。

13.15 定公问："一言而可以兴邦，有诸？"孔子对曰："言不可以若是其几也。人之言曰：'为君难，为臣不易。'如知为君之难也，不几乎一言而兴邦乎？"曰："一言而丧邦，有诸？"孔子对曰："言不可以若是其几也。人之言曰：'予无乐乎为君，唯其言而莫予违也。'如其善而莫之违也，不亦善乎？如不善而莫之违也，不几乎一言而丧邦乎？"

【译文】鲁定公问："一句话兴盛国家，有这事么？"孔子答道："说话不可以像这样地简单机械。不过，人家都说：'做君上很难，做臣子不容易。'假若知道做君上的艰难，[自然会谨慎认真地干去，]不近于一句话便兴盛国家么？"定公又道："一句话丧失国家，有这事么？"孔子答道："说话不可以像这样地简单机械。不过，大家都说：'我做国君没有别的快乐，只是我说什么话都没有人违抗我。'假若说的话正确而没有人违抗，不也好么？假若说的话不正确而也没有人违抗，不近于一句话便丧失国家么？"

13.16 叶公问政。子曰："近者悦，远者来。"

【译文】叶公问政治。孔子道："境内的人使他高兴，境外的人使他来投奔。"

13.17 子夏为莒父⑴宰，问政。子曰："无欲速，无见小利。欲速，则不达；见小利，则大事不成。"

【译文】子夏做了莒父的县长，问政治。孔子道："不要图快，不要顾小利。图快，反而不能达到目的；顾小利，就办不成大事。"

【注释】

⑴莒父——鲁国之一邑，现在已经不能确知其所在。《山东通志》认为在今山东高密县东南。

13.18 叶公语孔子曰："吾党有直躬者，其父攘羊，而子证⑴之。"孔子曰："吾党之直者异于是：父为子隐，子为父隐。——直在其中⑵矣。"

【译文】叶公告诉孔子道："我那里有个坦白直率的人，他父亲偷了羊，他便告发。"孔子道："我们那里坦白直率的人和你们的不同：父亲替儿子隐瞒，儿子替父亲隐瞒——直率就在这里面。"

【注释】

⑴证——《说文》云："证，告也。"正是此义。相当今日的"检举""揭发"，《韩非子·五蠹篇》述此事作"谒之吏"，《吕氏春秋·当务篇》述此事作"谒之上"，都可以说明正是其子去告发他父亲。"证明"的"证"，古书一般用"征"字为之。

⑵直在其中——孔子伦理哲学的基础就在于"孝"和"慈"，因之说父子相隐，直在其中。

13.19 樊迟问仁。子曰:"居处恭,执事敬,与人忠。虽之⑴夷狄,不可弃也。"

【译文】樊迟问仁。孔子道:"平日容貌态度端正庄严,工作严肃认真,为别人忠心诚意。这几种品德,纵到外国去,也是不能废弃的。"
【注释】
⑴之——动词,到也。

13.20 子贡问曰:"何如斯可谓之士矣?"子曰:"行己有耻,使于四方,不辱君命,可谓士矣。"曰:"敢问其次。"曰:"宗族称孝焉,乡党称弟焉。"曰:"敢问其次。"曰:"言必信,行必果,硁硁然小人哉!——抑亦可以为次矣。"曰:"今之从政者何如?"子曰:"噫!斗筲之人⑴,何足算也?"

【译文】子贡问道:"怎样才可以叫做'士'?"孔子道:"自己行为保持羞耻之心,出使外国,很好地完成君主的使命,可以叫做'士'了。"子贡道:"请问次一等的。"孔子道:"宗族称赞他孝顺父母,乡里称赞他恭敬尊长。"子贡又道:"请问再次一等的。"孔子道:"言语一定信实,行为一定坚决,这是不问是非黑白而只管自己贯彻言行的小人呀!但也可以说是再次一等的'士'了。"子贡道:"现在的执政诸公怎么样?"孔子道:"咳!这班器识狭小的人算得什么?"
【注释】
⑴斗筲之人——斗是古代的量名,筲音梢,shāo,古代的饭筐(《说

文》作箳），能容五升。斗筲譬如度量和见识的狭小。有人说，"斗筲之人"也可以译为"车载斗量之人"，言其不足为奇。

13.21 子曰："不得中行而与之，必也狂狷⁽¹⁾乎！狂者进取，狷者有所不为也。"

【译文】孔子说："得不到言行合乎中庸的人和他相交，那一定要交到激进的人和狷介的人罢，激进者一意向前，狷介者也不肯做坏事。"

【注释】

⑴狂狷——《孟子•尽心下》有一段话可以为本文的解释，录之于下："孟子曰：'孔子不得中道而与之，必也狂獧（同"狷"）乎！狂者进取，獧者有所不为也。孔子岂不欲中道哉？不可必得，故思其次也。''敢问何如斯可谓狂矣？'（此万章问词，下同。）曰：'如琴张、曾晳、牧皮者，孔子之所谓狂矣。''何以谓之狂也？'曰：'其志嘐嘐然，曰：古之人！古之人！夷考其行而不掩焉者也。狂者又不可得，欲得不屑不洁之士而与之，是獧也，是又其次也。'"孟子这话未必尽合孔子本意，但可备参考。

13.22 子曰："南人有言曰：'人而无恒，不可以作巫医⁽¹⁾。'善夫！""不恒其德⁽²⁾，或承之羞。"子曰："不占而已矣。"

【译文】孔子说："南方人有句话说：'人假若没有恒心，连巫医都做不了。'这句话很好呀！"《易经•恒卦》的《爻辞》说："三心二意，翻云覆雨，总有人招致羞耻。"孔子又说："这话的意思是叫无恒心的人不必去占卦罢了。"

【注释】

(1)巫医——巫医是一词，不应分为卜筮的巫和治病的医两种。古代常以禳祷之术替人治疗，这种人便叫巫医。

(2)不恒其德——这有两种意义：（甲）不能持久，时作时辍；（乙）没有一定的操守。译文用"三心二意"表示"不能持久"，用"翻云覆雨"表示"没有操守"。

13.23 子曰："君子和而不同，小人同而不和[1]。"

【译文】孔子说："君子用自己的正确意见来纠正别人的错误意见，使一切都做到恰到好处，却不肯盲从附和。小人只是盲从附和，却不肯表示自己的不同意见。"

【注释】

(1)和，同——"和"与"同"是春秋时代的两个常用术语，《左传》昭公二十年所载晏子对齐景公批评梁丘据的话，和《国语·郑语》所载史伯的话都解说得非常详细。"和"如五味的调和，八音的和谐，一定要有水、火、酱、醋各种不同的材料才能调和滋味；一定要有高下、长短、疾徐各种不同的声调才能使乐曲和谐。晏子说："君臣亦然。君所谓可，而有否焉，臣献其否以成其可；君所谓否，而有可焉，臣献其可以去其否。"因此史伯也说："以他平他谓之和。""同"就不如此，用晏子的话说："君所谓可，据亦曰可；君所谓否，据亦曰否；若以水济水，谁能食之？若琴瑟之专一，谁能听之？'同'之不可也如是。"我又认为这个"和"字与"礼之用和为贵"的"和"有相通之处。因此译文也出现了"恰到好处"的字眼。

13.24 子贡问曰:"乡人皆好之,何如?"子曰:"未可也⑴。""乡人皆恶之,何如?"子曰:"未可也;不如乡人之善者好之,其不善者恶之。"

【译文】子贡问道:"满乡村的人都喜欢他,这个人怎么样?"孔子道:"还不行。"子贡便又道:"满乡村的人都厌恶他,这个人怎么样?"孔子道:"还不行。最好是满乡村的好人都喜欢他,满乡村的坏人都厌恶他。"

【注释】

⑴未可也——如果一乡之人皆好之,便近乎所谓好好先生,孔孟叫他为"乡愿"。因之孔子便说:"众好之,必察焉;众恶之,必察焉。"(15.28)又说:"唯仁者能好人,能恶人。"(4.3)这可以为"善者好之,不善者恶之"的解释。

13.25 子曰:"君子易事⑴而难说也。说之不以道,不说也;及其使人也,器之。小人难事而易说也。说之虽不以道,说也;及其使人也,求备焉。"

【译文】孔子说:"在君子底下工作很容易,讨他的欢喜却难。不用正当的方式去讨他的欢喜,他不会欢喜的;等到他使用人的时候,却衡量各人的才德去分配任务。在小人底下工作很难,讨他的欢喜却容易。用不正当的方式去讨他的欢喜,他会欢喜的;等到他使用人的时候,便会百般挑剔,求全责备。"

【注释】

⑴易事——《说苑•雅言篇》说:"曾子曰:'夫子见人之一善而忘其百

非,是夫子之易事也。'"这话可以作"君子易事"的一个说明。

13.26 子曰:"君子泰而不骄[1],小人骄而不泰。"

【译文】孔子说:"君子安详舒泰,却不骄傲凌人;小人骄傲凌人,却不安详舒泰。"

【注释】

[1]泰,骄——皇侃《义疏》云:"君子坦荡荡,心貌怡平,是泰而不为骄慢也;小人性好轻凌,而心恒戚戚,是骄而不泰也。"李塨《论语传注》云:"君子无众寡,无小大,无敢慢(见20.2),何其舒泰!小人矜己傲物,惟恐失尊,何其骄侈,而安得泰?"译文正取此义。

13.27 子曰:"刚、毅、木、讷近仁。"

【译文】孔子说:"刚强、果决、朴质而言语不轻易出口,有这四种品德的人近于仁德。"

13.28 子路问曰:"何如斯可谓之士矣?"子曰:"切切偲偲[1],怡怡[2]如也,可谓士矣。朋友切切偲偲,兄弟怡怡。"

【译文】子路问道:"怎么样才可以叫做'士'了呢?"孔子道:"互相批评,和睦共处,可以叫做'士'了。朋友之间,互相批评;兄弟之间,和睦共处。"

【注释】
(1)切切偲偲——偲音思，sī。切切偲偲，互相责善的样子。
(2)怡怡——和顺的样子。

13.29 子曰："善人教民七年，亦可以即戎⁽¹⁾矣。"

【译文】孔子说："善人教导人民达七年之久，也能够叫他们作战了。"
【注释】
(1)即戎——"即"是"即位"的"即"，就也，往那里去的意思。"戎"是"兵戎"的意思。

13.30 子曰："以不教民⁽¹⁾战，是谓弃之。"

【译文】孔子道："用未经受过训练的人民去作战，这等于糟踏生命。"
【注释】
(1)不教民——"不教民"三字构成一个名词语，意思就是"不教之民"，正如《诗经·邶风·柏舟》"心之忧矣，如匪浣衣"的"匪浣衣"一样，意思就是"匪浣之衣"（不曾洗涤过的衣服）。

宪问篇第十四

共四十四章

宪问篇第十四

14.1 宪问耻。子曰:"邦有道,谷;邦无道,谷,耻也。""克、伐、怨、欲不行焉,可以为仁矣[1]?"子曰:"可以为难矣,仁则吾不知也。"

【译文】原宪问如何叫耻辱。孔子道:"国家政治清明,做官领薪俸;国家政治黑暗,做官领薪俸,这就是耻辱。"原宪又道:"好胜、自夸、怨恨和贪心四种毛病都不曾表现过,这可以说是仁人了吗?"孔子道:"可以说是难能可贵的了,若说是仁人,那我不能同意。"

【注释】
[1]可以为仁矣——这句话从形式上看应是肯定句,但从上下文看,实际应是疑问句,不过疑问只从说话者的语势来表示,不借助于别的表达形式而已。这一段可以和"邦有道,贫且贱焉,耻也;邦无道,富且贵焉,耻也"(8.13)互相发明。

14.2 子曰:"士而怀居[1],不足以为士矣。"

【译文】孔子说:"读书人而留恋安逸,便不配做读书人了。"

【注释】
[1]怀居——怀,怀思,留恋;居,安居。《左传》僖公二十三年记载着

晋文公的流亡故事，说他在齐国安居下来，有妻妾，有家财，便不肯再移动了。他老婆姜氏便对他说："行也！怀与安，实败名。"便和此意相近。

14.3 子曰："邦有道，危⁽¹⁾言危行；邦无道，危行言孙⁽²⁾。"

【译文】孔子说："政治清明，言语正直，行为正直；政治黑暗，行为正直，言语谦顺。"

【注释】
(1)危——《礼记·缁衣》注："危，高峻也。"意谓高于俗，朱熹《集注》用之，固然可通。但《广雅》云："危，正也。"王念孙《疏证》即引《论语》此文来作证，更为恰当，译文即用此解。
(2)孙——同逊。

14.4 子曰："有德者必有言，有言者不必有德。仁者必有勇，勇者不必有仁。"

【译文】孔子说："有道德的人一定有名言，但有名言的人不一定有道德。仁人一定勇敢，但勇敢的人不一定仁。"

14.5 南宫适⁽¹⁾问于孔子曰："羿⁽²⁾善射，奡⁽³⁾荡舟⁽⁴⁾，俱不得其死然。禹稷躬稼而有天下。"夫子不答。南宫适出，子曰："君子哉若人！尚德哉若人⁽⁵⁾！"

【译文】南宫适向孔子问道:"羿擅长射箭,奡擅长水战,都没有得到好死。禹和稷自己下地种田,却得到了天下。[怎样解释这些历史?]"孔子没有答复。南宫适退了出来。孔子道:"这个人,好一个君子!这个人,多么尊尚道德!"

【注释】

(1)南宫适——孔子学生南容。

(2)羿——音诣,yì。在古代传说中有三个羿,都是射箭能手。一为帝喾的射师,见于《说文》;二为唐尧时人,传说当时十个太阳同时出现,羿射落了九个,见《淮南子·本经训》;三为夏代有穷国的君主,见《左传》襄公四年。这里所指的和《孟子·离娄篇》所载的"逄蒙学射于羿"的羿,据说都是夏代的羿。

(3)奡——音傲,ào,也是古代传说中的人物,夏代寒浞的儿子。字又作"浇"。

(4)荡舟——顾炎武《日知录》云:"古人以左右冲杀为荡。陈其锐卒,谓之跳荡;别帅谓之荡主。荡舟盖兼此义。"译成现代汉语,就是用舟师冲锋陷阵。

(5)君子……尚德哉若人——南宫适托古代的事来问孔子,中心思想是当今尚力不尚德,但按之历史,尚力者不得善终,尚德者终有天下。因之孔子称赞他。

14.6 子曰:"君子(1)而不仁者有矣夫,未有小人(1)而仁者也。"

【译文】孔子说:"君子之中不仁的人有的罢,小人之中却不会有仁人。"

【注释】

(1)君子、小人——这个"君子""小人"的含义不大清楚。"君子""小人"若指有德者无德者而言,则第二句可以不说;看来,这里似乎是指在位者和老百姓而言。

14.7 子曰:"爱之,能勿劳乎⑴?忠焉,能勿诲乎?"

【译文】孔子说:"爱他,能不叫他劳苦吗?忠于他,能够不教诲他吗?"

【注释】

⑴能勿劳乎——《国语•鲁语下》说:"夫民劳则思,思则善心生;逸则淫,淫则忘善,忘善则恶心生。"可以为"能勿劳乎"的注脚。

14.8 子曰:"为命⑴,裨谌⑵草创之,世叔⑶讨论⑷之,行人子羽⑸修饰之,东里子产⑹润色之。"

【译文】孔子说:"郑国外交辞令的创制,裨谌拟稿,世叔提意见,外交官子羽修改,子产作文词上的加工。"

【注释】

⑴为命——《左传》襄公三十一年云:"郑国将有诸侯之事,子产乃问四国之为于子羽,且使多为辞令,与裨谌乘以适野,使谋可否,而告冯简子使断之。事成,乃授子太叔使行之,以应对宾客,是以鲜有败事。"可与《论语》此文相参校。《左传》所讲的过程和《论语》此文虽然有些出入,但主题是相同的,因此我把"命"译为"外交辞令",不作一般的政令讲。

⑵裨谌——音庇臣,bìchén,郑国大夫,见《左传》。

⑶世叔——即《左传》的子太叔(古代,"太"和"世"两字通用),名游吉。

(4)讨论——意义和今天的"讨论"不同,这是一个人去研究而后提意见的意思。

(5)行人子羽——行人,官名,即古代的外交官。子羽,公孙挥的字。

(6)东里子产——东里,地名,今在郑州市,子产所居。

14.9 或问子产。子曰:"惠人也。"问子西[1]。曰:"彼哉!彼哉[2]!"问管仲。曰:"人也。夺伯氏[3]骈邑[4]三百,饭疏食,没齿无怨言。"

【译文】有人向孔子问子产是怎样的人物。孔子道:"是宽厚慈惠的人。"又问到子西。孔子道:"他呀,他呀!"又问到管仲。孔子道:"他是人才。剥夺了伯氏骈邑三百户的采地,使伯氏只能吃粗粮,到死没有怨恨的话。"

【注释】

(1)子西——春秋时有三个子西,一是郑国的公孙夏,生当鲁襄公之世,为子产的同宗兄弟,子产便是继他而主持郑国政治的。二是楚国的斗宜申,生当鲁僖公、文公之世。三是楚国的公子申,和孔子同时。斗宜申去孔子太远,公子申又太近,这人所问的当是公孙夏。

(2)彼哉彼哉——《公羊传》定公八年记载阳虎谋杀季孙的事,说阳虎谋杀未成,在郊外休息,忽然望见公敛处父领着追兵而来,便道:"彼哉彼哉!"毛奇龄《论语稽求篇》因云:"此必古成语,而夫子引以作答者。"案:这是当时表示轻视的习惯语。

(3)伯氏——齐国的大夫,皇侃《义疏》云:"伯氏名偃。"不知何据。

(4)骈邑——地名。阮元曾得伯爵彝,说是乾隆五十六年出土于山东临朐县柳山寨。他在《积古斋钟鼎彝器款识》里说,柳山寨有古城的城基,即春秋的骈邑。用《水经·巨洋水·注》证之,阮氏之言很可信。

14.10 子曰:"贫而无怨难,富而无骄易。"

【译文】孔子说:"贫穷却没有怨恨,很难;富贵却不骄傲,倒容易做到。"

14.11 子曰:"孟公绰⁽¹⁾为赵魏老⁽²⁾则优⁽³⁾,不可以为滕、薛⁽⁴⁾大夫。"

【译文】孔子说:"孟公绰,若是叫他做晋国诸卿赵氏、魏氏的家臣,那是力有余裕的;却没有才能来做滕、薛这样小国的大夫。"

【注释】
(1)孟公绰——鲁国大夫,《左传》襄公二十五年记载着他的一段事。《史记·仲尼弟子列传》说他是孔子所尊敬的人。
(2)老——古代,大夫的家臣称老,也称室老。
(3)优——本意是"优裕",所以用"力有余裕"来译它。
(4)滕、薛——当时的小国,都在鲁国附近。滕的故城在今山东滕县西南十五里,薛的故城在今滕县南四十四里官桥公社处。

14.12 子路问成人。子曰:"若臧武仲⁽¹⁾之知,公绰之不欲,卞庄子⁽²⁾之勇,冉求之艺,文之以礼乐,亦可以为成人矣。"曰:"今之成人者何必然?见利思义,见危授命,久要⁽³⁾不忘平生之言,亦可以为成人矣。"

【译文】子路问怎样才是全人。孔子道:"智慧像臧武仲,清心寡欲像孟公绰,勇敢像卞庄子,多才多艺像冉求,再用礼乐来成就他的文采,也可以说是全人了。"等了一会,又道:"现在的全人哪里一定要这样?看见利益便能想起该得不该得,遇到危险便肯付出生命,经过长久的穷困日子都不忘记平日的诺言,也可以说是全人了。"

【注释】

(1)臧武仲——鲁大夫臧孙纥。他很聪明,逃到齐国之后,能预见齐庄公的被杀而设法辞去庄公给他的田。事见《左传》襄公二十三年。

(2)卞庄子——鲁国的勇士。《荀子·大略篇》和《韩诗外传》卷十都载有他的勇敢故事。

(3)久要——"要"为"约"的借字,"约",穷困之意。说见杨遇夫先生的《积微居小学述林》。

14.13 子问公叔文子[1]于公明贾[2]曰:"信乎,夫子不言,不笑,不取乎?"公明贾对曰:"以[3]告者过也。夫子时然后言,人不厌其言;乐然后笑,人不厌其笑;义然后取,人不厌其取。"子曰:"其然?岂其然乎?"

【译文】孔子向公明贾问到公叔文子,说:"他老人家不言语,不笑,不取,是真的吗?"公明贾答道:"这是传话的人说错了。他老人家到应说话的时候才说话,别人不厌恶他的话;高兴了才笑,别人不厌恶他的笑;应该取才取,别人不厌恶他的取。"孔子道:"如此的吗?难道真是如此的吗?"

【注释】

(1)公叔文子——卫国大夫,《檀弓》载有他的故事。

(2)公明贾——卫人,姓公明,名贾。贾音假,jiǎ。《左传》哀公十四年楚有芋贾也音假。

(3)以——代词,此也。例证可参考杨遇夫先生的《词诠》。

14.14 子曰:"臧武仲以防求为后于鲁⁽¹⁾,虽曰不要⁽²⁾君,吾不信也。"

【译文】孔子说:"臧武仲[逃到齐国之前,]凭借着他的采邑防城请求立其子弟嗣为鲁国卿大夫,纵然有人说他不是要挟,我是不相信的。"
【注释】
(1)臧武仲以防求为后于鲁——事见《左传》襄公二十三年。防,臧武仲的封邑,在今山东费县东北六十里之华城,离齐国边境很近。
(2)要——平声,音腰,yāo。

14.15 子曰:"晋文公⁽¹⁾谲⁽²⁾而不正,齐桓公⁽¹⁾正而不谲。"

【译文】孔子说:"晋文公诡诈好耍手段,作风不正派;齐桓公作风正派,不用诡诈,不耍手段。"
【注释】
(1)晋文公、齐桓公——晋文公名重耳,齐桓公名小白。齐桓、晋文是春秋时五霸中最有名声的两个霸主。
(2)谲——音决,jué,欺诈,玩弄权术阴谋。

14.16 子路曰:"桓公杀公子纠,召忽死之,管仲不死⁽¹⁾。"曰:"未仁乎?"子曰:"桓公九合⁽²⁾诸侯,不以兵车,管仲之力也。如其仁,如其仁⁽³⁾。"

【译文】子路道:"齐桓公杀了他哥哥公子纠,[公子纠的师傅]召忽因此自杀,[但是他的另一师傅]管仲却活着。"接着又道:"管仲该不是有仁德的吧?"孔子道:"齐桓公多次地主持诸侯间的盟会,停止了战争,都是管仲的力量。这就是管仲的仁德,这就是管仲的仁德。"

【注释】
(1)管仲不死——齐桓公和公子纠都是齐襄公的弟弟。齐襄公无道,两人都怕牵累,桓公便由鲍叔牙侍奉逃往莒国,公子纠也由管仲和召忽侍奉逃往鲁国。襄公被杀以后,桓公先入齐国,立为君,便兴兵伐鲁,逼迫鲁国杀了公子纠,召忽自杀以殉,管仲却做了桓公的宰相。这段历史可看《左传》庄公八年和九年。
(2)九合——齐桓公纠合诸侯共计十一次,这一"九"字实是虚数,不过表示其多罢了。
(3)如其仁——王引之《经传释词》云:"如犹乃也。"扬雄《法言》三次仿用这种句法,义同。

14.17 子贡曰:"管仲非仁者与?桓公杀公子纠,不能死,又相之。"子曰:"管仲相桓公,霸诸侯,一匡天下,民到于今受其赐。微⁽¹⁾管仲,吾其被⁽²⁾发左衽矣。岂若匹夫匹妇之为谅也,自经⁽³⁾于沟渎⁽⁴⁾而莫之知也?"

【译文】子贡道:"管仲不是仁人罢?桓公杀掉了公子纠,他不但不以身殉难,还去辅相他。"孔子道:"管仲辅相桓公,称霸诸侯,使天下一切得到匡正,人民到今天还受到他的好处。假若没有管仲,我们都会披散着头发,衣襟向左边开,[沦为落后民族]了。他难道要像普通老百姓一样守着小节小信,在山沟中自杀,还没有人知道的吗?"

【注释】

(1)微——假若没有的意思,只用于和既成事实相反的假设句之首。
(2)被——同"披"。
(3)自经——自缢。
(4)沟渎——犹《孟子·梁惠王》的"沟壑"。王夫之《四书稗疏》认为它是地名,就是《左传》的"句渎",《史记》的"笙渎",那么,孔子的匹夫匹妇就是指召忽而言,恐不可信。

14.18 公叔文子之臣大夫[1]僎与文子同升诸[2]公。子闻之,曰:"可以为'文'[3]矣。"

【译文】公叔文子的家臣大夫僎,[由于文子的推荐,]和文子一道做了国家的大臣。孔子知道这事,便道:"这便可以谥为'文'了。"

【注释】

(1)毛奇龄《四书剩言》云:"臣大夫即家大夫也。"把"臣大夫"三字不分,今不取。《后汉书·吴良传》李贤《注》说:"文子家臣名僎"云云,也可见唐初人不以"臣大夫"为一词。
(2)诸——用法同"于"。
(3)据《礼记·檀弓》,公叔文子实谥为贞惠文子。郑玄《礼记注》说:"不言'贞惠'者,'文'足以兼之。"

14.19 子言卫灵公之无道也,康子曰:"夫如是,奚而[1]不丧？"孔子曰："仲叔圉⁽²⁾治宾客，祝鮀治宗庙，王孙贾治军旅。夫如是，奚其丧？"

【译文】孔子讲到卫灵公的昏乱，康子道："既然这样，为什么不败亡？"孔子道："他有仲叔圉接待宾客，祝鮀管理祭祀，王孙贾统率军队，像这样，怎么会败亡？"

【注释】
⑴奚而——俞樾《群经平议》云："奚而犹奚为也。"
⑵仲叔圉——就是孔文子。

14.20 子曰："其言之不怍，则为之也难。"

【译文】孔子说："那个人大言不惭，他实行就不容易。"

14.21 陈成子⁽¹⁾弑简公⁽²⁾。孔子沐浴而朝⁽³⁾，告于哀公曰："陈恒弑其君，请讨之⁽⁴⁾。"公曰："告夫三子！"孔子曰⁽⁵⁾："以吾从大夫之后，不敢不告也。君曰'告夫三子'者！"之三子告，不可。孔子曰："以吾从大夫之后，不敢不告也。"

【译文】陈恒杀了齐简公。孔子斋戒沐浴而后朝见鲁哀公，报告道："陈恒杀了他的君主，请你出兵讨伐他。"哀公道："你向季孙、仲孙、孟孙三人去报告罢！"孔子〔退了出来，〕道："因为我曾忝为大夫，不敢不来报告，但是君上却对我说，'给那三人报告吧'！"孔子又去报告三位大臣,不肯出兵。孔子道:"因为我曾忝为大夫,不敢不报告。"

【注释】

(1)陈成子——就是陈恒。

(2)简公——齐简公,名壬。

(3)孔子沐浴而朝——这时孔子已经告老还家,特为这事来朝见鲁君。

(4)请讨之——孔子请讨陈恒,主要是由于陈恒以臣杀君,依孔子的学说,非讨不可。同时孔子也估计了战争的胜负。《左传》记载着孔子的话道:"陈恒弑其君,民之不与者半。以鲁之众加齐之半,可克也。"但这事仍可讨论。

(5)孔子曰——这是孔子退朝后的话,参校《左传》哀公十四年的记载便可以知道。

14.22 子路问事君。子曰:"勿欺也,而犯之。"

【译文】子路问怎样服侍人君。孔子道:"不要〔阳奉阴违地〕欺骗他,却可以〔当面〕触犯他。"

14.23 子曰:"君子上达(1),小人下达(1)。"

【译文】孔子说:"君子通达于仁义,小人通达于财利。"

【注释】

(1)上达、下达——古今学人各有解释,译文采取了皇侃《义疏》的说法。

14.24 子曰:"古之学者为己[1],今之学者为人[1]。"

【译文】孔子说:"古代学者的目的在修养自己的学问道德,现代学者的目的却在装饰自己,给别人看。"

【注释】

[1]为己、为人——如何叫做"为己"和"为人",译文采用了《荀子·劝学篇》、《北堂书钞》所引《新序》和《后汉书·桓荣传论》(俱见杨遇夫先生《论语疏证》)的解释。

14.25 蘧伯玉[1]使人于孔子。孔子与之坐而问焉,曰:"夫子何为?"对曰:"夫子欲寡其过[2]而未能也。"使者出。子曰"使乎!使乎!"

【译文】蘧伯玉派一位使者访问孔子。孔子给他座位,而后问道:"他老人家干些什么?"使者答道:"他老人家想减少过错却还没能做到。"使者辞了出来。孔子道:"好一位使者!好一位使者!"

【注释】

[1]蘧伯玉——卫国的大夫,名瑗。孔子在卫国之时,曾经住过他家。

[2]寡其过——《庄子·则阳篇》说:"蘧伯玉行年六十而六十化,未尝不始于是之,而卒诎之以非也;或未知今之所谓是之非五十九非也(六十之是或为五十九之非)。"《淮南子·原道篇》也说:"蘧伯玉年五十而知四十九年非。"大概这人是位求进甚急善于改过的人。使者之言既得其实,又不卑不亢,所以孔子连声称赞。

14.26 子曰:"不在其位,不谋其政⁽¹⁾。"曾子曰:"君子思不出其位。"

【译文】曾子说:"君子所思虑的不超出自己的工作岗位。"
【注释】
⑴见《泰伯篇》。

14.27 子曰:"君子耻其言而⁽¹⁾过其行。"

【译文】孔子说:"说得多,做得少,君子以为耻。"
【注释】
⑴而——用法同"之",说详《词诠》。皇侃所据本,日本足利本,这一"而"字都作"之"。

14.28 子曰:"君子道者三,我无能焉:仁者不忧,知者不惑,勇者不惧。"子贡曰:"夫子自道也。"

【译文】孔子说:"君子所行的三件事,我一件也没能做到:仁德的人不忧愁,智慧的人不迷惑,勇敢的人不惧怕。"子贡道:"这正是他老人家对自己的叙述哩。"

14.29 子贡方人⁽¹⁾。子曰:"赐也贤乎哉?夫我则不暇。"

【译文】子贡讥评别人。孔子对他道:"你就够好了吗?我却没有这闲工夫。"

【注释】

⑴方人——《经典释文》说,郑玄注的《论语》作"谤人",又引郑《注》云"谓言人之过恶"。因此译文译为"讥评"。《世说新语·容止篇》:"或以方谢仁祖不乃重者。"这"方"字作品评解,其用法可能出于此。

14.30 子曰:"不患人之不己知,患其不能也。"

【译文】孔子说:"不着急别人不知道我,只着急自己没有能力。"

14.31 子曰:"不逆诈,不亿不信,抑亦先觉者,是贤乎!"

【译文】孔子说:"不预先怀疑别人的欺诈,也不无根据地猜测别人的不老实,却能及早发觉,这样的人是一位贤者罢!"

14.32 微生亩⑴谓孔子曰:"丘何为是⑵栖栖者与?无乃为佞乎?"孔子曰:"非敢为佞也,疾固也。"

【译文】微生亩对孔子道:"你为什么这样忙忙碌碌的呢?不是要逞你的口才吗?"孔子道:"我不是敢逞口才,而是讨厌那种顽固不通的人。"

【注释】

(1)微生亩——"微生"是姓,"亩"是名。

(2)是——这里作副词用,当"如此"解。

14.33 子曰:"骥不称其力,称其德也。"

【译文】孔子说:"称千里马叫做骥,并不是赞美它的气力,而是赞美它的品质。"

14.34 或曰:"以德报怨[1],何如?"子曰:"何以报德?以直报怨,以德报德。"

【译文】有人对孔子道:"拿恩惠来回答怨恨,怎么样?"孔子道:"拿什么来酬答恩惠呢?拿公平正直来回答怨恨,拿恩惠来酬答恩惠。"

【注释】

(1)以德报怨——《老子》也说:"大小多少,报怨以德。"可能当日流行此语。

14.35 子曰:"莫我知也夫!"子贡曰:"何为其莫知子也?"子曰:"不怨天,不尤人,下学而上达[1]。知我者其天乎!"

【译文】孔子叹道:"没有人知道我呀!"子贡道:"为什

么没有人知道您呢？"孔子道："不怨恨天，不责备人，学习一些平常的知识，却透彻了解很高的道理。知道我的，只是天罢！"

【注释】

(1)下学而上达——这句话具体的意义是什么，古今颇有不同解释，译文所言只能备参考。皇侃《义疏》云："下学，学人事；上达，达天命。我既学人事，人事有否有泰，故不尤人。上达天命，天命有穷有通，故我不怨天也。"全部意思都贯通了，虽不敢说合于孔子本意，无妨录供参考。

14.36 公伯寮[1]愬[2]子路于季孙。子服景伯[3]以告，曰："夫子固有惑志于公伯寮，吾力犹能肆诸市朝[4]。"子曰："道之将行也与，命也；道之将废也与，命也。公伯寮其如命何！"

【译文】公伯寮向季孙毁谤子路。子服景伯告诉孔子，并且说："他老人家已经被公伯寮所迷惑了，可是我的力量还能把他的尸首在街头示众。"孔子道："我的主张将实现吗，听之于命运；我的主张将永不实现吗，也听之于命运。公伯寮能把我的命运怎样呢！"

【注释】

(1)公伯寮——《史记·仲尼弟子列传》作"公伯僚"云"字子周"。

(2)愬——同"诉"。

(3)子服景伯——鲁大夫，名何。

(4)市朝——古人把罪人之尸示众，或者于朝廷，或者于市集。

14.37 子曰:"贤者辟⁽¹⁾世,其次辟地,其次辟色,其次辟言。"子曰:"作者七人矣。"

【译文】孔子说:"有些贤者逃避恶浊社会而隐居,次一等的择地而处,再次一等的避免不好的脸色,再次一等的回避恶言。"孔子又说:"像这样的人已经有七位了。"

【注释】
⑴辟——同"避"。

14.38 子路宿于石门⁽¹⁾。晨门曰:"奚自?"子路曰:"自孔氏。"曰:"是知其不可而为之者与?"

【译文】子路在石门住了一宵,〔第二天清早进城,〕司门者道:"从哪儿来?"子路道:"从孔家来。"司门者道:"就是那位知道做不到却定要去做的人吗?"

【注释】
⑴石门——《后汉书·张皓王龚传论》注引郑玄《论语注》云:"石门,鲁城外门也。"

14.39 子击磬于卫,有荷蒉而过孔氏之门者,曰:"有心哉,击磬乎!"既而曰:"鄙哉,硁硁乎!莫己知也,斯己而已矣。深则厉,浅则揭⁽¹⁾。"子曰:"果哉!末之难矣。"

【译文】孔子在卫国,一天正敲着磬,有一个挑着草筐子的汉子恰在门前走过,便说道:"这个敲磬是有深意的呀!"等一会又说道:"磬声硁硁的,可鄙呀![它好像在说,没有人知道我呀!]没有人知道自己,这就罢休好了。水深,索性连衣裳走过去;水浅,无妨撩起衣裳走过去。"孔子道:"好坚决!没有办法说服他了。"

【注释】

(1)深厉浅揭——两句见于《诗经•邶风•匏有苦叶》。这是比喻。水深比喻社会非常黑暗,只得听之任之;水浅比喻黑暗的程度不深,还可以使自己不受沾染,便无妨撩起衣裳,免得濡湿。

14.40 子张曰:"《书》云:'高宗谅阴[1],三年不言。'何谓也?"子曰:"何必高宗,古之人皆然。君薨,百官总己以听于冢宰三年。"

【译文】子张道:"《尚书》说:'殷高宗守孝,住在凶庐,三年不言语。'这是什么意思?"孔子道:"不仅仅高宗,古人都是这样:国君死了,继承的君王三年不问政治,各部门的官员听命于宰相。"

【注释】

(1)谅阴——居丧时所住的房子,又叫"凶庐"。两语见《无逸篇》。

14.41 子曰:"上好礼,则民易使也。"

【译文】孔子说:"在上位的人若遇事依礼而行,就容易使百姓听从指挥。"

14.42 子路问君子。子曰:"修己以敬。"曰:"如斯而已乎?"曰:"修己以安人(1)。"曰:"如斯而已乎?"曰:"修己以安百姓。修己以安百姓(2),尧舜其犹病诸?"

【译文】子路问怎样才能算是一个君子。孔子道:"修养自己来严肃认真地对待工作。"子路道:"这样就够了吗?"孔子道:"修养自己来使上层人物安乐。"子路道:"这样就够了吗?"孔子道:"修养自己来使所有老百姓安乐。修养自己来使所有老百姓安乐,尧舜大概还没有完全做到哩!"

【注释】

(1)人——这个"人"字显然是狭义的"人"(参见1.5注4),没有把"百姓"包括在内。

(2)修己以安百姓——《雍也篇》说:"博施于民……尧舜其犹病诸。"(6.30)这里说:"修己以安百姓,尧舜其犹病诸。"可见这里的"修己以安百姓"就是"博施于民"。

14.43 原壤(1)夷俟(2)。子曰:"幼而不孙弟(3),长而无述焉,老而不死,是为贼。"以杖叩其胫。

【译文】原壤两腿像八字一样张开坐在地上,等着孔子。孔子骂道:"你幼小时候不懂礼节,长大了毫无贡献,老了还白吃粮食,真是个害人精。"说完,用拐杖敲了敲他的小腿。

【注释】

(1)原壤——孔子的老朋友,《礼记·檀弓》记载他一段故事,说他母亲死了,孔子去帮助他治丧,他却站在棺材上唱起歌来了,孔子也只好装作没听见。大概这人是一位另有主张而立意反对孔子的人。

(2)夷俟——夷,箕踞;俟,等待。

(3)孙弟——同逊悌。

14.44 阙党[1]童子将命。或问之曰:"益者与?"子曰:"吾见其居于位[2]也,见其与先生并行[3]也。非求益者也,欲速成者也。"

【译文】阙党的一个童子来向孔子传达信息。有人问孔子道:"这小孩是肯求上进的人吗?"孔子道:"我看见他[大模大样地]坐在位上,又看见他同长辈并肩而行。这不是个肯求上进的人,只是一个急于求成的人。"

【注释】

(1)阙党——顾炎武的《日知录》说:"《史记·鲁世家》'炀公筑茅阙门',盖阙门之下,其里即名阙里,夫子之宅在焉。亦谓之阙党。"案顾氏此说很对(阎若璩《四书释地》的驳论不对),《荀子·儒效篇》也有孔子"居于阙党"的记载,可见阙党为孔子所居之地名。

(2)居于位——根据《礼记·玉藻》的记载,"童子无事则立主人之北,南面",则"居于位"是不合当日礼节的。

(3)与先生并行——《礼记·曲礼》上篇说"五年以长,则肩随之"("肩随"就是与之并行而稍后),而童子的年龄相差甚远,依当日礼节,不能和成人并行。

卫灵公篇第十五

共四十二章

卫灵公篇第十五

15.1 卫灵公问陈[1]于孔子。孔子对曰:"俎豆之事[2],则尝闻之矣;军旅之事,未之学也。"明日遂行。

【译文】卫灵公向孔子问军队陈列之法。孔子答道:"礼仪的事情,我曾经听到过;军队的事情,从来没学习过。"第二天便离开卫国。

【注释】
(1)陈——就是今天的"阵"字。
(2)俎豆之事——俎和豆都是古代盛肉食的器皿,行礼时用它,因之借以表示礼仪之事。这种用法和《泰伯篇第八》的"笾豆之事"相同。

15.2 在陈绝粮,从者病,莫能兴。子路愠见曰:"君子亦有穷乎?"子曰:"君子固穷,小人穷斯滥矣。"

【译文】孔子在陈国断绝了粮食,跟随的人都饿病了,爬不起床来。子路很不高兴地来见孔子,说道:"君子也有穷得毫无办法的时候吗?"孔子道:"君子虽然穷,还是坚持着;小人一穷便无所不为了。"

15.3 子曰:"赐也,女以予为多学而识之者与?"对曰:

"然,非与?"曰:"非也,予一以贯之⑴。"

【译文】孔子道:"赐!你以为我是多多地学习又能够记得住的吗?"子贡答道:"对呀,难道不是这样吗?"孔子道:"不是的,我有一个基本观念来贯串它。"

【注释】

⑴一以贯之——这和《里仁篇》的"夫子之道,忠恕而已矣"(4.15)的"一贯"相同。从这里可以看出,子贡他们所重视的,是孔子的博学多才,因之认为他是"多学而识之";而孔子自己所重视的,则在于他的以忠恕之道贯穿于其整个学行之中。

15.4 子曰:"由!知德者鲜矣。"

【译文】孔子对子路道:"由!懂得'德'的人可少啦。"

15.5 子曰:"无为而治⑴者其舜也与?夫何为哉?恭己正南面而已矣。"

【译文】孔子说:"自己从容安静而使天下太平的人大概只有舜罢?他干了什么呢?庄严端正地坐朝廷罢了。"

【注释】

⑴无为而治——舜何以能如此?一般儒者都以为他能"所任得其人,故优游而自逸也"(《三国志•吴志•楼玄传》)。如《大戴礼•主言篇》云:"昔者舜左禹而右皋陶,不下席而天下治。"《新序•杂事三》云:"故王者劳于求人,佚于得贤。舜举众贤在位,垂衣裳恭己无为而天下治。"赵岐《孟子注》也说:"言任官得其人,故无为而治。"

15.6 子张问行。子曰:"言忠信,行笃敬,虽蛮貊之邦,行矣。言不忠信,行不笃敬,虽州里,行乎哉?立则见其参于前也,在舆则见其倚于衡也,夫然后行。"子张书诸绅。

【译文】子张问如何才能使自己到处行得通。孔子道:"言语忠诚老实,行为忠厚严肃,纵到了别的部族国家,也行得通。言语欺诈无信,行为刻薄轻浮,就是在本乡本土,能行得通吗?站立的时候,就〔仿佛〕看见'忠诚老实忠厚严肃'几个字在我们面前;在车厢里,也〔仿佛〕看见它刻在前面的横木上;〔时时刻刻记着它,〕这才能使自己到处行得通。"子张把这些话写在大带上。

15.7 子曰:"直哉史鱼(1)!邦有道,如矢;邦无道,如矢。君子哉蘧伯玉(2)!邦有道,则仕;邦无道,则可卷而怀之。"

【译文】孔子说:"好一个刚直不屈的史鱼!政治清明也像箭一样直,政治黑暗也像箭一样直。好一个君子蘧伯玉!政治清明就出来做官,政治黑暗就可以把自己的本领收藏起来。"

【注释】
(1)史鱼——卫国的大夫史䲡,字子鱼。他临死时嘱咐他的儿子,不要"治丧正室",以此劝告卫灵公进用蘧伯玉,斥退弥子瑕,古人叫为"尸谏",事见《韩诗外传》卷七。
(2)蘧伯玉——事可参见《左传》襄公十四年和二十六年。

15.8 子曰:"可与言而不与之言,失人;不可与言而与之言,失言。知者不失人,亦不失言。"

【译文】孔子说:"可以同他谈,却不同他谈,这是错过人才;不可以同他谈,却同他谈,这是浪费言语。聪明人既不错过人才,也不浪费言语。"

15.9 子曰:"志士仁人,无求生以害仁,有杀身以成仁。"

【译文】孔子说:"志士仁人,不贪生怕死因而损害仁德,只勇于牺牲来成全仁德。"

15.10 子贡问为仁。子曰:"工欲善其事,必先利其器。居是邦也,事其大夫之贤者,友其士⁽¹⁾之仁者。"

【译文】子贡问怎样去培养仁德。孔子道:"工人要搞好他的工作,一定先要搞好他的工具。我们住在一个国家,就要敬奉那些大官中的贤人,结交那些士人中的仁人。"

【注释】

⑴士——《论语》中的"士",有时指有一定修养的人,如"士志于道"(4.9)的"士"。有时指有一定社会地位的人,如"使于四方,不辱君命,可谓士矣"的"士"(13.20)。此处和"大夫"并言,可能是"士、大夫"之"士",即已做官而位置下于大夫的人。

15.11 颜渊问为邦。子曰:"行夏之时⑴,乘殷之辂⑵,服周之冕⑶,乐则《韶》《舞》⑷。放郑声⑸,远佞人。郑声淫,佞人殆。"

【译文】颜渊问怎样去治理国家。孔子道:"用夏朝的历法,坐殷朝的车子,戴周朝的礼帽,音乐就用《韶》和《武》。舍弃郑国的乐曲,斥退小人。郑国的乐曲靡曼淫秽,小人危险。"

【注释】

⑴行夏之时——据古史记载,夏朝用的自然历,以建寅之月(旧历正月)为每年的第一月,春、夏、秋、冬合乎自然现象。周朝则以建子之月(旧历十一月)为每年的第一月,而且以冬至日为元日。这个虽然在观测天象方面比较以前进步,但实用起来却不及夏历方便于农业生产。就是在周朝,也有很多国家是仍旧用夏朝历法。

⑵乘殷之辂——辂音路,商代的车子,比周代的车子自然朴质些。所以《左传》桓公二年也说:"大辂、越席,昭其俭也。"

⑶服周之冕——周代的礼帽自然又比以前的华美,孔子是不反对礼服的华美的,赞美禹"致美乎黻冕"可见。

⑷《韶》《舞》——《韶》是舜时的音乐,"舞"同"武",周武王时的音乐。

⑸放郑声——"郑声"和"郑诗"不同。郑诗指其文辞,郑声指其乐曲。说本明人杨慎《丹铅总录》、清人陈启源《毛诗稽古篇》。

15.12 子曰:"人无远虑,必有近忧。"

【译文】孔子说:"一个人没有长远的考虑,一定会有眼前的忧患。"

15.13 子曰:"已矣乎!吾未见好德如好色⑴者也。"

【译文】孔子说:"完了吧!我从没见过像喜欢美貌一般地喜欢美德的人哩。"

【注释】

(1)好色——据《史记·孔子世家》,孔子"居卫月余,灵公与夫人(南子)同车,宦者雍渠参乘出,使孔子为次乘,招摇市过之"。孔子因发这一感叹。

15.14 子曰:"臧文仲(1)其窃位者与!知柳下惠(2)之贤而不与立(3)也。"

【译文】孔子说:"臧文仲大概是个做官不管事的人,他明知柳下惠贤良,却不给他官位。"

【注释】

(1)臧文仲——鲁国的大夫臧孙辰,历仕庄、闵、僖、文四朝。
(2)柳下惠——鲁国贤者,本名展获,字禽,又叫展季。"柳下"可能是其所居,因以为号;据《列女传》,"惠"是由他的妻子的倡议给他的私谥(不由国家授予的谥号叫私谥)。
(3)立——同"位",说详俞樾《群经平议》。

15.15 子曰:"躬自厚(1)而薄责于人,则远怨矣。"

【译文】孔子说:"重责备自己,而轻责备别人,怨恨自然不会来了。"

【注释】

(1)躬自厚——本当作"躬自厚责","责"字探下文"薄责"之"责"而省略。说详拙著《文言语法》。"躬自"是一双音节的副词,和《诗经·卫风·氓》的"静言思之,躬自悼矣"的"躬自"用法一样。

15.16 子曰:"不曰'如之何⑴,如之何'者,吾末如之何也已矣。"

【译文】孔子说:"[一个人]不想想'怎么办,怎么办'的,对这种人,我也不知道怎么办了。"
【注释】
⑴如之何——"不曰如之何"意思就是不动脑筋。《荀子·大略篇》说:"天子即位,上卿进曰,如之何,忧之长也。"则说如之何的,便是深忧远虑的人。

15.17 子曰:"群居终日,言不及义,好行小慧,难矣哉!"

【译文】孔子说:"同大家整天在一块,不说一句有道理的话,只喜欢卖弄小聪明,这种人真难教导!"

15.18 子曰:"君子义以为质,礼以行之,孙以出之⑴,信以成之。君子哉!"

【译文】孔子说:"君子[对于事业],以合宜为原则,依礼节实行它,用谦逊的言语说出它,用诚实的态度完成它。真是位君子呀!"

【注释】

⑴孙以出之——"出"谓出言。何晏《论语集解》引郑玄《注》云:"孙以出之谓言语。"

15.19 子曰:"君子病无能焉,不病人之不己知也。"

【译文】孔子说:"君子只惭愧自己没有能力,不怨恨别人不知道自己。"

15.20 子曰:"君子疾没世而名不称焉。"

【译文】孔子说:"到死而名声不被人家称述,君子引以为恨。"

15.21 子曰:"君子求诸己,小人求诸人。"

【译文】孔子说:"君子要求自己,小人要求别人。"

15.22 子曰:"君子矜而不争,群而不党[1]。"

【译文】孔子说:"君子庄矜而不争执,合群而不闹宗派。"
【注释】

⑴群而不党——"群而不党"可能包含着"周而不比"(2•14)以及"和而不同"(13•23)两个意思。

15.23 子曰:"君子不以言举人,不以人废言。"

【译文】孔子说:"君子不因为人家一句话[说得好]便提拔他,不因为他是坏人而鄙弃他的好话。"

15.24 子贡问曰:"有一言而可以终身行之者乎?"子曰:"其恕⑴乎!己所不欲,勿施于人。"

【译文】子贡问道:"有没有一句可以终身奉行的话呢?"孔子道:"大概是'恕'罢!自己所不想要的任何事物,就不要加给别人。"

【注释】
⑴恕——"忠"(己欲立而立人,己欲达而达人)是有积极意义的道德,未必每个人都有条件来实行。"恕"只是"己所不欲,勿施于人",则谁都可以这样做,因之孔子在这里言"恕"不言"忠"。《礼记·大学》篇的"絜矩之道"就是"恕"道。可是在阶级社会里,也只能是幻想。

15.25 子曰:"吾之于人也,谁毁谁誉?如有所誉者,其有所试矣。斯民也,三代之所以直道而行也。"

【译文】孔子说:"我对于别人,诋毁了谁?称赞了谁?假若我有所称赞,必然是曾经考验过他的。夏、商、周三代的人都如此,所以三代能直道而行。"

15.26 子曰:"吾犹及史之阙文也。有马者借人乘之,今亡矣夫!"

【译文】孔子说:"我还能够看到史书存疑的地方。有马的人〔自己不会训练,〕先给别人使用,这种精神,今天也没有了吧!"

【注释】
"史之阙文"和"有马借人乘之",其间有什么关连,很难理解。包咸的《论语章句》和皇侃的《义疏》都把它们看成两件不相关的事。宋叶梦得《石林燕语》却根据《汉书·艺文志》的引文无"有马"等七个字,因疑这七个字是衍文。其他穿凿的解释很多,依我看来,还是把它看为两件事较妥当。又有人说这七字当作"有焉者晋人之乘"(见《诂经精舍六集》卷九方赞尧《有马者借人乘之解》),更是毫无凭据的臆测。

15.27 子曰:"巧言乱德。小不忍(1),则乱大谋。"

【译文】孔子说:"花言巧语足以败坏道德。小事情不忍耐,便会败坏大事情。"

【注释】
(1)小不忍——"小不忍"不仅是不忍小愤怒,也包括不忍小仁小恩,没有"蝮蛇螫手,壮士断腕"的勇气,也包括吝财不忍舍,以及见小利而贪。

15.28 子曰:"众恶之,必察焉(1);众好之,必察焉。"

【译文】孔子说:"大家厌恶他,一定要去考察;大家喜爱他,也一定要去考察。"

【注释】

(1)必察焉——《子路篇》有这样一段:"子贡问曰:'乡人皆好之,何如?'子曰:'未可也。''乡人皆恶之,何如?'子曰:'未可也。不如乡人之善者好之,其不善者恶之。'"(13.24)可以和这段话互相发明。

15.29 子曰:"人能弘道,非道弘人⑴。"

【译文】孔子说:"人能够把道廓大,不是用道来廓大人。"

【注释】

(1)这一章只能就字面来翻译,孔子的真意何在,又如何叫做"非道弘人",很难体会。朱熹曾经强为解释,而郑皓的《论语集注述要》却说,"此章最不烦解而最可疑",则我们也只好不加臆测。《汉书•董仲舒传》所载董仲舒的对策和《礼乐志》所载的平当对策都引此二句,都以为是治乱兴废在于人的意思,但细加思考,仍未必相合。

15.30 子曰:"过而不改,是谓过矣⑴。"

【译文】孔子说:"有错误而不改正,那个错误便真叫做错误了。"

【注释】

(1)是谓过矣——《韩诗外传》卷三曾引孔子的话说:"过而改之,是不过也。"

15.31 子曰:"吾尝终日不食,终夜不寝,以思,无益,不如学也。"

【译文】孔子说:"我曾经整天不吃,整晚不睡,去想,没有益处,不如去学习。"

15.32 子曰:"君子谋道不谋食。耕也,馁在其中矣;学也,禄在其中⁽¹⁾矣。君子忧道不忧贫。"

【译文】孔子说:"君子用心力于学术,不用心力于衣食。耕田,也常常饿着肚皮;学习,常常得到俸禄。君子只着急得不到道,不着急得不到财。"

【注释】
⑴禄在其中——这一章可以和"樊迟请学稼"章(13.4)结合着看。

15.33 子曰:"知及之⁽¹⁾,仁不能守之;虽得之,必失之。知及之,仁能守之。不庄以莅之,则民不敬。知及之,仁能守之,庄以莅之,动之不以礼,未善也。"

【译文】孔子说:"聪明才智足以得到它,仁德不能保持它;就是得到,一定会丧失。聪明才智足以得到它,仁德能保持它。不用严肃态度来治理百姓,百姓也不会认真[地生活和工作]。聪明才智足以得到它,仁德能保持它,能用严肃的态度来治理百姓,假若不合理合法地动员百姓,是不够好的。"

【注释】

⑴知及之——"知及之"诸"之"字究竟何指,原文未曾说出。以"不庄以莅之""动之不以礼"诸句来看,似是小则指卿大夫士的禄位,大则指天下国家。不然,不会涉及临民和动员人民的。

15.34 子曰:"君子不可小知而可大受也,小人不可大受而可小知也。"

【译文】孔子道:"君子不可以用小事情考验他,却可以接受重大任务;小人不可以接受重大任务,却可以用小事情考验他。"

15.35 子曰:"民之于仁也,甚于水火⑴。水火,吾见蹈而死者矣,未见蹈仁而死者也。"

【译文】孔子说:"百姓需要仁德,更急于需要水火。往水火里去,我看见因而死了的,却从没有看见践履仁德因而死了的。"

【注释】

⑴甚于水火——《孟子•尽心上》说:"民非水火不生活。"译文摘取此意,故加"需要"两字。

15.36 子曰:"当仁,不让于师。"

【译文】孔子说:"面临着仁德,就是老师,也不同他谦让。"

15.37 子曰:"君子贞⑴而不谅⑵。"

【译文】孔子说:"君子讲大信,却不讲小信。"
【注释】
⑴贞——《贾子·道术篇》云:"言行抱一谓之贞。"所以译文以"大信"译之。
⑵谅——朱骏声《说文通训定声》说这"谅"字假借为"勍",犹固执也。则他把这"贞"字解为《伪古文尚书·太甲》"万邦以贞"的"贞",正也。似不妥。

15.38 子曰:"事君,敬其事而后其食⑴。"

【译文】孔子说:"对待君上,认真工作,把拿俸禄的事放在后面。"
【注释】
⑴而后其食——据宋晁公武《郡斋读书志》的记载,蜀《石经》作"而后食其禄"。

15.39 子曰:"有教无类⑴。"

【译文】孔子说:"人人我都教育,没有〔贫富、地域等等〕区别。"
【注释】
⑴无类——"自行束脩以上,吾未尝无诲焉"(7.7),便是"有教无类。"

15.40 子曰:"道不同,不相为谋。"

【译文】孔子说:"主张不同,不互相商议。"

15.41 子曰:"辞达⑴而已矣。"

【译文】孔子说:"言辞,足以达意便罢了。"
【注释】
⑴辞达——可以和"文胜质则史"(6.18)参看。过于浮华的词藻,是孔子所不同意的。

15.42 师冕⑴见,及阶,子曰:"阶也。"及席,子曰:"席也。"皆坐,子告之曰:"某在斯,某在斯。"师冕出。子张问曰:"与师言之道与?"子曰:"然;固相师之道也。"

【译文】师冕来见孔子,走到阶沿,孔子道:"这是阶沿啦。"走到坐席旁,孔子道:"这是坐席啦。"都坐定了,孔子告诉他说:"某人在这里,某人在这里。"师冕辞了出来。子张问道:"这是同瞎子讲话的方式吗?"孔子道:"对的;这本来是帮助瞎子的方式。"
【注释】
⑴师冕——师,乐师,冕,这人之名。古代乐官一般用瞎子充当。

季氏篇第十六

共十四章

16.1 季氏将伐颛臾⁽¹⁾。冉有、季路见于孔子曰:"季氏将有事⁽²⁾于颛臾。"孔子曰:"求!无乃尔是过⁽³⁾与?夫颛臾,昔者先王以为东蒙⁽⁴⁾主,且在邦域之中矣,是社稷之臣也。何以伐为?"冉有曰:"夫子欲之,吾二臣者皆不欲也。"孔子曰:"求!周任⁽⁵⁾有言曰:'陈力就列,不能者止。'危而不持,颠而不扶,则将焉用彼相矣?且尔言过矣,虎兕出于柙,龟玉毁于椟中,是谁之过与?"冉有曰:"今夫颛臾,固而近于费⁽⁶⁾。今不取,后世必为子孙忧。"孔子曰:"求!君子疾夫舍曰欲之而必为之辞。丘也闻有国有家者,不患寡当作贫而患不均,不患贫当作寡而患不安⁽⁷⁾。盖均无贫,和无寡,安无倾。夫如是,故远人不服,则修文德以来之。既来之,则安之。今由与求也,相夫子,远人不服,而不能来也;邦分崩离析,而不能守也;而谋动干戈于邦内。吾恐季孙之忧,不在颛臾,而在萧墙之内⁽⁸⁾也。"

【译文】季氏准备攻打颛臾。冉有、子路两人谒见孔子,说道:"季氏准备对颛臾使用兵力。"孔子道:"冉求!这难道不应该责备你吗?颛臾,上代的君王曾经授权他主持东蒙山的祭祀,而且它的国境早在我们最初被封时的疆土之中,这正是和鲁国共安危存亡的藩属,为什么要去攻打它呢?"冉有道:"季孙要这么干,我们两人本来都是不同意的。"孔子道:"冉求!周任有句话说:'能够贡献自己的力量,这再任职；如果不行，就该辞职。'譬如瞎子遇到危险，不去扶持；将要摔倒了，不去搀扶，那又何必用助手呢？你的话是错了。老虎犀牛从槛里逃了出来，龟壳美玉在匣子里毁坏了，这是谁的责任呢？"冉有道："颛臾，城墙既然坚牢，而且离季孙的采邑费地很近。现今不把它占领，日子久了，一定会给子孙留下祸害。"孔子道："冉求！君子就讨厌[那种态度，]不说自己贪心无厌，却一定另找借口。我听说过：无论是诸侯或者大夫，不必着急财富不多，只需着急财富不均；不必着急人民太少，只需着急境内不安。若是财富平均，便无所谓贫穷；境内和平团结，便不会觉得人少；境内平安，便不会倾危。做到这样，远方的人还不归服，便再修仁义礼乐的政教来招致他们。他们来了，就得使他们安心。如今仲由和冉求两人辅相季孙，远方之人不归服，却不能招致；国家支离破碎，却不能保全；反而想在国境以内使用兵力。我恐怕季孙的忧愁不在颛臾，却在鲁君哩。"

【注释】

(1)颛臾——鲁国的附庸国家，现在山东省费县西北八十里有颛臾村，当是古颛臾之地。

(2)有事——《左传》成公十三年，"国之大事，在祀与戎"。这"有事"即指用兵。

(3)尔是过——不能解作"尔之过"，因为古代人称代词表示领位极少再加别的虚词的（像《尚书·康诰》"朕其弟小子封"只是极个别的例子）。这里"过"字可看作动词，"是"字是表示倒装之用的词，顺装便是"过尔"，"责备你""归罪于你"的意思。

(4)东蒙——即蒙山，在今山东蒙阴县南，接费县界。

(5)周任——古代的一位史官。

(6)费——音秘，bì，鲁国季氏采邑，今山东费县西南七十里有费城。

(7) 不患寡而患不均，不患贫而患不安——当作"不患贫而患不均，不患寡而患不安"，"贫"和"均"是从财富着眼，下文"均无贫"可以为证；"寡"和"安"是从人民着眼，下文"和无寡"可以为证。说详俞樾《群经平议》。

(8) 萧墙之内——"萧墙"是鲁君所用的屏风。人臣至此屏风，便会肃然起敬，所以叫做萧墙（萧字从肃得声）。"萧墙之内"指鲁君。当时季孙把持鲁国政治，和鲁君矛盾很大，也知道鲁君想收拾他以收回主权，因此怕颛臾凭借有利的地势起而帮助鲁国，于是要先下手为强，攻打颛臾。孔子这句话，深深地刺中了季孙的内心。

16.2 孔子曰："天下有道，则礼乐征伐自天子出；天下无道，则礼乐征伐自诸侯出。自诸侯出，盖十世希不失矣；自大夫出，五世希不失矣；陪臣执国命，三世希不失矣[1]。天下有道，则政不在大夫。天下有道，则庶人不议。"

【译义】孔子说："天下太平，制礼作乐以及出兵都决定于天子；天下昏乱，制礼作乐以及出兵便决定于诸侯。决定于诸侯，大概传到十代，很少还能继续的；决定于大夫，传到五代，很少还能继续的；若是大夫的家臣把持国家政权，传到三代很少还能继续的。天下太平，国家的最高政治权力就不会掌握在大夫之手。天下太平，老百姓就不会议论纷纷。"

【注释】

(1) 孔子这一段话可能是从考察历史，尤其是当日时事所得出的结论。"自天子出"，孔子认为尧、舜、禹、汤以及西周都如此的；"天下无道"则自齐桓公以后，周天子已无发号施令的力量了。齐自桓公称霸，历孝公、昭公、懿公、惠公、顷公、灵公、庄公、景公、悼公、简公十公,至简公而为陈恒所杀,孔子亲身见之;晋自文公称霸,历襄公、灵公、成公、景公、厉公、平公、昭公、顷公九公,六卿专权,也是孔子所亲见的。所以说"十世希不失"。鲁自季友专政,历文子、武子、平子、桓子而为阳虎所执,更是孔子所亲见的。所以说"五世希不失"。至于鲁季氏家臣南蒯、公山弗扰、阳虎之流都当身而败,不曾到过三世。当时各国家臣有专政的,孔子言"三世希不失",盖宽言之。这也是历史演变的必然,愈近变动时代,权力再分配的斗争,一定愈加激烈。这却是孔子所不明白的。

16.3 孔子曰:"禄之去公室五世[1]矣,政逮于大夫四世[1]矣,故夫三桓[2]之子孙微矣。"

【译文】孔子说:"国家政权离开了鲁君,[从鲁君来说,]已经五代了;政权到了大夫之手,[从季氏来说,]已经四代了,所以桓公的三房子孙现在也衰微了。"

【注释】

(1)五世、四世——自鲁君丧失政治权力到孔子说这段话的时候,经历了宣公、成公、襄公、昭公、定公五代;自季氏最初把持鲁国政治到孔子说这段话时,经历了文子、武子、平子、桓子四代。说本毛奇龄《论语稽求篇》。

(2)三桓——鲁国的三卿,仲孙(即孟孙)、叔孙、季孙都出于鲁桓公,故称"三桓"。

16.4 孔子曰:"益者三友,损者三友。友直,友谅[1],友多闻,益矣。友便辟,友善柔,友便佞,损矣。"

【译文】孔子说:"有益的朋友三种,有害的朋友三种。同正直的人交友,同信实的人交友,同见闻广博的人交友,便有益了。同谄媚奉承的人交友,同当面恭维背面毁谤的人交友,同夸夸其谈的人交友,便有害了。"

【注释】

⑴谅——《说文》:"谅,信也。""谅"和"信"有时意义相同,这里便如此。有时意义有别。如《宪问篇第十四》"岂若匹夫匹妇之为谅也"的"谅"只是"小信"的意思。

16.5 孔子曰:"益者三乐,损者三乐。乐节礼乐,乐道人之善,乐多贤友,益矣。乐骄乐,乐佚游,乐宴乐,损矣。"

【译文】孔子说:"有益的快乐三种,有害的快乐三种。以得到礼乐的调节为快乐,以宣扬别人的好处为快乐,以交了不少有益的朋友为快乐,便有益了。以骄傲为快乐,以游荡忘返为快乐,以饮食荒淫为快乐,便有害了。"

16.6 孔子曰:"侍于君子有三愆:言未及之而言谓之躁,言及之而不言谓之隐,未见颜色而言谓之瞽。"

【译文】孔子说:"陪着君子说话容易犯三种过失:没轮到他说话,却先说,叫做急躁;该说话了,却不说,叫做隐瞒;不看看君子的脸色便贸然开口,叫做瞎眼睛。"

16.7 孔子曰："君子有三戒：少之时，血气未定，戒之在色；及其壮也，血气方刚，戒之在斗；及其老也，血气既衰，戒之在得⑴。"

【译文】孔子说："君子有三件事情应该警惕戒备：年轻的时候，血气未定，便要警戒，莫迷恋女色；等到壮大了，血气正旺盛，便要警戒，莫好胜喜斗；等到年老了，血气已经衰弱，便要警戒，莫贪求无厌。"

【注释】

⑴孔安国《注》云："得，贪得。"所贪者可能包括名誉、地位、财货在内。《淮南子•诠言训》："凡人之性，少则猖狂，壮则强暴，老则好利。"意本于此章，而以"好利"释得，可能涵义太狭。

16.8 孔子曰："君子有三畏：畏天命，畏大人⑴，畏圣人之言。小人不知天命而不畏也，狎大人，侮圣人之言。"

【译文】孔子说："君子害怕的有三件事：怕天命，怕王公大人，怕圣人的言语。小人不懂得天命，因而不怕它；轻视王公大人，轻侮圣人的言语。"

【注释】

⑴大人——古代对于在高位的人叫"大人"，如《易•乾卦》"利见大人"，《礼记•礼运》"大人世及以为礼"，《孟子•尽心下》"说大人，则藐之"。对于有道德的人也可以叫"大人"，如《孟子•告子上》"从其大体为大人"。这里的"大人"是指在高位的人，而"圣人"则是指有道德的人。

16.9 孔子曰:"生而知之者上也,学而知之者次也;困而学之,又其次也;困而不学,民斯为下矣。"

【译文】孔子说:"生来就知道的是上等,学习然后知道的是次一等;实践中遇见困难,再去学它,又是再次一等;遇见困难而不学,老百姓就是这种最下等的了。"

16.10 孔子曰:"君子有九思:视思明,听思聪,色思温,貌思恭,言思忠,事思敬,疑思问,忿思难,见得思义。"

【译文】孔子说:"君子有九种考虑:看的时候,考虑看明白了没有,听的时候,考虑听清楚了没有;脸上的颜色,考虑温和么;容貌态度,考虑庄矜么;说的言语,考虑忠诚老实么;对待工作,考虑严肃认真么;遇到疑问,考虑怎样向人家请教;将发怒了,考虑有什么后患;看见可得的,考虑我是否应该得。"

16.11 孔子曰:"见善如不及,见不善如探汤。吾见其人矣,吾闻其语矣。隐居以求其志,行义以达其道。吾闻其语矣,未见其人也。"

【译文】孔子说:"看见善良,努力追求,好像赶不上似的;遇见邪恶,使劲避开,好像将伸手到沸水里。我看见这样的人,也听过这样的话。避世隐居求保全他的意志,依义而行来贯彻他的主张。我听过这样的话,却没有见过这样的人。"

16.12 齐景公有马千驷⑴，死之日，民无德而称焉。伯夷叔齐饿于首阳⑵之下，民到于今称之。其斯之谓与⑶？

【译文】齐景公有马四千匹，死了以后，谁都不觉得他有什么好行为可以称述。伯夷、叔齐两人饿死在首阳山下，大家到现在还称颂他。那就是这个意思吧！

【注释】

⑴千驷——古代一般用四匹马驾一辆车，所以一驷就是四匹马。《左传》哀公八年："鲍牧谓群公子曰：'使女有马千乘乎？'"这"千乘"就是景公所遗留的"千驷"。鲍牧用此来诱劝群公子争夺君位，可见"千乘"是一笔相当富厚的私产。

⑵首阳——山名，现在何地，古今传说纷歧，总之，已经难于确指。

⑶其斯之谓与——这一章既然没有"子曰"字样，而且"其斯之谓与"的上面无所承受，程颐以为《颜渊篇第十二》的"诚不以富，亦只以异"两句引文应该放在此处"其斯之谓与"之上，但无证据。朱熹《答江德功书》云："此章文势或有断续，或有阙文，或非一章，皆不可考。"

16.13 陈亢⑴问于伯鱼曰："子亦有异闻乎？"对曰："未也。尝独立，鲤趋而过庭。曰：'学诗乎？'对曰：'未也。''不学诗，无以言。'鲤退而学诗。他日，又独立，鲤趋而过庭。曰：'学礼乎？'对曰：'未也。''不学礼，无以立。'鲤退而学礼。闻斯二者。"陈亢退而喜曰："问一得三，闻诗，闻礼，又闻君子之远其子也。"

【译文】陈亢向孔子的儿子伯鱼问道："您在老师那儿，也得着与众不同的传授吗？"答道："没有。他曾经一个人站在庭中，我恭敬地走过。他问我道：'学诗没有？'我道：'没有。'他便道：'不学诗就不会说话。'我退回便学诗。过了几天，他又一个人站在庭中，我又恭敬地走过。他问道：'学礼没有？'我答：'没有。'他道：'不学礼，便没有立足社会的依据。'我退回便学礼。只听到这两件。"陈亢回去非常高兴地道："我问一件事，知道了三件事。知道诗，知道礼，又知道君子对他儿子的态度。"

【注释】

(1)陈亢——就是陈子禽。

16.14 邦君之妻，君称之曰夫人，夫人自称曰小童；邦人称之曰君夫人，称诸异邦曰寡小君；异邦人称之亦曰君夫人(1)。

【译文】国君的妻子，国君称她为夫人，她自称为小童；国内的人称她为君夫人，但对外国人便称她为寡小君；外国人称她也为君夫人。

【注释】

(1)这章可能也是孔子所言，却遗落了"子曰"两字。有人疑心这是后人见竹简有空白处，任意附记的。殊不知书写《论语》的竹简不过八寸，短者每章一简，长者一章数简，断断没有多大空白能书写这四十多字。而且这一章既见于《古论》，又见于《鲁论》（《鲁论》作"国君之妻"），尤其可见各种古本都有之，决非后人所掺入。

阳货篇第十七

共二十六章

17.1 阳货⁽¹⁾欲见孔子，孔子不见，归孔子豚⁽²⁾孔子时其亡也，而往拜之。遇诸途。谓孔子曰："来！予与尔言。"曰⁽³⁾："怀其宝而迷其邦，可谓仁乎？"曰："不可。——好从事而亟⁽⁴⁾失时，可谓知乎？"曰："不可。——日月逝矣，岁不我与。"孔子曰："诺；吾将仕矣⁽⁵⁾。"

【译文】阳货想要孔子来拜会他，孔子不去，他便送孔子一个[蒸熟了的]小猪，[使孔子到他家来道谢]。孔子探听他不在家的时候，去拜谢。两人在路上碰着了。他叫着孔子道："来！我同你说话。"[孔子走了过去。]他又道："自己有一身的本领，却听任着国家的事情糊里糊涂，可以叫做仁爱吗？"[孔子没吭声。]他便自己接口道："不可以。——一个人喜欢做官，却屡屡错过机会，可以叫做聪明吗？"[孔子仍然没吭声。]他又自己接口道："不可以。——时光一去，就不再回来了呀。"孔子这才说道："好吧；我打算做官了。"

【注释】
(1)阳货——又叫阳虎，季氏的家臣。季氏几代以来把持鲁国的政治，阳货这时正又把持季氏的权柄。最后因企图削除三桓而未成，逃往晋国。
(2)归孔子豚——"归"同"馈"，赠送也。《孟子•滕文公下》对这事有一段说明，他说，当时，"大夫有赐于士，不得受于其家，则往拜其门"。阳货便利用这一礼俗，趁孔子不在家，送一个蒸熟了的小猪去。孔子也就趁阳货不在家才去登门拜谢。

(3)曰——自此以下的几个"曰"字，都是阳货的自为问答。说本毛奇龄《论语稽求篇》引明人郝敬之说。俞樾《古书疑义举例》卷二有"一人之辞而加曰字例"，对这种修辞方式更有详细引证。

(4)亟——去声，音气，qì，屡也。

(5)吾将仕矣——孔子于阳虎当权之时，并未仕于阳虎。可参《左传》定公八、九年传。

17.2 子曰："性相近也，习相远也。"

【译文】孔子说："人性情本相近，因为习染不同，便相距悬远。"

17.3 子曰："唯上知与下愚(1)不移。"

【译文】孔子说："只有上等的智者和下等的愚人是改变不了的。"

【注释】

(1)上知、下愚——关于"上知""下愚"的解释，古今颇有异说。《汉书·古今人表》说："可与为善，不可与为恶，是谓上智。可与为恶，不可与为善，是谓下愚。"则是以其品质言。孙星衍《问字堂集》说："上知谓生而知之，下愚谓困而不学。"则是兼以其知识与品质而言。译文仅就字面译出。但孔子说过"生而知之者上也"（16.9），这里的"上知"可能就是"生而知之"的人。当然这种人是不会有的。可是当时的人却以为一定有，甚至孔子都曾否认地说过"我非生而知之者"（7.20）。

17.4 子之武城，闻弦歌之声。夫子莞尔而笑，曰："割鸡焉用牛刀？"子游对曰："昔者偃也闻诸夫子曰：'君子学道则爱人，小人学道则易使也。'"子曰："二三子！偃之言是也。前言戏之耳。"

【译文】孔子到了［子游作县长］的武城，听到了弹琴瑟唱诗歌的声音。孔子微微笑着，说道："宰鸡，何必用宰牛的刀？［治理这个小地方，用得着教育吗？］"子游答道："以前我听老师说过，做官的学习了，就会有仁爱之心；老百姓学习了，就容易听指挥，听使唤。［教育总是有用的。］"孔子便向学生们道："二三子！言偃的这话是正确的。我刚才那句话不过同他开玩笑罢了。"

17.5 公山弗扰⑴以费畔⑵，召，子欲往。子路不说，曰："末之也，已⑶，何必公山氏之之⑷也？"子曰："夫召我者，而岂徒哉⑸？如有用我者，吾其为东周乎？"

【译文】公山弗扰盘踞在费邑图谋造反，叫孔子去，孔子准备去。子路很不高兴，说道："没有地方去便算了，为什么一定要去公山氏那里呢？"孔子道："那个叫我去的人，难道是白白召我吗？假若有人用我，我将使周文王、武王之道在东方复兴。"

【注释】
⑴公山弗扰——疑即《左传》定公五年、八年、十二年及哀公八年之公山不狃（唯陈天祥的《四书辨疑》认为是两人）。不过《论语》所叙之事不见于《左传》，而《左传》定公十二年所叙的公山不狃反叛鲁

国的事，不但没有叫孔子去，而且孔子当时正为司寇，命人打败了他。因此赵翼的《陔馀丛考》、崔述的《洙泗考信录》都疑心这段文字不可信。但是其后又有一些人，如刘宝楠《论语正义》，则说赵、崔不该信《左传》而疑《论语》。我们于此等处只能存疑。

(2)畔——毛奇龄说，"畔是谋逆"，译文取这一义。

(3)末之也已——旧作一句读，此依武亿《经读考异》作两句读。"末"，没有地方的意思；"之"，动词，往也；"已"，止也。

(4)何必公山氏之之也——"何必之公山氏也"的倒装。"之之"的第一个"之"字只是帮助倒装用的结构助词，第二个"之"字是动词。

(5)而岂徒哉——"徒"下省略动宾结构，说完全是"而岂徒召我哉"。

17.6 子张问仁于孔子。孔子曰："能行五者于天下为仁矣。""请问之。"曰："恭，宽，信，敏，惠。恭则不侮，宽则得众，信则人任焉，敏则有功，惠则足以使人。"

【译文】子张向孔子问仁。孔子道："能够处处实行五种品德，便是仁人了。"子张道："请问哪五种。"孔子道："庄重，宽厚，诚实，勤敏，慈惠。庄重就不致遭受侮辱，宽厚就会得到大众的拥护，诚实就会得到别人的任用，勤敏就会工作效率高、贡献大，慈惠就能够使唤人。"

17.7 佛肸[1]召，子欲往。子路曰："昔者由也闻诸夫子曰：'亲于其身为不善者，君子不入也。'佛肸以中牟[2]畔，子之往也，如之何？"子曰："然，有是言也。不曰坚乎，磨而不磷[3]；不曰白乎，涅[4]而不缁。吾岂匏瓜[5]也哉？焉能系而不食？"

【译文】佛肸叫孔子,孔子打算去。子路道:"从前我听老师说过:'亲自做坏事的人那里,君子不去的。'如今佛肸盘踞中牟谋反,您却要去,怎么说得过去呢?"孔子道:"对,我有过这话。但是,你不知道吗?最坚固的东西,磨也磨不薄;最白的东西,染也染不黑。我难道是匏瓜吗?哪里能够只是被悬挂着而不给人吃食呢?"

【注释】
(1)佛肸——晋国赵简子攻打范中行,佛肸是范中行的家臣,为中牟的县长,因此依据中牟来抗拒赵简子。
(2)中牟——春秋时晋邑,故址当在今日河北省邢台和邯郸之间,跟河南的中牟了不相涉。
(3)磷——音吝,lìn,薄也。
(4)涅——音聂,niè,本是一种矿物,古人用作黑色染料,这里作动词,染黑之意。
(5)匏瓜——即匏子,古有甘、苦两种,苦的不能吃,但因它比水轻,可以系于腰,用以泅渡。《国语•鲁语》:"苦瓠不材,于人共济而已。"《庄子•逍遥游》:"今子有五石之匏,何不虑以为大樽,而浮乎江湖。"皆可以为证。

17.8 子曰:"由也!女闻六言(1)六蔽矣乎?"对曰:"未也。""居!吾语女。好仁不好学(2),其蔽也愚(3);好知不好学,其蔽也荡(4);好信不好学,其蔽也贼(5);好直不好学,共蔽也绞;好勇不好学,其蔽也乱;好刚不好学,其蔽也狂。"

【译文】孔子说:"仲由!你听过有六种品德便会有六种弊病吗?"子路答道:"没有。"孔子道:"坐下!我告诉你。爱仁德,却不爱学问,那种弊病就是容易被人愚弄;爱耍聪明,却不爱学问,那种弊病就是放荡而无基础;爱诚实,却不爱学问,那种弊病就是[容易被人利用,反而]害了自己;爱直率,却不爱学问,那种弊病就是说话尖刻,刺痛人心;爱勇敢,却不爱学问,那种弊病就是捣乱闯祸;爱刚强,却不爱学问,那种弊病就是胆大妄为。"

【注释】

(1) 言——这个"言"字和"有一言而可以终身行之"(15.24)的"言"相同,名曰"言",实是指"德"。"一言",孔子拈出"恕"字;"六言",孔子拈出"仁""知""信""直""勇""刚"六字。后代"五言诗""七言诗"以一字为"言"之义盖本于此。

(2) 不好学——不学则不能明其理。

(3) 愚——朱熹《集注》云:"愚若可陷可罔之类。"译文取之。

(4) 荡——孔安国云:"荡,无所适守也。"译文取之。

(5) 贼——管同《四书纪闻》云:"大人之所以不必信者,唯其为学而知义之所在也。苟好信不好学,则唯知重然诺而不明事理之是非,谨厚者则硁硁为小人;苟又挟以刚勇之气,必如周汉刺客游侠,轻身殉人,扦文网而犯公义,自圣贤观之,非贼而何?"这是根据春秋侠勇之士的事实,又根据儒家明哲保身的理论所发的议论,似乎近于孔子本意。

17.9 子曰:"小子何莫学夫诗?诗,可以兴,可以观,可以群,可以怨。迩之事父,远之事君;多识于鸟兽草木之名。"

【译文】孔子说:"学生们为什么没有人研究诗?读诗,可以培养联想力,可以提高观察力,可以锻炼合群性,可以学得讽刺方法。近呢,可以运用其中道理来侍奉父母;远呢,可以用来服侍君上;而且多多认识鸟兽草木的名称。"

17.10 子谓伯鱼曰:"女为《周南》《召南》⁽¹⁾矣乎?人而不为《周南》《召南》,其犹正墙面而立⁽²⁾也与?"

【译文】孔子对伯鱼说道:"你研究过《周南》和《召南》了吗?人假若不研究《周南》和《召南》,那会像面正对着墙壁而站着罢!"

【注释】

(1)《周南》、《召南》——现存《诗经·国风》中。但沈括《梦溪笔谈》卷三说:"《周南》《召南》,乐名也。……有乐有舞焉,学者之事。……所谓为《周南》《召南》者,不独诵其诗而已。"

(2)正墙面而立——朱熹云:"言即其至近之地,而一物无所见,一步不可行。"

17.11 子曰:"礼云礼云,玉帛云乎哉?乐云乐云,钟鼓云乎哉?"

【译文】孔子说:"礼呀礼呀,仅是指玉帛等等礼物而说的吗?乐呀乐呀,仅是指钟鼓等等乐器而说的吗?"

17.12 子曰:"色厉而内荏,譬诸小人,其犹穿窬之盗也与?"

【译文】孔子说:"颜色严厉,内心怯弱,若用坏人作比喻,怕像个挖洞跳墙的小偷罢!"

17.13 子曰:"乡愿⑴,德之贼也。"

【译文】孔子说:"没有真是非的好好先生是足以败坏道德的小人。"

【注释】

⑴乡愿——愿,《孟子》作"原"。《孟子•尽心下》对"乡愿"有一段最具体的解释:"何以是嘐嘐也?言不顾行,行不顾言,则曰:'古之人,古之人,行何为踽踽凉凉?生斯世也,为斯世也,善斯可矣。'阉然媚于世者,是乡原也。"又说:"非之无举也,刺之无刺也。同乎流俗,合乎污世。居之似忠信,行之似廉洁。众皆悦之,自以为是,而不可与入尧舜之道。故曰'德之贼'也。"

17.14 子曰:"道听而途说,德之弃也。"

【译文】孔子说:"听到道路传言就四处传播,这是应该革除的作风。"

17.15 子曰:"鄙夫可与⑴事君也与哉?其未得之也,患得之当作患不得之⑵。既得之,患失之。苟患失之,无所不至矣。"

【译文】孔子说:"鄙夫,难道能同他共事吗?当他没有得到职位的时候,生怕得不着;已经得着了,又怕失去。假若生怕失去,会无所不用其极了。"

【注释】

⑴可与——王引之《释词》谓即"可以",今不取。

(2)患得之——王符《潜夫论•爱日篇》云:"孔子疾夫未之得也,患不得之;既得之,患失之者。"可见东汉人所据的本子有"不"字。《荀子•子道篇》说:"孔子曰……小人者,其未得也,则忧不得;既已得之,又恐失之。"(《说苑杂言篇》同)此虽是述意,"得"上也有"不"字。宋人沈作喆《寓简》云:"东坡解云,'患得之'当作'患不得之'。"可见宋人所见的本子已脱此"不"字。

17.16 子曰:"古者民有三疾,今也或是之亡也。古之狂也肆,今之狂也荡;古之矜也廉⁽¹⁾,今之矜也忿戾;古之愚也直,今之愚也诈而已矣。"

【译文】孔子说:"古代的人民还有三种[可贵的]毛病,现在呢,或许都没有了。古代的狂人肆意直言,现在的狂人便放荡无羁了;古代自己矜持的人还有些不能触犯的地方,现在自己矜持的人却只是一味老羞成怒,无理取闹罢了;古代的愚人还直率,现在的愚人却只是欺诈耍手段罢了。"

【注释】

(1)廉——"廉隅"的"廉",本义是器物的棱角,人的行为方正有威也叫"廉"。

17.17 子曰:"巧言令色,鲜矣仁⁽¹⁾。"

【注释】

(1)见《学而篇》。

17.18 子曰:"恶紫之夺朱⁽¹⁾也,恶郑声之乱雅乐也,恶利口之覆邦家者。"

【译文】孔子说:"紫色夺去了大红色的光彩和地位,可憎恶;郑国的乐曲破坏了典雅的乐曲,可憎恶;强嘴利舌颠覆国家,可憎恶。"

【注释】

⑴紫之夺朱——春秋时候,鲁桓公和齐桓公都喜欢穿紫色衣服。从《左传》哀公十七年卫浑良夫"紫衣狐裘"而被罪的事情看来,那时的紫色可能已代替了朱色而变为诸侯衣服的正色了。

17.19 子曰:"予欲无言。"子贡曰:"子如不言,则小子何述焉?"子曰:"天何言哉?四时行焉,百物生焉,天何言哉?"

【译文】孔子说:"我想不说话了。"子贡道:"您假若不说话,那我们传述什么呢?"孔子道:"天说了什么呢?四季照样运行,百物照样生长,天说了什么呢?"

17.20 孺悲⁽¹⁾欲见孔子,孔子辞以疾⁽²⁾。将命者出户,取瑟而歌,使之闻之。

【译文】孺悲来,要会晤孔子,孔子托言有病,拒绝接待。传命的人刚出房门,孔子便把瑟拿下来弹,并且唱着歌,故意使孺悲听到。

【注释】

(1)孺悲——鲁国人。《礼记·杂记》云:"恤由之丧,哀公使孺悲之孔子学士丧礼,《士丧礼》于是乎书。"

(2)辞以疾——《孟子·告子下》说:"教亦多术矣。予不屑之教诲也者,是亦教诲之而已矣。"孔子故意不接见孺悲,并且使他知道,是不是也是如此的呢?

17.21 宰我问:"三年之丧,期已久矣。君子三年不为礼,礼必坏;三年不为乐,乐必崩。旧谷既没,新谷既升,钻燧改火(1),期(2)可已矣。"子曰:"食夫稻(3),衣夫锦,于女安乎?"曰:"安。""女安,则为之!夫君子之居丧,食旨不甘,闻乐不乐,居处不安(4),故不为也。今女安,则为之!"宰我出,子曰:"予之不仁也!子生三年,然后免于父母之怀。夫三年之丧,天下之通丧也,予也有三年之爱于其父母乎!"

【译文】宰我问道:"父母死了,守孝三年,为期也太久了。君子有三年不去习礼仪,礼仪一定会废弃掉;三年不去奏音乐,音乐一定会失传。陈谷既已吃完了,新谷又已登场;打火用的燧木又经过了一个轮回,一年也就可以了。"孔子道:"[父母死了,不到三年,]你便吃那个白米饭,穿那个花缎衣,你心里安不安呢?"宰我道:"安。"孔子便抢着道:"你安,你就去干吧!君子的守孝,吃美味不晓得甜,听音乐不觉得快乐,住在家里不以为舒适,才不这样干。如今你既然觉得心安,便去干好了。"宰我退了出来。孔子道:"宰予真不仁呀!儿女生下地来,三年以后才能完全脱离父母的怀抱。替父母守孝三年,天下都是如此的。宰予难道就没有从他父母那里得着三年怀抱的爱护吗?"

【注释】

(1)钻燧改火——古代用的是钻木取火的方法,被钻的木,四季不同,所谓"春取榆柳之火,夏取枣杏之火,季夏取桑柘之火,秋取柞楢之火,冬取槐檀之火"(马融引《周书·月令篇》文),一年一轮回。

(2)期——音基。jī,一年。

(3)稻——古代北方以稷(小米)为主要粮食,水稻和粱(精细的小米)是珍品,而稻的耕种面积更小,所以这里特别提出它来和"锦"为对文。

(4)居处不安——古代孝子要"居倚庐,寝苫枕块",就是住临时用草料木料搭成的凶庐,睡在用草编成的藁垫上,用土块做枕头。这里的"居处"是指平日的居住生活而言。

17.22 子曰:"饱食终日,无所用心,难矣哉!不有博(1)弈者乎?为之,犹贤乎已(2)。"

【译文】孔子说:"整天吃饱了饭,什么事也不做,不行的呀!不是有掷采下弈的游戏吗?干干也比闲着好。"

【注释】

(1)博——古代的一种棋局。焦循的《孟子正义》说:"盖弈但行棋,博以掷采(骰子)而后行棋。"又说:"后人不行棋而专掷采,遂称掷采为博(赌博),博与弈益远矣。"

(2)犹贤乎已——句法与意义和《墨子·法仪篇》的"犹逾(同愈)已",《孟子·尽心上》的"犹愈于已"全同。"已"是不动作的意思。

17.23 子路曰:"君子尚(1)勇乎?"子曰:"君子义以为上(1),

君子有勇而无义为乱，小人有勇而无义为盗。"

【译文】子路问道："君子尊贵勇敢不？"孔子道："君子认为义是最可尊贵的，君子只有勇，没有义，就会捣乱造反；小人只有勇，没有义，就会做土匪强盗。"

【注释】
(1)尚、上——"尚勇"的"尚"和"上"相同，不过用作动词。

17.24 子贡曰："君子亦有恶乎？"子曰："有恶：恶称人之恶者，恶居下流(1)流字衍文而讪上者，恶勇而无礼者，恶果敢而窒者。"曰："赐也亦有恶乎？""恶徼以为知者，恶不孙以为勇者，恶讦以为直者。"

【译文】子贡道："君子也有憎恨的事吗？"孔子道："有憎恨的事：憎恨一味传播别人的坏处的人，憎恨在下位而毁谤上级的人，憎恨勇敢却不懂礼节的人，憎恨勇于贯彻自己的主张，却顽固不通、执拗到底的人。"孔子又道："赐，你也有憎恶的事吗？"子贡随即答道："我憎恨偷袭别人的成绩却作为自己的聪明的人，憎恨毫不谦虚却自以为勇敢的人，憎恨揭发别人阴私却自以为直率的人。"

【注释】
(1)下流——根据惠栋的《九经古义》和冯登府的《论语异文考证》，证明了晚唐以前的本子没有这个"流"字。案文义，这个"流"字也是不应该有的。但苏轼《上韩太尉书》引此文时已有"流"字，可见北宋时已经误衍。

17.25 子曰:"唯女子与小人为难养也,近之则不孙,远之则怨。"

【译文】孔子道:"只有女子和小人是难得同他们共处的,亲近了,他会无礼;疏远了,他会怨恨。"

17.26 子曰:"年四十而见恶焉,其终也已⑴。"

【译文】孔子说:"到了四十岁还被厌恶,他这一生也就完了。"

【注释】
⑴其终也已——"已"是动词,和"末之也已"(17•4)"斯害也已"(2.16)的"已"字相同,句法更和"斯害也已"一致。"其终也""斯害也"为主语;"已"为动词,谓语。如在"其终也"下作一停顿,文意便显豁了。

微子篇第十八

共十一章

18.1 微子⁽¹⁾去之,箕子为之奴⁽²⁾,比干谏而死⁽³⁾。孔子曰:"殷有三仁焉。"

【译文】[纣王昏乱残暴,]微子便离开了他,箕子做了他的奴隶,比干谏劝而被杀。孔子说:"殷商末年有三位仁人。"

【注释】
⑴微子——名启,纣王的同母兄,不过当他出生时,他的母亲尚为帝乙之妾,其后才立为妻,然后生了纣,所以帝乙死后,纣得嗣立,而微子不得立。事见《吕氏春秋·仲冬纪》。古书中唯《孟子·告子篇》认为微子是纣的叔父。
⑵箕子为之奴——箕子,纣王的叔父。纣王无道,他曾进谏而不听,便披发佯狂,降为奴隶。
⑶比干谏而死——比干也是纣的叔父,力谏纣王,纣王说,我听说圣人的心有七个孔,便剖开他的心而死。

18.2 柳下惠为士师,三黜。人曰:"子未可以去乎?"曰:"直道而事人,焉往而不三黜?枉道而事人,何必去父母之邦?"

【译文】柳下惠做法官,多次地被撤职。有人对他说:"您不可以离开鲁国吗?"他道:"正直地工作,到哪里去不多次被撤职?不正直地工作,为什么一定要离开祖国呢?"

18.3 齐景公待孔子曰:"若季氏,则吾不能;以季、孟之间待之。"曰:"吾老矣,不能用也。"孔子行。

【译文】齐景公讲到对待孔子的打算时说:"用鲁君对待季氏的模样对待孔子,那我做不到;我要用次于季氏而高于孟氏的待遇来对待他。"不久,又说道:"我老了,没有什么作为了。"孔子离开了齐国。

18.4 齐人归女乐[1],季桓子[2]受之,三日不朝,孔子行。

【译文】齐国送了许多歌姬舞女给鲁国,季桓子接受了,三天不问政事,孔子就离职走了。

【注释】

(1)齐人归女乐——"归"同"馈"。此事可参阅《史记·孔子世家》和《韩非子·内储说》。

(2)季桓子——季孙斯,鲁国定公以至哀公初年时的执政上卿,死于哀公三年。

18.5 楚狂接舆[1]歌而过孔子曰:"凤兮凤兮!何德之衰?往者不可谏,来者犹可追[2]。已而,已而!今之从政者殆而!"孔子下,欲与之言。趋而辟之,不得与之言。

【译文】楚国的狂人接舆一面走过孔子的车子,一面唱着歌,道:"凤凰呀,凤凰呀!为什么这么倒霉?过去的不能再挽回,未来的还可不再着迷。算了吧,算了吧!现在的执政诸公危乎其危!"孔子下车,想同他谈谈,他却赶快避开,孔子没法同他谈。

【注释】

(1)接舆——曹之升《四书摭余说》云:"《论语》所记隐士皆以其事名之。门者谓之'晨门',杖者谓之'丈人',津者谓之'沮''溺',接孔子之舆者谓之'接舆',非名亦非字也。"

(2)犹可追——赶得上、来得及的意思,译文因图押韵,故用意译法。

18.6 长沮、桀溺耦而耕(1),孔子过之,使子路问津焉。长沮曰:"夫执舆(2)者为谁?"子路曰:"为孔丘。"曰:"是鲁孔丘与?"曰:"是也。"曰:"是知津矣。"问于桀溺。桀溺曰:"子为谁?"曰:"为仲由。"曰:"是鲁孔丘之徒与?"对曰:"然。"曰:"滔滔者天下皆是也,而谁以(3)易之?且而(4)与其从辟(5)人之士也,岂若从辟世之士哉?"耰(6)而不辍。子路行以告。夫子怃(7)然曰:"鸟兽不可与同群,吾非斯人之徒与而谁与?天下有道,丘不与易也。"

【译文】长沮、桀溺两人一同耕田,孔子在那儿经过,叫子路去问渡口。长沮问子路道:"那位驾车子的是谁?"子路道:"是孔丘。"他又道:"是鲁国的那位孔丘吗?"子路道:"是的。"他便道:"他么,早晓得渡口在哪儿了。"去问桀溺。桀溺道:"您是谁?"子路道:"我是仲由。"桀溺道:"您是鲁国孔丘的门徒吗?"答道:"对的。"他便道:"像洪水一样的坏东西到处都是,你们同谁去改革它呢?你与其跟着[孔丘那种]逃避坏人的人,为什么不跟着[我们这些]逃避整个社会的人呢?"说完,仍旧不停地做田里工夫。子路回来报告给孔子。孔子很失望地道:"我们既然不可以同飞禽走兽合群共处,若不同人群打交道,又同什么去打交道呢?如果天下太平,我就不会同你们一道来从事改革了。"

【注释】

(1)长沮、桀溺耦而耕——"长沮""桀溺"不是真姓名。其姓名当时已经不暇询问,后世更无由知道了。耦耕是古代耕田的一种方法。春秋时代已经用牛耕田,不但由冉耕字伯牛、司马耕字子牛的现象可以看出,《国语·晋语》云:"其子孙将耕于齐,宗庙之牺为畎亩之勤。"尤为确证。耦耕的方法说法不少,都难说很精确。下文又说"耰而不辍",则这耦耕未必是执耒,像夏炘《学礼管释·释二耜为耦》所说的。估计这个耦耕不过说二人做庄稼活罢了。1959年科学出版社《农史研究集刊》万国钧《耦耕考》对此有解释,上海中华书局《中华文史论丛》第三辑何兹全《谈耦耕》对万说有补充,也只能作参考。

(2)执舆——就是执辔(拉马的缰绳)。本是子路做的,因子路已下车,所以孔子代为驾御。

(3)以——与也,和下文"不可与同群","斯人之徒与而谁与","丘不与易也"诸"与"字同义。

(4)而——同"尔"。

(5)辟——同"避"。

(6)耰——音忧,yōu,播种之后,再以土覆之,摩而平之,使种入土,鸟不能啄,这便叫耰。

(7)怃——音舞,wǔ,怃然,怅惘失意之貌。

18.7 子路从而后,遇丈人,以杖荷蓧[1]。子路问曰:"子见夫子乎?"丈人曰:"四体不勤,五谷不分[2]。孰为夫子?"植其杖而芸。子路拱而立。止子路宿,杀鸡为黍[3]而食之,见其二子焉。明日,子路行以告。子曰:"隐者也。"使子路反见之。至,则行矣。子路曰:"不仕无义。长幼之节,不可废也;君臣之义,如之何其废之?欲洁其身,而乱大伦。君子之仕也,行其义也。道之不行,已知之矣。"

【译文】子路跟随着孔子,却远落在后面,碰到一个老头,用拐杖挑着除草用的工具。子路问道:"您看见我的老师吗?"老头道:"你这人,四肢不劳动,五谷不认识,谁晓得你的老师是什么人?"说完,便扶着拐杖去锄草。子路拱着手恭敬地站着。他便留子路到他家住宿,杀鸡、做饭给子路吃,又叫他两个儿子出来相见。第二天,子路赶上了孔子,报告了这件事。孔子道:"这是位隐士。"叫子路回去再看看他。子路到了那里,他却走开了。子路便道:"不做官是不对的。长幼间的关系,是不可能废弃的;君臣间的关系,怎么能不管呢?你原想不玷污自身,却不知道这样隐居便是忽视了君臣间的必要关系。君子出来做官,只是尽应尽之责。至于我们的政治主张行不通,早就知道了。"

【注释】
(1)蓧——音掉,diào,古代除田中草所用的工具。《说文》作"莜"。
(2)四体不勤,五谷不分——这二句,宋吕本中《紫微杂说》以至清朱彬《经传考证》、宋翔凤《论语发微》都说是丈人说自己。其余更多人主张说是丈人责子路。译文从后说。
(3)为黍——黍就是现在的黍子,也叫黄米。它比当时的主要食粮稷(小米)的收获量小,因此在一般人中也算是比较珍贵的主食。杀鸡做菜,为黍做饭,这在当时是很好的招待了。

18.8 逸[1]民:伯夷、叔齐、虞仲、夷逸、朱张、柳下惠、少连[2]。子曰:"不降其志,不辱其身,伯夷、叔齐与!"谓"柳下惠、少连,降志辱身矣,言中伦,行中虑,其斯而已矣。"谓:"虞仲、夷逸,隐居放言,身中清,废中权。我则异于是,无可无不可。"

【译文】古今被遗落的人才有伯夷、叔齐、虞仲、夷逸、朱张、柳下惠、少连。孔子道:"不动摇自己意志,不辱没自己身份,是伯夷、叔齐罢!"又说,"柳下惠、少连降低自己意志,屈辱自己身份了,可是言语合乎法度,行为经过思虑,那也不过如此罢了。"又说:"虞仲、夷逸逃世隐居,放肆直言。行为廉洁,被废弃也是他的权术。我就和他们这些人不同,没有什么可以,也没有什么不可以。"

【注释】
(1)逸——同"佚",《论语》两用"逸民",义都如此。《孟子•公孙丑上》云:"柳下惠……遗佚而不怨,厄穷而不悯。"这一"逸"正是《孟子》"遗佚"之义。说本黄式三《论语后案》。
(2)虞仲、夷逸、朱张、少连——四人言行多已不可考。虞仲前人认为就是吴太伯之弟仲雍,不可信。夷逸曾见《尸子》,有人劝他做官,他不肯。少连曾见《礼记•杂记》,孔子说他善于守孝。夏炘《景紫堂文集》卷三有《逸民虞仲夷逸朱张皆无考说》,于若干附会之说有所驳正。

18.9 大师挚(1)适齐,亚饭干适楚,三饭缭适蔡,四饭缺适秦(2),鼓方叔入于河,播鼗武入于汉,少师阳、击磬襄入于海。

【译文】太师挚逃到了齐国,二饭乐师干逃到了楚国,三饭乐师缭逃到了蔡国,四饭乐师缺逃到了秦国,打鼓的方叔入居黄河之滨,摇小鼓的武入居汉水之涯,少师阳和击磬的襄入居海边。

【注释】
(1)大师挚——《泰伯篇第八》有"师挚之始",不知是不是此人。
(2)亚饭——古代天子诸侯用饭都得奏乐,所以乐官有"亚饭""三饭""四饭"之名。这些人究竟是何时人,已经无法肯定。

18.10 周公谓鲁公(1)曰:"君子不施(2)其亲,不使大臣怨乎不以。故旧无大故,则不弃也。无求备于一人!"

【译文】周公对鲁公说道:"君子不怠慢他的亲族,不让大臣抱怨没被信用。老臣故人没有发生严重过失,就不要抛弃他。不要对某一人求全责备!"

【注释】
(1)周公、鲁公——周公,周公旦,孔子心目中的圣人。鲁公是他的儿子伯禽。
(2)施——同"弛",有些本子即作"弛"。

18.11 周有八士:伯达、伯适、仲突、仲忽、叔夜、叔夏、季随、季䯄(1)。

【译文】周朝有八个有教养的人:伯达、伯适、仲突、仲忽、叔夜、叔夏、季随、季骒。

【注释】

(1)伯达等八人——此八人已经无可考。前人看见此八人两人一列,依伯、仲、叔、季排列,而且各自押韵(达适一韵,突忽一韵,夜夏韵,随骒一韵),便说这是四对双生子。

子张篇第十九

共二十五章

子张篇第十九

19.1 子张曰:"士见危致命,见得思义,祭思敬,丧思哀,其可已矣。"

【译文】子张说:"读书人看见危险便肯豁出生命,看见有所得便考虑是否该得,祭祀时候考虑严肃恭敬,居丧时候考虑悲痛哀伤,那也就可以了。"

19.2 子张曰:"执德不弘(1),信道不笃,焉能为有?焉能为亡(2)?"

【译文】子张说:"对于道德,行为不坚强,信仰不忠实,〔这种人,〕有他不为多,没他不为少。"
【注释】
(1)弘——此"弘"字就是今之"强"字,说见章炳麟《广论语骈枝》。
(2)焉能为有,焉能为亡——这两句疑是当日成语。何晏《论语集解》
　　云:"言无所轻重。"所以译文也用今日俗语来表达此意。

19.3 子夏之门人问交于子张。子张曰:"子夏云何?"对曰:"子夏曰:'可者与之,其不可者拒之。'"子张曰:"异乎吾所闻:君子尊贤而容众,嘉善而矜不能。我之大贤与,于人何所不容？我之不贤与，人将拒我，如之何其拒人也？"

【译文】子夏的学生向子张问怎样去交朋友。子张道："子夏说了些什么？"答道："子夏说，可以交的去交他，不可以交的拒绝他。"子张道："我所听到的与此不同：君子尊敬贤人，也接纳普通人；鼓励好人，可怜无能的人。我是非常好的人吗，对什么人不能容纳呢？我是坏人吗，别人会拒绝我，我怎能去拒绝别人呢？"

19.4 子夏曰："虽小道，必有可观者焉；致远恐泥，是以君子不为也。"

【译文】子夏说道："就是小技艺，一定有可取的地方；恐怕它妨碍远大事业，所以君子不从事于它。"

19.5 子夏曰："日知其所亡，月无忘其所能，可谓好学也已矣。"

【译文】子夏说："每天知道所未知的，每月复习所已能的，可以说是好学了。"

19.6 子夏曰："博学而笃志[1]，切问而近思，仁在其中矣。"

【译文】子夏说："广泛地学习，坚守自己志趣；恳切地发问,多考虑当前的问题,仁德就在这中间了。"

【注释】

⑴志——孔注以为"志"与"识"同,那么,"博学笃志"便是"博闻强记"之意,说虽可通,但不及译文所解恰切。

19.7 子夏曰:"百工居肆以成其事,君子学以致其道。"

【译文】子夏说:"各种工人居住于其制造场所完成他们的工作,君子则用学习获得那个道。"

19.8 子夏曰:"小人之过也必文。"

【译文】子夏说:"小人对于错误一定加以掩饰。"

19.9 子夏曰:"君子有三变:望之俨然,即之也温,听其言也厉。"

【译文】子夏说:"君子有三变:远远望着,庄严可畏;向他靠拢,温和可亲;听他的话,严厉不苟。"

19.10 子夏曰:"君子信而后劳其民;未信,则以为厉己也。信而后谏;未信,则以为谤己也。"

【译文】子夏说:"君子必须得到信仰以后才去动员百姓;否则百姓会以为你在折磨他们。必须得到信任以后才去进谏,否则君上会以为你在毁谤他。"

19.11 子夏曰:"大德不逾闲,小德出入可也。"

【译文】子夏说:"人的重大节操不能逾越界限,作风上的小节稍稍放松一点是可以的。"

19.12 子游曰:"子夏之门人小子,当洒扫应对进退,则可矣,抑末也。本之则无,如之何?"子夏闻之,曰:"噫!言游过矣!君子之道,孰先传焉?孰后倦焉?譬诸草木,区以别矣。君子之道,焉可诬也?有始有卒者,其惟圣人乎!"

【译文】子游道:"子夏的学生,叫他们做做打扫、接待客人、应对进退的工作,那是可以的;不过这只是末节罢了。探讨他们的学术基础却没有,怎样可以呢?"子夏听了这话,便道:"咳!言游说错了!君子的学术,哪一项先传授呢?哪一项最后讲述呢?学术犹如草木,是要区别为各种各类的。君子的学术,如何可以歪曲?〔依照一定的次序去传授而〕有始有终的,大概只有圣人罢!"

19.13 子夏曰:"仕而优则学,学而优则仕。"

【译文】子夏说:"做官了,有余力便去学习;学习了,有余力便去做官。"

19.14 子游曰:"丧致乎哀而止。"

【译文】子游说:"居丧,充分表现了他的悲哀也就够了。"

19.15 子游曰:"吾友张也为难能也,然而未仁。"

【译文】子游说:"我的朋友子张是难能可贵的了,然而还不能做到仁。"

19.16 曾子曰:"堂堂⑴乎张也,难与并为仁矣。"

【译文】曾子说:"子张的为人高得不可攀了,难以携带别人一同进入仁德。"

【注释】

⑴堂堂——这是叠两字而成的形容词,其具体意义如何,古今解释纷纭。《荀子·非十二子篇》云:"弟佗其冠,衶襌其辞,禹行而舜趋,是子张氏之贱儒也。"这是对子张学派的具体描写,因此我把"堂堂"译为"高不可攀"。根据《论语》和后代儒家诸书,可以证明曾子的学问重在"正心诚意",而子张则重在言语形貌,所以子游也批评子张"然而未仁"。

19.17 曾子曰:"吾闻诸夫子:人未有自致者也,必也亲丧乎!"

【译文】曾子说:"我听老师说过,平常时候,人不可能来自动地充分发挥感情,〔如果有,〕一定在父母死亡的时候罢!"

19.18 曾子曰:"吾闻诸夫子:孟庄子⑴之孝也,其他可能也;其不改父之臣与父之政,是难能也。"

【译文】曾子说:"我听老师说过:孟庄子的孝,别的都容易做到;而留用他父亲的僚属,保持他父亲的政治设施,是难以做到的。"

【注释】

⑴孟庄子——鲁大夫孟献子仲孙蔑之子,名速。其父死于鲁襄公十九年,本人死于二十三年,相距仅四年。这一章可以和"三年无改于父之道可谓孝矣"(1.11)结合来看。

19.19 孟氏使阳肤⑴为士师,问于曾子。曾子曰:"上失其道,民散⑵久矣。如得其情,则哀矜而勿喜!"

【译文】孟氏任命阳肤做法官,阳肤向曾子求教。曾子道:"现今在上位的人不依规矩行事,百姓早就离心离德了。你假若能够审出罪犯的真情,便应该同情他,可怜他,切不要自鸣得意!"

【注释】

⑴阳肤——旧注说他是曾子弟子。

⑵散——黄家岱《𡟛艺轩杂著·论语多齐鲁方言述》云:"散训犯法,与上下文义方接。扬氏《方言》:'虔散,杀也。东齐曰散,青、徐、淮、楚之间曰虔。'虔散为贼杀义。曰民散久矣,用齐语也。"译文未取此说,录之以备参考。

19.20 子贡曰:"纣⑴之不善,不如是之甚也。是以君子恶居下流,天下之恶皆归焉。"

【译文】子贡说:"商纣的坏,不像现在传说的这么厉害。所以君子憎恨居于下流,一居下流,天下的什么坏名声都会集中在他身上了。"

【注释】

⑴纣——殷商最末之君,为周武王所伐,自焚而死。

19.21 子贡曰:"君子之过也,如日月之食焉:过也,人皆见之;更也,人皆仰之。"

【译文】子贡说:"君子的过失好比日蚀月蚀:错误的时候,每个人都看得见;更改的时候,每个人都仰望着。"

19.22 卫公孙朝⑴问于子贡曰:"仲尼焉学?"子贡曰:"文武之道,未坠于地,在人。贤者识其大者,不贤者识其小者。莫不有文武之道焉。夫子焉不学？而亦何常师之有？"

【译文】卫国的公孙朝向子贡问道："孔仲尼的学问是从哪里学来的？"子贡道："周文王、武王之道，并没有失传，散在人间。贤能的人便抓住大处，不贤能的人只抓些末节。没有地方没有文王、武王之道。我的老师何处不学，又为什么要有一定的老师，专门的传授呢？"

【注释】

(1)卫公孙朝——翟灏《四书考异》云："春秋时鲁有成大夫公孙朝，见昭二十六年《传》；楚有武城尹公孙朝，见哀十七年《传》；郑子产有弟曰公孙朝，见《列子》。记者故系'卫'以别之。"

19.23 叔孙武叔(1)语大夫于朝曰："子贡贤于仲尼。"子服景伯以告子贡。子贡曰："譬之宫墙(2)，赐之墙也及肩，窥见室家之好。夫子之墙数仞(3)，不得其门而入，不见宗庙之美，百官(4)之富。得其门者或寡矣。夫子之云，不亦宜乎！"

【译文】叔孙武叔在朝廷中对官员们说："子贡比他老师仲尼要强些。"子服景伯便把这话告诉子贡。子贡道："拿房屋的围墙作比喻罢：我家的围墙只有肩膀那么高，谁都可以探望到房屋的美好。我老师的围墙却有几丈高，找不到大门走进去，就看不到他那宗庙的雄伟，房舍的多种多样。能够找着大门的人或许不多罢，那么，武叔他老人家的这话，不也是自然的吗？"

【注释】

(1)叔孙武叔——鲁大夫，名州仇。

(2)宫墙——"宫"有围障的意义,如《礼记•丧大记》:"君为庐宫之。""宫墙"当系一词,犹如今天的"围墙"。

(3)仞——七尺曰仞(此从程瑶田《通艺录•释仞》之说)。

(4)官——"官"字的本义是房舍,其后才引申为官职之义,说见俞樾《群经平议》卷三及遇夫先生《积微居小学金石论丛》卷一。这里也是指房舍而言。

19.24 叔孙武叔毁仲尼。子贡曰:"无以⁽¹⁾为也!仲尼不可毁也。他人之贤者,丘陵也,犹可逾也;仲尼,日月也,无得而逾焉。人虽欲自绝,其何伤于日月乎?多⁽²⁾见其不知量也⁽³⁾。"

【译文】叔孙武叔毁谤仲尼。子贡道:"不要这样做!仲尼是毁谤不了的。别人的贤能,好比山丘,还可以超越过去;仲尼,简直是太阳和月亮,不可能超越他。人家纵是要自绝于太阳月亮,那对太阳月亮有什么损害呢?只是表示他不自量罢了。"

【注释】

(1)以——此也,这里作副词用。

(2)多——副词,只也,适也。

(3)不知量也——皇侃《义疏》解此句为"不知圣人之度量",译文从朱熹《集注》。"也",用法同"耳"。

19.25 陈子禽谓子贡曰:"子为恭也,仲尼岂贤于子乎?"子贡曰:"君子一言以为知,一言以为不知,言不可不慎也。夫子之不可及也,犹天之不可阶而升也。夫子之得邦家者,所谓立之斯立,道之斯行,绥之斯来,动之斯和。其生也荣,其死也哀,如之何其可及也?"

【译文】陈子禽对子贡道:"您对仲尼是客气罢,是谦让罢,难道他真比您还强吗?"子贡道:"高贵人物由一句话表现他的有知,也由一句话表现他的无知,所以说话不可不谨慎。他老人家的不可以赶得上,犹如青天的不可以用阶梯爬上去。他老人家如果得国而为诸侯,或者得到采邑而为卿大夫,那正如我们所说的一叫百姓人人能立足于社会,百姓自会人人能立足于社会;一引导百姓,百姓自会前进;一安抚百姓,百姓自会从远方来投靠;一动员百姓,百姓自会同心协力。他老人家,生得光荣,死得可惜,怎么样能够赶得上呢?"

尧曰篇第二十

共三章

20.1 尧曰："咨！尔舜！天之历数在尔躬，允执其中。四海困穷，天禄永终。"舜亦以命禹⑴。

【译文】尧［让位给舜的时候，］说道："啧啧！你这位舜！上天的大命已经落到你的身上了，诚实地保持着那正确罢！假若天下的百姓都陷于困苦贫穷，上天给你的禄位也会永远地终止了。"舜［让位给禹的时候，］也说了这一番话。

【注释】
⑴这一章的文字前后不相连贯，从宋朝苏轼以来便有许多人疑心它有脱落。我只得把它分为若干段落，逐段译注，以便观览。

曰："予小子履⑴敢用玄牡，敢昭告于皇皇后帝：有罪不敢赦。帝臣不蔽⑵，简在帝心。朕躬有罪，无以万方；万方有罪，罪在朕躬。"

【译文】［汤］说："我履谨用黑色牡牛作牺牲，明明白白地告于光明而伟大的天帝：有罪的人［我］不敢擅自去赦免他。您的臣仆［的善恶］我也不隐瞒掩盖，您心里也是早就晓得的。我本人若有罪，就不要牵连天下万方；天下万方若有罪，都归我一个人来承担。"

尧曰篇第二十

【注释】

(1)予小子履——"予小子"和"予一人"都是上古帝王自称之词。从《史记·殷本纪》中知道汤名天乙,甲骨卜辞作"大乙",相传汤又名履。

(2)帝臣不蔽——《墨子·兼爱下篇》此句作"有善不敢蔽",但郑玄注此句云:"言天简阅其善恶也。"译文从郑。《墨子·兼爱下篇》和《吕氏春秋·顺民篇》都说这是成汤战胜夏桀以后,遭逢大旱,向上天祈祷求雨之词。《国语·周语上》引《汤誓》"余一人有罪,无以万夫",和这"朕躬有罪,无以万方"义近。

周有大赉,善人是富。"虽有周亲,不如仁人。百姓有过,在予一人(1)。"

【译文】周朝大封诸侯,使善人都富贵起来。"我虽然有至亲,却不如有仁德之人。百姓如果有罪过,应该由我来担承。"

【注释】

(1)虽有周亲……一人——刘宝楠《论语正义》引宋翔凤说,"虽有周亲"四句是周武王封诸侯之辞,尤其像封姜太公于齐之辞。

谨权量,审法度(1),修废官(2),四方之政行焉。兴灭国,继绝世,举逸民,天下之民归心焉。

【译文】检验并审定度量衡,修复已废弃的机关工作,全国的政令就都会通行了。恢复被灭亡的国家,承续已断绝的后代,提拔被遗落的人才,天下的百姓就都会心悦诚服了。

【注释】

(1) 谨权量，审法度——权就是量轻重的衡量，量就是容量，度就是长度。"法度"不是法律制度之意。《史记•秦始皇本纪》和秦权、秦量的刻辞中都有"法度"一词，都是指长度的分、寸、尺、丈、引而言。所以"谨权量，审法度"两句只是"齐一度量衡"一个意思。这一说法，清初阎若璩的《四书释地又续》已发其端。

(2) 废官——赵佑《四书温故录》云："或有职而无其官，或有官而不举其职，皆曰废。"这以下都是孔子的话。从文章的风格来看，也和尧告舜、成汤求雨、武王封诸侯的文诰体不同。历代注释家多以为是孔子的话，大致可信。但是刘宝楠《正义》引《汉书•律历志》"孔子陈后王之法曰，谨权量，审法度，修废官，举逸民，四方之政行矣"说，"据《志》此文，是'谨权量'以下皆孔子语，故何休《公羊》昭三十二年注引此节文冠以孔子曰"云云，则不足为证。因为汉人引《论语》，不论是否孔子之言，多称"孔子曰"。《困学纪闻》曾举出《汉书•艺文志》引"小道可观"（19.4），《后汉书•蔡邕传》引"致远恐泥"（同上）皆以子夏之言为孔子，其实不止于此，如后汉章帝长水校尉樊儵奏言引"博学而笃志"三句（19.6），也以子夏之言为孔子之言；《史记•田叔传赞》曰"孔子称居是国必闻其政"，又以子禽之问（1.10）为孔子之言；刘向《说苑》引"孔子曰，君子务本"，又引"孔子曰，恭近于礼"，则以有子之言为孔子之言。甚至郑玄注《曲礼》《玉藻》，以及王充著《论衡》，引《乡党篇》之文，都冠以"孔子曰"。则可见《论语》之书当时似别称"孔子"，如"孟子书"之称《孟子》者然。翟灏《四书考异》据《尸子•广泽篇》"墨子贵兼，孔子贵公，皇子贵衷"云云，以为先儒以孔子杂诸子中；又据《论衡•率性篇》云"孔子道德之祖，诸子中最卓者也"谓当时等孔子于诸子，其言不为无据（说本《诂经精舍三集》吴承志《汉人引孔门诸子言皆称孔子说》）。若此，则刘氏所举不足为证矣。

所重：民、食、丧、祭。

【译文】所重视的：人民、粮食、丧礼、祭祀。

宽则得众，信则民任焉[1]此五字衍文，敏则有功，公则说。

【译文】宽厚就会得到群众的拥护，勤敏就会有功绩，公平就会使百姓高兴。

【注释】

(1)信则民任焉——《汉石经》无此五字，《天文本校勘记》云："皇本、唐本、津藩本、正平本均无此句。"足见这一句是因《阳货篇》"信则人任焉"而误增的。《阳货篇》作"人"，"人"是领导。此处误作"民"。"民"指百姓。有信实，就会被百姓任命，这种思想绝非孔子所能有，尤其可见此句不是原文。

20.2 子张问于孔子曰："何如斯可以从政矣？"子曰："尊五美，屏[1]四恶，斯可以从政矣。"子张曰："何谓五美？"子曰："君子惠而不费，劳而不怨，欲而不贪[2]，泰而不骄，威而不猛。"子张曰："何谓惠而不费？"子曰："因民之所利而利之，斯不亦惠而不费乎？择可劳而劳之，又谁怨？欲仁而得仁，又焉贪？君子无众寡，无小大，无敢慢，斯不亦泰而不骄乎？君子正其衣冠，尊其瞻视，俨然人望而畏之，斯不亦威而不猛乎？"子张曰："何谓四恶？"子曰："不教而杀谓之虐；不戒视成谓之暴；慢令致期谓之贼；犹之[3]与人也，出纳[4]之吝谓之有司[5]。"

【译文】子张向孔子问道:"怎样就可以治理政事呢?"孔子道:"尊贵五种美德,排除四种恶政,这就可以治理政事了。"子张道:"五种美德是些什么?"孔子道:"君子给人民以好处,而自己却无所耗费;劳动百姓,百姓却不怨恨;自己欲仁欲义,却不能叫做贪;安泰矜持却不骄傲;威严却不凶猛。"子张道:"给人民以好处,自己却无所耗费,这应该怎么办呢?"孔子道:"就着人民能得利益之处因而使他们有利,这也不是给人民以好处而自己却无所耗费吗?选择可以劳动的〔时间、情况和人民〕再去劳动他们,又有谁来怨恨呢?自己需要仁德便得到了仁德,又贪求什么呢?无论人多人少,无论势力大小,君子都不敢怠慢他们,这不也是安泰矜持却不骄傲吗?君子衣冠整齐,目不斜视,庄严地使人望而有所畏惧,这也不是威严却不凶猛吗?"子张道:"四种恶政又是些什么呢?"孔子道:"不加教育便加杀戮叫做虐;不加申诫便要成绩叫做暴;起先懈怠,突然限期叫做贼;同是给人以财物,出手悭吝,叫做小家子气。"

【注释】

(1)屏——音丙,bǐng,屏除。

(2)欲而不贪——下文云:"欲仁而得仁,又焉贪?"可见此"欲"字是指欲仁欲义而言,因之皇侃《义疏》云:"欲仁义者为廉,欲财色者为贪。"译文本此。

(3)犹之——王引之《释词》云:"犹之与人,均之与人也。"

(4)出纳——出和纳(入)是两个意义相反的词,这里虽然在一起连用,却只有"出"的意义,没有"纳"的意义。说本俞樾《群经平议》。

(5)有司——古代管事者之称,职务卑微,这里意译为"小家子气"。

20.3 孔子曰:"不知命,无以为君子也;不知礼,无以立也;不知言⑴,无以知人也。"

【译文】孔子说:"不懂得命运,没有可能作为君子;不懂得礼,没有可能立足于社会;不懂得分辨人家的言语,没有可能认识人。"

【注释】
⑴知言——这里"知言"的意义和《孟子•公孙丑上》的"我知言"的"知言"相同,善于分析别人的言语,辨其是非善恶的意思。

论语

Theory on Literary Translation of the Chinese School

The theory on literary translation of the Chinese school owes its origin to traditional Chinese culture, including the Confucian and the Taoist school of thought respectively represented by *Thus Spoke the Master* and *Laws Divine and Human*.

It is said in the first chapter of *Laws Divine and Human* that truth can be known, but it may not be the truth you know, and that things may be named, but names are not the things. When applied to literary translation, this may mean that the theory on literary translation can be known, but it may not the unproven theory on the one hand, nor the scientific theory on the other, for neither literary translation nor its theory is science. As the names are not equal to the things, the translation cannot be equal to the original. As there is more difference than equivalence between the Chinese and the English language, the principle of equivalence can not be applied to the translation between them as between two occidental languages.

It is said in the last chapter of *Laws Divine and Human* that truthful words may not be beautiful and beautiful words may not be truthful. That is to say, there is contradiction between truth and beauty or between equivalence and excellence. A translation where equivalents are used may be called a faithful or truthful translation. When no equivalent can be found between two languages, the translator should make use of the best expressions or excellent expressions of the target language. That may be called theory of excellence.

In *Thus Spoke the Master*, Confucius said, "At seventy, I can do what I will without going beyond what is right." Professor Zhu Guangqian said that this has shown the mature state of an artist. I think it may also show the mature state of a literary translator. The literal translator has used the equivalents without going beyond the original in sound; the liberal translator has described the image without going beyond the original in sense; the literary translator has described the scene without going beyond reality. Not to go beyond the original is to be truthful or faithful, and the translator has reached the ordinary level of translation. To do what one will without going beyond the original is not only to be faithful but also to make his translation beautiful, in that case the translator has attained a higher level. To excel the original without going beyond the reality it describes is to attain the highest level.

What is literary translation? It is an art of solving the contradiction between faithfulness (or truth) and beauty. How to solve it? There are three methods, namely, equalization, generalization and particularization. When there is little or no contradition between truth and beauty, equalization or equivalents may be used. When there is contradction between them, generalization may be used to make the meaning clear, and particularization to make a deeper impression.

Confucius said in *Thus Spoke the Master* that it would be good to be understandable, better to be enjoyable and best to be delectable or delightful. When applied to literary translation, this principle means that an understandable translation is good, an enjoyable one is better and a delightful one is best. The ontology or theory of contradition between truth and beauty, the methodology or theory of equalization, generalization and particularization, and the teleology or theory of the understandable, the enjoyable and the delectable, all owe their origin to the Confucian and Taoist schools of thoughts.

But Confucius said less about what delight is and more about how to be delightful. In the beginning of *Thus Spoke the Master* he said it is delightful to acquire knowledge and put it into practice; In Chapter Six he told us how Yan Hui could find delight in reading though living in a humble lane with only a handful of rice to eat and a gourdful of water to drink; In Chapter Eleven, Zeng Xi told us his delight in an spring excursion. From these examples we can see Confucius' theory on delight or teleology, and his theory on practice or methodology. His theory is not scientific but artistic. Since literary translation is an art but not a branch of science, his theory can not only be applied to the practice but also to the theory of literary translation. As his theory has stood the test of time, it is as durable as scientific theories. A theorist on science who studies truth and the truthful should not go beyond what is truthful. A theorist on art or an artist who studies beauty and the beautiful may go beyond what is truthful and faithful.

The contradiction between truth and beauty in Chinese theory on literary translation has developed into a contradiction between equivalence and excellence. As Keats said, "Beauty is truth, truth beauty," we may even say beauty is a virtue, a kind of excellence. When we cannot find the equivalent, we may resort to generalization or particularization.

In short, literary translation is an art to create the beautiful.

This is the epistemology of the Chinese school. The contradition between truth and beauty or between equivalence and excellence is its ontology; the theory on equalization, generalization and particularization is its triple methodology; and the theory of the understandable, the enjoyable and the delectable or delightful is its triple teleology.

Xu Yuanchong
Oct. 2011

代后记：中国学派的文学翻译理论

中国学派的文学翻译理论源自中国的传统文化，主要包括儒家思想和道家思想，儒家思想的代表著作是《论语》，道家思想的代表著作是《老子道德经》。

《老子道德经》第一章开始就说："道可道，非常道；名可名，非常名。"联系到翻译理论上来，就是说：翻译理论是可以知道的，是可以说得出来的，但不是只说得出来而经不起实践检验的空头理论，这就是中国学派翻译理论中的实践论。其次，文学翻译理论不能算科学理论（自然科学），与其说是社会科学理论，不如说是人文学科或艺术理论，这就是文学翻译的艺术论，也可以说是相对论。后六个字"名可名，非常名"应用到文学翻译理论上来，可以有两层意思：第一层是原文的文字是描写现实的，但并不等于现实，文字和现实之间还有距离，还有矛盾；第二层意思是译文和原文之间也有距离，也有矛盾，译文和原文所描写的现实之间，自然还有距离，还有矛盾。译文应该发挥译语优势，运用最好的译语表达方式，来和原文展开竞赛，使译文和现实的距离或矛盾小于原文和现实之间的矛盾，那就是超越原文了。这就是文学翻译理论中的优势论或优化论，超越论或竞赛论。文学翻译理论应该解决的不只是译文和原文在文字方面的矛盾，还要解决译文和原文所反映的现实之间的矛盾，这是文学翻译的本体论。

一般翻译只要解决"真"或"信"或"似"的问题，文学翻译却要解决"真"或"信"和"美"之间的矛盾。原文反映的现实不只是言内之意，还有言外之意。中国的文学语言往往有言外之意，甚至还有言外之情。文学翻译理论也要解决译文和原文的言外之意、言外之情的矛盾。

《论语》说："知之者不如好之者，好之者不如乐之者。"知之，好之，乐之，这"三之论"是对艺术论的进一步说明。艺术论第一条原则要求译文忠实于原文所反映的现实，求的是真，可以使人知之；第二条原则要求用"三化"法来优化译文，求的是美，可以使人好之；第三条原则要求用"三美"来优化译文，尤其是译诗词，求的是意美、音美和形美，可以使人乐之。如果"不逾矩"的等化译文能使人知之（理解），那就达到了文学翻译的低标准，如从心所欲而不逾矩的浅化或深化的译文既能使人知之，又能使人好之（喜欢），那就达到了中标准；如果从心所欲的译文不但能使人知之，好之，还能使人乐之（愉快），那才达到了文学翻译的高标准。这也是中国译者对世界译论作出的贡献。

翻译艺术的规律是从心所欲而不逾矩。"矩"就是规矩，规律。但艺术规律却可以依人的主观意志而转移，是因为得到承认才算正确的。所以贝多芬说：为了更美，没有什么清规戒律不可打破。他所说的戒律不是科学规律，而是艺术规律。不能用科学规律来评论文学翻译。

孔子不大谈"什么是"(What?)而多谈"怎么做"(How?)。这是中国传统的方法论，比西方流传更久，影响更广，作用更大，并且经过了两三千年实践的考验。《论语》第一章中说："学而时习之，不亦说（悦，乐）乎！""学"是取得知识，"习"是实践。孔子只说学习实践可以得到乐趣，却不说什么是"乐"。这就是孔子的方法论，是中国文学翻译理论的依据。

总而言之，中国学派的文学翻译理论是研究老子提出的

"信"(似)"美"(优)矛盾的艺术(本体论),但"信"不限原文,还指原文所反映的现实,这是认识论,"信"由严复提出的"信达雅"发展到鲁迅提出"信顺"的直译,再发展到陈源的"三似"(形似,意似,神似),直到傅雷的"重神似不重形似",这已经接近"美"了。"美"发展到鲁迅的"三美"(意美,音美,形美),再发展到林语堂提出的"忠实,通顺,美",转化为朱生豪"传达原作意趣"的意译,直到茅盾提出的"美的享受"。孔子提出的"从心所欲"发展到郭沫若提出的创译论(好的翻译等于创作),以及钱钟书说的译文可以胜过原作的"化境"说,再发展到优化论,超越论,"三化"(等化,浅化,深化)方法论。孔子提出的"不逾矩"和老子说的"信言不美,美言不信"有同有异。老子"信美"并重,孔子"从心所欲"重于"不逾矩",发展为朱光潜的"艺术论",包括郭沫若说的"在信达之外,愈雅愈好。所谓'雅'不是高深或讲修饰,而是文学价值或艺术价值比较高。"直到茅盾说的:"必须把文学翻译工作提高到艺术创造的水平。"孔子的"乐之"发展为胡适之的"愉快"说(翻译要使读者读得愉快),再发展到"三之"(知之,好之,乐之)目的论。这就是中国学派的文学翻译理论发展为"美化之艺术"("三美","三化","三之"的艺术)的概况。

许渊冲
2011年10月

图书在版编目（CIP）数据

论语：汉英对照 / 许渊冲译. —2版. —北京: 五洲传播出版社, 2019.3
（2021.5重印）
ISBN 978-7-5085-4123-5

Ⅰ.①论… Ⅱ.①许… Ⅲ.①儒家－汉、英 Ⅳ.①B222.21

中国版本图书馆CIP数据核字(2019)第041106号

论语

译　　者：	许渊冲
策划编辑：	荆孝敏　郑　磊
责任编辑：	王　峰
中文译注：	杨伯峻
中文编辑：	朱立峰
英文编辑：	马培武　张祯隆
装帧设计：	北京正视文化艺术有限责任公司
出版发行：	五洲传播出版社
地　　址：	北京市海淀区北三环中路31号生产力大楼B座6层
邮　　编：	100088
电　　话：	010-82005927，010-82007837
网　　址：	http://www.cicc.org.cn　http://www.thatsbooks.com
印　　刷：	中煤（北京）印务有限公司
版　　次：	2012年1月第1版 2021年5月第2版第2次印刷
开　　本：	140mm×210mm　1/32
印　　张：	14.25
字　　数：	400千字
书　　号：	ISBN 978-7-5085-4123-5
定　　价：	108.00元